The Spanish Economy

The Spanish Economy

A General Equilibrium Perspective

Edited by

José E. Boscá, Rafael Doménech,
Javier Ferri and Juan Varela

First published in 2011 by
PALGRAVE MACMILLAN

Palgrave Macmillan in the UK is an imprint of Macmillan Publishers Limited, registered in England, company number 785998, of Houndmills, Basingstoke, Hampshire RG21 6XS.

Palgrave Macmillan in the US is a division of St Martin's Press LLC, 175 Fifth Avenue, New York, NY 10010.

Palgrave Macmillan is the global academic imprint of the above companies and has companies and representatives throughout the world.

Palgrave® and Macmillan® are registered trademarks in the United States, the United Kingdom, Europe and other countries.

ISBN 978–0–230–284654

This book is printed on paper suitable for recycling and made from fully managed and sustained forest sources. Logging, pulping and manufacturing processes are expected to conform to the environmental regulations of the country of origin.

A catalogue record for this book is available from the British Library.

A catalog record for this book is available from the Library of Congress.

10 9 8 7 6 5 4 3 2 1
20 19 18 17 16 15 14 13 12 11

Printed and bound in the United States of America

Contents

List of Tables   viii

List of Figures   ix

Preface   xiii

Foreword   xviii

Editors' Biographies   xx

List of Contributors   xxii

1   **Long-Run and Business Cycle Factors of the
    Spanish Economy**   1
    *J. E. Boscá, A. Díaz, R. Doménech, J. Ferri, E. Pérez, L. Puch
    and J. Varela*
    1.1   Introduction   1
    1.2   Economic growth and productivity in Spain   3
    1.3   The determinants of labour productivity   11
    1.4   Cyclical regularities of the Spanish economy   18
    1.5   Conclusions   27

2   **REMS: A Rational Expectations Model for Simulation
    and Policy Evaluation of the Spanish Economy**   30
    J. E. Boscá, A. Díaz, R. Doménech, J. Ferri, E. Pérez and L. Puch
    2.1   Introduction   30
    2.2   Theoretical framework   31
    2.3   Model solution method and parameterisation   55
    2.4   Simulations   60
    2.5   Conclusions   65

3   **Job Creation in Spain: Productivity Growth, Labour
    Market Reforms or Both?**   69
    J. Andrés, J. E. Boscá, R. Doménech and J. Ferri
    3.1   Introduction   69
    3.2   The Spanish growth model   71
    3.3   Growth model and job creation: the example of EU-10   83

| | 3.4 | General equilibrium evaluation of job creation with the new growth model | 87 |
| | 3.5 | Concluding remarks | 94 |

4 | **Productivity and Competitiveness: The Economic Impact of the Services Directive** | | **97**
C. Cuerpo, R. Doménech and L. González-Calbet
	4.1	Introduction	97
	4.2	International evidence on the effects of the Services Directive	108
	4.3	Economic impact of the Services Directive in Spain	112
	4.4	Conclusions	117

5 | **The Effects of Public Investment** | | **120**
A. de la Fuente and R. Doménech
	5.1	Introduction	120
	5.2	Public investment and public capital stocks in the OECD	120
	5.3	Infrastructures and productivity: a brief survey	127
	5.4	Effects of a permanent increase in public investment	135
	5.5	Conclusions	141

6 | **On Ricardian Equivalence and Twin Divergence** | | **144**
M. Cardoso and R. Doménech
	6.1	Introduction	144
	6.2	Fiscal policy and the current account: a shock in public consumption	148
	6.3	A temporary increase in public investment	150
	6.4	A temporary reduction of labour income taxes	152
	6.5	Sensitivity analysis	154
	6.6	Conclusions	157

7 | **Tax Reforms and Economic Performance** | | **160**
J. E. Boscá, R. Doménech and J. Ferri
	7.1	Introduction	160
	7.2	Macroeconomic performance, taxes and the labour market	162
	7.3	Tax reform and economic performance in Spain	169
	7.4	Sensitivity analysis	176
	7.5	Conclusions	179

8 | **Conclusions** | | **181**
J. E. Boscá, R. Doménech, J. Ferri and J. Varela

Appendix 1 Dataset for International Comparisons   189
    A.1.1   Definitions and sources of international data   189
    A.1.2   Estimation of the capital stocks   190

Appendix 2 The REMS Database (REMSDB)   192
    A.2.1   Data sources   193
    A.2.2   Description of the series   193

Appendix 3 Nash Bargaining with RoT Consumers   198
    A.3.1   Maximisation problem   198
    A.3.2   Solution for hours   199
    A.3.3   Solution for wages   199

Appendix 4 Net Foreign Asset Accumulation   201

Appendix 5 Using Behavioural Equations to Produce Non-observable Data   204

Appendix 6 Tax Reforms and Economic Performance: Transitional Dynamics   207

References   211

Index   223

Tables

1.1 First and second moments (HP-filtered) properties of main
    macroeconomic aggregates, 1980–2009   24
2.1 Parameter values   56
2.2 Steady state   57
3.1 Evaluation of the new growth model   89
3.2 Correspondence between reforms and REMS   92
3.3 Evaluation of labour market reforms   93
4.1 Labour productivity and firm size, 2005   103
4.2 Long-run effects of the Services Directive   113
5.1 Summary of results on infrastructures and growth   132
5.2 Long-run effects of public investment   137
5.3 Impact effects of a permanent increase in public investment   140
6.1 Sensitivity analysis   155
7.1 Long-run benefits of lowering tax wedges in Spain   170
7.2 Long-run effects of increasing capital taxes in Spain   173
7.3 Sensitivity of long-run benefits of lowering tax wedges in
    Spain   177
7.4 Sensitivity of long-run effects of increasing capital taxes in
    Spain   177

Figures

1.1	Relative per capita GDP, EU-12 and Spain, 1960–2009 (USA = 1)	4
1.2	Working-age population as a percentage of total population, 1960–2009	5
1.3	Participation rate (L^s/L^{16-64}), 1960–2005	5
1.4	Employment rate (L^d/L^s), 1960–2009	6
1.5	Annual hours worked per employed worker (H/L^d), 1960–2009	7
1.6	GDP per hour worked, 1960–2009 (USA = 1)	8
1.7	Logarithmic differences of the determinants of per capita income in Spain compared with the USA, 1960–2009	9
1.8	Logarithmic differences of determinants of per capita income in the EU-12 compared with the USA, 1960–2009	10
1.9	Private productive capital per hour worked (in logs), 1960–2009	13
1.10	Private productive capital over GDP, 1960–2009	13
1.11	Years of schooling per adult (S), 1960–2009	14
1.12	Years of schooling of adult population compared with the USA (S_i/S_{USA}), 1960–2009	15
1.13	Contribution of private productive capital (K/H), human capital (S) and total factor productivity (PTF) to the labour productivity differential (GDP/H) of the EU compared with the USA, 1960–2009	17
1.14	Contribution of private productive capital (K/H), human capital (S) and total factor produtivity (PTF) to the labour productivity differential (GDP/H) of Spain compared with the USA, 1960–2009	17
1.15	HP trend of GDP in logs	19
1.16	Hours per adult	20
1.17	Capital–output ratio	21
1.18	Vacancies per adult	21
1.19	Money (M1) velocity	22
1.20	Unemployment rate and its trend (dotted line)	23
1.21	Cyclical unemployment (solid line) and output gap (dotted line)	23
1.22	Trend and cycle decomposition of GDP and GDP per adult	25

1.23   Trend and cycle components of private consumption
       (level and per adult)   25
1.24   Trend and cycle components of investment (level and per
       adult)   26
1.25   Trend and cycle components of public consumption
       (level and per adult)   26
2.1   Effects of a transitory technological shock   61
2.2   Effects of a technology shock on full-time equivalent
       employment   63
2.3   Effects of a transitory public consumption shock   64
2.4   Effects of a public consumption shock on full-time
       equivalent employment   65
3.1   Employment growth, annual rates, 1992–2008   72
3.2   Unemployment rate, 1991–2009   73
3.3   Evolution of productivity per worker, 1991–2008   74
3.4   Annual rates of growth of productivity per worker,
       1992–2008   74
3.5   Okun's law   78
3.6   Okun's law in Spain in 1960–83 and 1984–2008, and in
       EU-15 1960–83   80
3.7   Okun's law in Spain in 1960–83 and 1984–2008, and in
       EU-15 1984–2008   80
3.8   Productivity across sectors, averages 2003–7   81
3.9   Distribution of employment across sectors, averages 2003–7   82
3.10   Simulated employment (levels) versus observed
       employment, 1991–2007   85
3.11   Simulated employment, index 1991 = 100   86
3.12   Simulated growth of value added, 1991–2007   87
3.13   Simulation of Okun's curves under different scenarios   90
4.1   Inflation in Spain and the EMU, 1997–2010   98
4.2   Per capita income and consumer price levels in the EMU,
       2007 (EMU = 100)   99
4.3   Inflation and the productivity growth gap between
       tradable and non-tradable goods, 1999–2008 averages   100
4.4   Current account balance and GDP per capita, 2002–8
       averages   101
4.5   Share of Spanish exports and imports in world trade,
       1980–2008   102
4.6   Product market regulations in 2003 and structural
       unemployment (NAIRU) in 2005   104
4.7   Product market regulations in 2003 and share of
       employment in firms with fewer than 20 employees in 2006   105

4.8   Correlation between product market regulations
      indicators from the OECD and the World Bank (Doing
      Business)   106
4.9   Contribution of profit margins to inflation differentials
      and the interaction of GDP growth and the Doing
      Business indicator of product market regulations,
      averages 1999–2007   107
4.10 Inflation in services, annual growth rates, 1991–2010   107
4.11 Transitional dynamics after permanent reduction in
      intermediate sector's mark-up   115
4.12 Transitional dynamics after permanent reduction in final
      goods sector mark-up, using QUEST III; periods = years   118
5.1   Public investment as a fraction of GDP, evolution over
      time, 1950–2005   122
5.2   Public investment as a fraction of GDP, averages for 2000–5   122
5.3   Public investment as a fraction of total investment,
      evolution over time, 1950–2005   123
5.4   Public investment as a fraction of total investment,
      averages for 2000–5   123
5.5   Stock of public capital per capita, evolution over time   124
5.6   Stock of public capital per capita in 2005   125
5.7   Public capital as a fraction of the total stock of capital,
      evolution over time, 1950–2005   125
5.8   Public capital as a fraction of the total stock of capital in
      2005   126
5.9   Stock of public capital as a fraction of GDP, evolution
      over time, 1950–2005   126
5.10 Stock of public capital as a fraction of GDP in 2005   127
5.11 Optimal public investment rate as a function of the
      output elasticity of public capital (solid line)   136
5.12 Impulse–response functions to a permanent increase in
      government investment equivalent to 1 per cent of GDP   138
6.1   Household saving and investment rates (% of GDP),
      Spain, SD1987–2009   145
6.2   General government balance (% of GDP), Spain, 1995–2009   145
6.3   Current account (% of GDP), Spain, 1987–2009   146
6.4   Current account and the budget surplus (% of GDP),
      quarterly frequency, 1981–2009   146
6.5   Impulse–response functions after a temporary shock in
      public consumption   148

6.6   The response of saving, investment and public
        consumption rates after a temporary shock in public
        consumption, absolute deviations from their steady-state
        values   150
6.7   Impulse–response functions after a temporary shock in
        public investment   151
6.8   The response of saving, investment and public
        investment rates (% of GDP) after a temporary shock in
        public investment, absolute deviations from their
        steady-state values   152
6.9   Impulse–response functions after a temporary reduction
        in the labour income tax rate   153
6.10   The response of saving and investment rates, and
        revenues from labour income taxes over GDP after a
        temporary reduction of the labour income tax rate,
        absolute deviations from their steady-state values   154
7.1   GDP over working-age population, relative to the United
        States, 1960–2010   163
7.2   Productivity, hours worked per employee, and
        employment and participation rates in relative terms to
        the United States, 1960–2010   164
7.3   Taxes on consumption and labour income, social security
        contributions and the overall tax wedge in Spain, EU-15
        and the United States, 1965–2007   165
7.4   Capital tax   166
7.5   Intensive (hours per employee) and extensive margins
        (employed per adult population) in Spain, relative to the
        United States, 1960–2007   168
7.6   Intensive (hours per employee) and extensive (employed
        per adult population) margins in EU-15, relative to the
        United States, 1960–2007   169
7.7   Transitional dynamics after a permanent reduction in the
        overall tax wedge   174
7.8   Dynamics of consumption after a permanent reduction
        in the overall tax wedge   176
A6.1   Transitional dynamics after a permanent reduction in the
        consumption tax rate   207
A6.2   Transitional dynamics after a permanent increase in
        labour tax rate   208
A6.3   Transitional dynamics after a permanent reduction in
        social security contributions   209
A6.4   Transitional dynamics after a permanent increase in
        capital tax rate   210

Preface

In 2005 we initiated a joint research project with the Ministry of Economic Affairs and Finance, the Fundación Rafael del Pino and the University of Valencia. The aim of this project was to develop a robust analytical tool for simulation and policy evaluation of the Spanish economy, in line with recent advances in macroeconomics. Many years ago, in the late 1980s, the Ministry of Economic Affairs and Finance developed a simulation model for the Spanish economy (MOISEES) that at that time brought macroeconomic modelisation in Spain to the international frontier. MOISEES was a disequilibrium model in which aggregate demand played a determinant role in both the short and the long run. Although the empirical implementation of the model relied on long-run co-integration relationships, the model did not impose the long-run restrictions implied by neoclassical models. Additionally, as was common practice at that time with most large-scale models, the solution of MOISEES relied on a backward-looking specification instead of considering the forward-looking nature of multiple economic decisions.

In the past 20 years macroeconomic modelisation has witnessed the development of new tools that have allowed the introduction of many short-run Keynesian features into the basic framework of neoclassical dynamic general equilibrium models.[1] The new dynamic macroeconomic models are based on a consistent general equilibrium framework, derived from the optimising behaviour of households and firms and subject to budget and technological constraints, which is empirically implemented to match key cyclical and long-run features of macroeconomic aggregates. Thus most international economic institutions, such as the ECB, the European Commission, the Fed or the IMF, now use this kind of model intensively for evaluation of alternative economic policies and shocks. Given this trend at international level, it seemed evident that the Spanish economy needed comparable tools for economic analysis. In fact, not surprisingly, similar initiatives appeared more or less at the same time. In 2007 we completed the specification, estimation and calibration of REMS, the acronym for the Rational Expectations Model of the Spanish economy. One year earlier Andrés et al. (2006; 2010b) developed BEMOD for the Bank of Spain, and in 2007 Burriel et al. (2010) started the elaboration of MEDEA for the Economic Bureau of the Prime Minister.

During the time in which REMS became fully operational, it seemed obvious that it would be very useful to write a book with many examples of simulations undertaken during the past years of the use of this model. This is the objective of this book: to take advantage of some of the simulations and policy evaluations done with REMS to offer a comprehensive and careful overview of the Spanish economy.

During this process the Spanish economy has gone from being considered as one of the European growth miracles to the most important recession in its recent economic history. Although the book is not about the Spanish economic crisis, initiated after the subprime financial crisis in 2007, it offers a different analysis on the simulation effects of stabilisation policies and structural reforms that have been discussed or implemented during the present crisis. In this vein the book focuses more on the effects of alternative demand and supply-side policies, some of them implemented in the past two years, rather than in explaining the determinants and characteristics of the Spanish economic crisis.[2] Besides the policy evaluation and simulations described in the following chapters, many others analysed with REMS such as the effects of the increase in risk premia, interest rates and oil prices, the substitution of social security contribution by higher VAT rates, and the fall in taxes on firms' profits could have been included in this book. The specific contents of the book are as follows.

In the first chapter, J. E. Boscá, A. Díaz, R. Doménech, J. Ferri, E. Pérez, L. Puch and J. Varela deal with the long-run and cyclical behaviour of Spain's main macroeconomic aggregates such as GDP, per capita GDP, employment, private productive capital, human capital or productivity. This chapter traces the determinants of economic growth and compares their behaviour with those in the USA and in the EU in order to identify the factors driving the convergence or the divergence process that the economy has exhibited in different periods. The part devoted to the cyclical patterns uses a new database for the Spanish economy (the REMSDB dataset) to analyse the cyclical properties of the Spanish economy since 1980.

In the second chapter, J. E. Boscá, A. Díaz, R. Doménech, J. Ferri, E. Pérez and L. Puch explain REMS in detail, offering all the equations and the economic intuition behind them. The results from two standard simulations are presented: a productivity shock and a fiscal shock. The chapter ends with some comments about possible avenues to improve the model in different dimensions to address future specific policy areas.

In the third chapter, J. Andrés, J. E. Boscá, R. Doménech and J. Ferri examine the relationship between output and unemployment in Spain, i.e. the Okun curve, and try to explain this relationship. Then the trade-off between employment and productivity growth for the Spanish economy is explained. By means of an accounting exercise, the employment effects of a model for more productivity growth for Spain are explored. Finally, the authors shift from a partial equilibrium analysis to a general equilibrium approach introducing shocks to productivity growth. For this purpose they use REMS, which gives the effects on key labour market variables of a productivity shock with and without labour market reforms.

In Chapter 4, C. Cuerpo, R. Doménech and L. González-Calbet use REMS to simulate the dynamic effects of applying the Services Directive of the European Union, another important policy affecting aggregate supply and firms' mark-ups. As can be seen, the expectations about the positive effects of this liberalisation initiative through enhanced competition are both great and justified.

In the fifth chapter, A. de la Fuente and R. Doménech analyse the relevance of public investment and the public capital stock in the economy. After exposing the importance of public investment in Spain and revising the evidence of its effects on output growth in a number of countries, the REMS model is used to simulate the aggregate effects of a positive permanent shock to public investment, with the aim of stimulation of fiscal policies in Spain following the crisis.

In Chapter 6, M. Cardoso and R. Doménech explore the forces at work behind the rapid correction in private imbalances following the dramatic deterioration in public accounts and the sharp improvement in the current account in Spain that have characterised the economic crisis after 2007. The two hypotheses tested with the REMS model are Ricardian Equivalence and Twin Divergence. The authors find in this small open-economy framework that Ricardian Equivalence holds only partially and that quick correction of the current account in 2009 associated with the large public deficit cannot be explained by the Twin Divergence hypothesis.

In Chapter 7, J. E. Boscá, R. Doménech and J. Ferri present an interesting exercise that consists of simulating what would happen to the economy if the tax structure in Spain was changed, in particular if the tax wedge was lowered to the same level as in the US. By so doing the authors can test the evidence offered by some economists who find that taxes explain much of the difference between the US and Europe as regards hours worked per adult.

Finally, the main conclusions drawn by the authors from the analysis of the Spanish economy in this publication are summarised.

We are extremely grateful to all the contributors to this book. Most of them were part of the research team that constructed REMS. Others provided and still give insightful suggestions to improve and to use this model. Neither the model nor this book would have been possible without their generous and skilful collaboration.

This book is a very good example of a joint project between the different institutions that have been actively involved. This research project benefited from the financing of Fundación Rafael del Pino and from the continuous support and encouragement of its management, particularly Amadeo Petitbó and Vicente Montes. Miguel Ángel Fernández Ordoñez and Carlos Ocaña, the two State Secretaries for Finances and Budget during this project, David Vegara and José Manuel Campa, State Secretaries for Economic Policy, David Taguas, former Director of the Economic Bureau of the Prime Minister, as well as the two Directors General for the Budget, Luis Espadas and Fernando Rojas, made possible the development of REMS and its use as a tool for simulation and policy evaluation in the public administration. We also acknowledge support from the University of Valencia, which contributed to make this book possible in the last two years. We acknowledge the financial contribution from the European Regional Development Fund (ERDF) and by CICYT grants SEJ2005-01365, ECO2008-04669 and and ECO2009-09569.

We gratefully thank the generous comments and contributions made by G. Ascari, L. Boone, P. Burriel, S. Castillo, G. Coenen, J. C. Conesa, F. Corrales, M. Correa, M. Díaz, J. Escribá, A. García, J. R. García, A. Gavilán, S. Gnocchi, V. Gómez, A. G. Gómez-Plana, M. Jiménez, J. F. Jimeno, T. Kehoe, M. Ledo, C. Leith, E. Leeper, F. Lores, C. Martínez-Mongay, Á. Melguizo, M. J. Murgui, E. Pappa, E. Pedreira, V. Pou, E. Prades, J. A. Rojas, P. Ruiz, Á. Sanmartín, C. Ulloa and participants at various seminars and conferences. The work of Andrés de Bustos and José Ramón García with the dataset has been invaluable.

Among other meetings and seminars, a previous version of Chapter 2 was presented at the workshop on Lisbon methodology organised by the EU Commission and at the XXXII SAE, at the OCDE, at the XI Applied Economics Meeting and at the joint Bank of Spain and *SERIEs Structural Dynamic Stochastic Models for the Spanish Economy* meeting. A previous version of this chapter was published in *SERIEs, the Journal of the Spanish Economic Association*.

Chapter 3 was presented at the 2008 UIMP Conference in Santander, at the XVII Public Economics Meeting and at the 9th Journées Louis-André Gérard-Varet Conference in Public Economics in Marseille. A previous version of this chapter was published in Spanish in *Papeles de Economía Española*.

A previous version of Chapter 6 was prepared for the ECFIN Workshop on *External Imbalances and Public Finances in the EU*, Brussels, 27 November 2009. The papers presented at this conference were edited by S. Barrios, S. Deroose, S. Langedijk, and L. Pench in a special issue of *European Economy Occasional Papers*. This chapter was also presented at the Bank of Spain conference *Interactions between Monetary and Fiscal Policies*, Madrid, 25–26 February 2010.

A previous version of Chapter 7 was prepared for the XXI Symposium of *Moneda y Crédito* in 2008 and published in that journal in 2009.

Finally, we would like to thank our families for their support and understanding. This book is dedicated to them.

José E. Boscá, Rafael Doménech, Javier Ferri and Juan Varela

Notes

1. See, for example, Blanchard (2009), Woodford (2009), Chari et al. (2009), Galí (2008), Smets et al. (2010), Karagedikli et al. (2009), and Kremer et al. (2006) and the references therein.
2. De la Dehesa (2009), Suarez (2010) or Estrada, Jimeno and Malo de Molina (2010) offer excellent analyses of the Spanish economic crisis.

Foreword

Before the present crisis, economists felt quite confident about their ability to forecast economic events in the short-term or even in long-term trends thanks to the development of complex microfounded general equilibrium models. However, the crisis, which these models had trouble identifying, has attracted a lot of criticisms about economic science in general terms and particularly about the usefulness of macroeconomic modelling.

Despite these critiques, economic modelling is a very helpful tool to analyse economic policy, although it usually works far better looking back than looking forward. However, we should not forget its obvious limitations. First, reality is always more complex than we can mathematically represent. In the same way, economics, as other social sciences, is a field where the observer has the ability to change the reality he or she observes. Second, the accuracy of each model directly depends on the validity of the hypotheses on which it is founded.

Rather than putting the blame for our own failures on macroeconomic modelling, this tool should remain an important reference for policymakers. At the Spanish Ministry of Economic Affairs and Finance we have been working for a long time in modelling the Spanish economy as a fundamental basis for making economic policy decisions, but always taking into account its unavoidable limitations.

Following these works, in January 2008, a team of economists from Universidad de Valencia, Universidad Complutense de Madrid and the Ministry of Economic Affairs and Finance completed the specification, estimation and calibration of a macroeconomic model of the Spanish economy. The model, called Rational Expectations Model for Simulation and Policy Evaluation of the Spanish Economy (REMS), is a small open-economy dynamic general equilibrium model that attempts to feature the main characteristics of our economy. This project benefited from the financing of Fundación Rafael del Pino and therefore it has been an example of collaboration between the Public Administration, the University and the private sector to provide the Ministry of Economic Affairs and Finance and all research centres with a tool to simulate the economic impact of alternative policy measures over the medium term. Most of the authors of this book belong to the team that constructed the model. Others provided and still provide insightful advice for improving it and using it to evaluate economic policy measures.

The making of the REMS model is the continuation of a long-term modelling project at the Ministry of Economic Affairs and Finance which was mentioned above. By doing so we have managed to become endowed with a state-of-the-art model in the vein of New-Neoclassical-Keynesian synthesis with microfounded forward-looking behavioural equations that are derived from intertemporal optimisation by households and firms. We think that this kind of model provides a good representation of the Spanish economy by assuming that it behaves in the long run with the flexibility that characterises the Real Business Cycle paradigm, but with short-run frictions in goods, labour and financial markets. These frictions are due to the fact that firms perform in an imperfect competition context and that contracts in the labour market are achieved through a costly matching process. The model also departs from the standard Neoclassical framework in that it assumes a fraction of the consumers to be liquidity-constrained.

This book presents a series of essays on the Spanish economy, mostly based on simulations with the REMS model and with its database (REMSDB). It is not about the Spanish economic crisis initiated after the subprime financial crisis in 2007. On the contrary, this book offers very interesting analytical tools to evaluate the kind of stabilisation policies and structural reforms implemented during the crisis. Therefore the book focuses more on the effects of alternative demand and supply-side policies, some of them implemented in the past two years, than in explaining the determinants and characteristics of the Spanish economic crisis, which have been well explained by other authors.

The research herein exposed highlights the usefulness of economic modelling for designing policies and for understanding the working of the economy. It also reveals the need to continue this work in order to improve the REMS model by better characterising specific areas that would allow a capturing of the microeconomic effects which are triggered by different policy measures, especially structural reforms.

Carlos Ocaña Pérez de Tudela
State Secretary for Finances and Budget
Ministry of Economic Affairs and Finance

Editors' Biographies

José E. Boscá is Professor of Economics and Director of the International Economic Institute at the University of Valencia. He holds an advanced Studies Certificate in International Economic Policy (Kiel Institute for the World Economy, Germany) and a PhD in Economics (University of Valencia). He is also an external researcher at the Spanish Ministry of Economic Affairs and Finance and the Fundación Rafael del Pino. He has been Vice-Dean of International Relations at the Faculty of Economics, University of Valencia. He has published numerous articles in international journals on economic growth, business cycles, regional economics and fiscal policies.

Rafael Doménech is Chief Economist for Spain and Europe of BBVA Research and Full Professor of Economics at BBVA Research Department and the University of Valencia. He holds an MSc in Economics (London School of Economics) and a PhD in Economics (University of Valencia). He is the Director General and Deputy Director of the Economic Bureau of the Spanish Prime Minister (2007–8). He has been Director of the International Economic Institute and member of the Advisory Board of the University of Valencia, external researcher at the Spanish Ministry of Economic Affairs and Finance and the Fundación Rafael del Pino and board member of the Spanish Economy Association. He has published many articles in international academic journals on economic growth, human capital, business cycles and fiscal and monetary policies.

Javier Ferri is Professor of Economics at the University of Valencia. He holds an MSc in Economics (University College London), PhD in Economics (University of Valencia). He is an external researcher at the Spanish Ministry of the Economy and Finance and the Fundación Rafael del Pino. His research has combined microeconometrics, CGE and DSGE models. He has published numerous articles in international journals on education, immigration, taxation and the labour market. Currently he maintains a fruitful line of research on business cycles.

Juan Varela is Deputy Director of Economic Analysis and Programming in the General Directorate of the Budget, Ministry of Economic Affairs and Finances, Spain. He has held several posts at the Ministry of

Economic Affairs and Finance since joining the Spanish Civil Service as member of the Body of Economists of the State in 1983. Much of his professional career has involved conducting research on the Spanish economy and representing the Ministry of Economic Affairs and Finances at international meetings and conferences. He holds a Bachelor's Degree in Economics (Universidad Complutense de Madrid, Spain) and a Master's in Economics (Boston College, USA).

Contributors

Javier Andrés, Full Professor of Economics, University of Valencia, Valencia, Spain.

Miguel Cardoso, Chief Economist for Spain, BBVA Research, Madrid, Spain.

Carlos Cuerpo, Advisor to the Director General for Macroeconomic Analysis and International Economy, Ministry of Economic Affairs and Finance, Madrid, Spain.

Ángel de la Fuente, Tenured Scientist, Instututo de Análisis Económico, CSIC, Barcelona, Spain.

Antonio Díaz, Advisor to the Director General of the Budget Office, Ministry of Economic Affairs and Finance, Madrid, Spain.

Luis González-Calbet, Deputy Director General for Economic Modeling, Ministry of Economic Affairs and Finance, Madrid, Spain.

Esther Pérez, Economist, European Department, EU Policies and Regional Studies, International Monetary Fund, Washington, United States.

Luis Puch, Associate Professor of Economics, Universidad Computense de Madrid, Madrid, Spain.

1
Long-Run and Business Cycle Factors of the Spanish Economy

J. E. Boscá, A. Díaz, R. Doménech, J. Ferri, E. Pérez, L. Puch and J. Varela

1.1 Introduction

The construction of a model for simulation and policy evaluation of the Spanish economy constitutes a far-reaching project. This research task involves the specification of the behavioural equations that better describe the economy, as will be explained in the next chapter. Growth and cyclical regularities impose several restrictions on the specification and calibration of a useful general equilibrium model. For this reason much effort is needed in the analysis of the long- and short-run stylised factors of the Spanish economy. Thus throughout this chapter we shall study what has been behind the pattern of growth of the Spanish economy in recent decades, what has determined its labour productivity and what are the special features characterising business cycles in Spain.

From 1995 until 2007 the Spanish economy enjoyed one of the longest recent periods of economic growth with an average growth rate of 3.7 per cent. This rate has been higher than in the majority of the Economic Union's economies (2.1 per cent in the EU-12).[1] Total population in Spain also grew more during this period (1.0 against 0.3 per cent in the EU-12) in a process that has been compatible with per capita income convergence, since Spain has reduced the gap with the European average by 8 points, from 83.8 per cent of the EU-12 average in 1995 to 91.7 per cent in 2007, a figure that is equivalent to 67.1 per cent of the per capita income of the United States.

However, this period of sizeable economic growth has also been characterised by some elements that raised doubts and concerns about the quality of growth in the Spanish economy. The first was the persistent inflation differential with respect to the Economic and Monetary Union

(EMU) which, with a monetary policy determined by the European Central Bank (ECB) according to the behaviour of the euro-zone as a whole, gave rise to ex-post real interest rates that were exceptionally low and even negative for some years. As shown by Gavilán *et al.* (2010), negative real interest rates and intense population growth, as a result of immigration, induced a significant residential investment boom, with immense consequences. The second imbalance was the increasing current account deficit, which went from balanced to 10 per cent of GDP in 2008. The third issue was the weak growth in productivity in the latter period (1995–2007). Productivity per worker had converged to the EU level in the second half of the twentieth century, reaching 99.5 per cent of the EU-12 in 1995, but from that year until 2006 it diminished again to as low as 89 per cent. This performance is even more noticeable if we take into account that in this period productivity in the United States was outstandingly dynamic, growing at higher rates than in Europe. Therefore in the decade of the 2000s Europe lagged behind the United States in terms of productivity, and Spain underperformed to an even greater extent. To many economists these three problems of inflation differential, external imbalance and weak increase in productivity are linked: it is frequently said that the inflation differential and a high current account deficit are the consequence of weak productivity growth.[2]

In 2007 some of the drivers of economic growth in recent years were almost exhausted or heading towards exhaustion. The benefits derived from economic integration and the stability of monetary and fiscal policies had already materialised. Spain gradually stopped being a net beneficiary of European cohesion policies which had contributed very much to public capital accumulation and therefore also to the improvement in infrastructures. Finally, there was little margin for improvement in participation rates (except in the case of women) as they have converged towards the levels prevailing in advanced economies such as the United States or the European Union. Under these circumstances the accumulated imbalances were not sustainable for a longer period. Additionally, the adjustment of these imbalances has coincided with the deepest international crisis since the Great Depression, inducing an intense fall in activity particularly in employment. The consequence has been a rapid increase of the unemployment rate to 20 per cent of the labour force, reaching in just two years the levels of the previous recession of 1993/4. Given the experience of the current crisis, it is clear that future growth cannot be based on the same determinants as in the economic expansion from 1995 to 2007. On the contrary, future improvements in

Spanish per capita income will require larger increases in labour productivity, and in particular in total factor productivity and human capital, an issue that has caught the attention of many authors.[3]

This chapter begins with a characterisation of the long-run growth of the Spanish economy and ends with an analysis of its cyclical properties. With respect to the long run, in section 1.2 we summarise the macroeconomic evidence on the evolution of growth and productivity in Spain from 1960 to 2009, updating the growth analysis done by Doménech *et al.* (2008), and in section 1.3 we carry out an empirical analysis on the contribution of the classical determinants of labour productivity. With respect to the business cycle, in section 1.4 we analyse the cyclical behaviour of the main macroeconomic variables by characterising the first and second moments of key macroeconomic aggregates. Finally, in section 1.5 we present the main conclusions.

1.2 Economic growth and productivity in Spain

As is widely known, labour productivity is one of the basic determinants of per capita income levels in an economy and therefore of its welfare. To show this in a simple algebraic way, we can decompose per capita GDP using the following identity:

$$\frac{GDP_t}{L_t} \equiv \frac{GDP_t}{H_t} \frac{H_t}{L_t^d} \frac{L_t^d}{L_t^s} \frac{L_t^s}{L_t^{16-64}} \frac{L_t^{16-64}}{L_t} \tag{1.1}$$

where H_t is total hours worked, L_t^d is the number of occupied workers, L_t^s is labour supply and L_t^{16-64} is the working-age population. The first factor on the right-hand side of Equation 1.1 is productivity per hour worked. The second is the average number of hours worked by an occupied person. The third term is the employment rate; that is, the percentage of individuals who actively participate in the labour market and who are employed. The fourth is the participation rate; that is, the percentage of the working-age population that participates actively in the labour market. Finally, the last term is a ratio that refers to the age structure of the population.

Figure 1.1 represents per capita income levels in Spain and the EU-12 relative to the United States for the period 1960–2009. As can be seen, until 1975 the trend for Europe and Spain was positive meaning that the gap of both Europe and Spain with the US narrowed significantly. In this vein, Europe approached the United States by more than five percentage points, whereas Spain also slashed its wedge with respect to the EU-12.

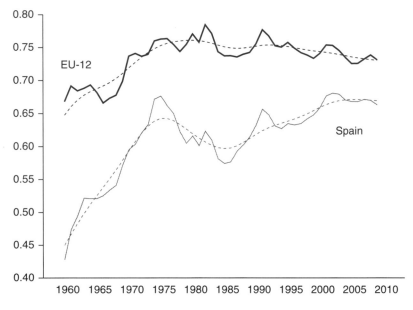

Figure 1.1   Relative per capita GDP, EU-12 and Spain, 1960–2009 (USA = 1)

However, not much progress has occurred since 1975 and Europe's per capita income has even fallen slightly with respect to the United States. The Spanish economy moved away in the decade up to 1985, but since its accession to the EU it progressed again as regards the EU-12 and by 2000 had recovered its relative pre-1975 level compated to the United States. According to the trend components, in 2009 Spain was very close to the average of the EU-12, but these countries register levels of income per capita which on average are 25 per cent lower than in the United States.[4]

According to the different factors on the right-hand side of Equation (1.1), one of the main reasons explaining the differences in per capita GDP among the economies analysed could be the different age structure. But Figure 1.2 shows that, despite the fact that this variable has exhibited different trends in the three areas (because the baby boom took place at different times, and migration flows have not coincided), average levels are not very different at present, with the working-age population converging at between 65 per cent and 67 per cent of total population in the long run for all three economies.

In contrast, participation rates (L^s/L^{16-64}) record marked differences, as can be seen in Figure 1.3. The participation rate fell considerably in Spain between 1975 and 1985, to close to 60 per cent, as a consequence of

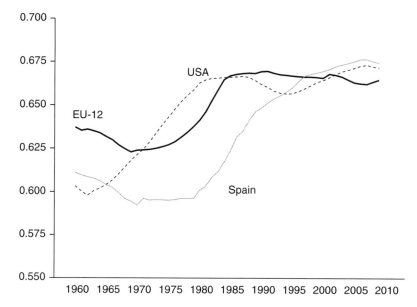

Figure 1.2 Working-age population as a percentage of total population, 1960–2009

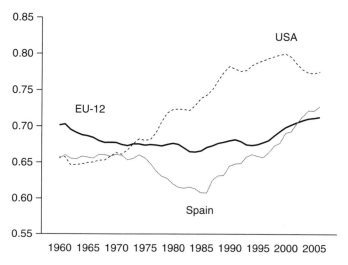

Figure 1.3 Participation rate (L^s/L^{16-64}), 1960–2005

the significant decrease in the likelihood of finding a job and the industrial restructuring that took place in Spain, in a process that brought the
Spanish economy in line with the standards of most modern societies.
Since then the Spanish economy has raised its participation rate considerably, thanks to the incorporation of women into the labour market
and the posterior increase in immigration.[5] This rate is already on a par
with Europe, though it remains below that of the United States. Looking
at the recent evolution of the participation rate in Spain, convergence
towards the rates in the United States (which have remained relatively
stable at around 78 per cent for nearly two decades) seems plausible in the
future, though this will probably require additional structural changes
in European labour markets.

The higher rate of structural unemployment has also contributed to
the differences in per capita income over the years.[6] In Figure 1.4 it can
be seen that the employment rate in Spain fell at the end of the 1970s and
stayed well below that of the EU-12 for more than thirty years. Also the
unemployment rate was still lower in the United States than in the EU-12,
especially among young people, women and those aged between 60 and
65, as pointed out by Dolado *et al.* (2001). As shown in Equation (1.1)

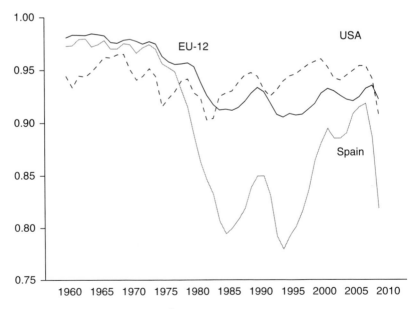

Figure 1.4   Employment rate (L^d/L^s), 1960–2009

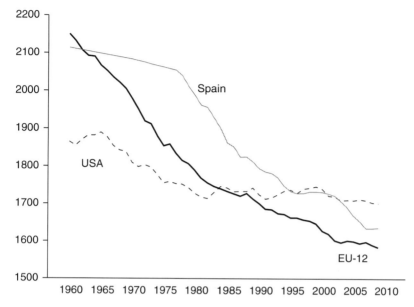

Figure 1.5 Annual hours worked per employed worker (H/L^d), 1960–2009

the different equilibrium unemployment rate is a crucial factor when explaining why per capita income is higher in the United States than in Europe and Spain.

Hours worked by employees also partly explain per capita income differentials. In 2009, Spain held an intermediate position between the USA and the EU-12, as can be seen in Figure 1.5. However, trends have differed. While in the United States the number of hours per worker has remained relatively stable since 1975, in Europe and Spain this variable has displayed a downward trend. Some authors point out that this downward trend is the aftermath of the higher tax burden on European economies (Prescott, 2004). For other authors, fiscal structure is not the relevant variable (Blanchard, 2004, 2006), but rather Europeans' preference for leisure. Doménech and Pérez (2006) have analysed this issue with a general equilibrium model with unemployment *a la* Diamond Mortensen Pissarides. They find that tax increases can to some extent explain an important reduction in the number of hours in the extensive margin because the effects of taxes on unemployment are relatively light, in line with the results obtained by Nickell *et al.* (2005). In Chapter 7 we

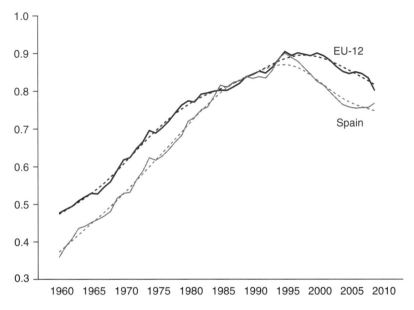

Figure 1.6 GDP per hour worked, 1960–2009 (USA = 1)

use a general equilibrium rational expectations model to answer the question of how the different tax structure in Spain and the United States can influence the number of hours at both the intensive and the extensive margin.

Productivity per hour worked is the last component of the Equation (1.1) and is represented in Figure 1.6. In Spain, this component was seen to rise to a similar level to that in the EU-12 in the mid-1980s and maintained this situation for a decade. However, from 1995 onwards, relative productivity diminished at an even faster pace than in Europe, dropping to 77 per cent of US productivity in 2009. This downward trend in productivity lasted longer than a phase of the business cycle (the expansion in the second half of the 1990s, the slowdown that began in 2001 and the subsequent recovery) and has followed a similar path to its trend component with a decline of approximately 12 percentage points. In this vein, while productivity per hour in the United States grew on average by 2.2 per cent between 1995 and 2009, in Spain this growth rate was barely above 0.6 per cent. However, in 2008-9 it accelerated significantly as a result of employment destruction, narrowing the distance with respect to the US economy. This evidence that has raised a great

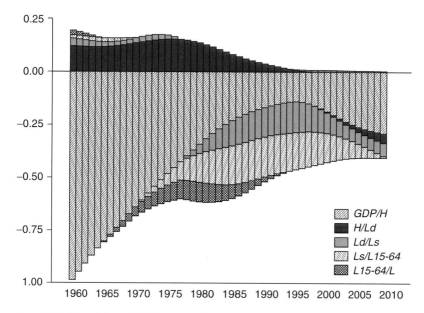

Figure 1.7 Logarithmic differences of the determinants of per capita income in Spain compared with the USA, 1960–2009

deal of concern over the recent evolution of productivity: the inability of the Spanish economy to generate employment without adversely affecting the relative growth rate of productivity.

Figures 1.7 and 1.8 summarise the relative importance of each of the determinants into which the observed differential in per capita income between Spain and the European Union has been decomposed. To do so, we take logs in Equation (1.1)

$$\ln \frac{GDP_t}{L_t} \equiv \ln \frac{GDP_t}{H_t} + \ln \frac{H_t}{L_t^d} + \ln \frac{L_t^d}{L_t^s} + \ln \frac{L_t^s}{L_t^{16-64}} + \ln \frac{L_t^s}{L_t^{16-64}} + \ln \frac{L_t^{16-64}}{L_t}$$

(1.2)

and calculate the difference with respect to the United States for each of the trend components of these variables.

From Figures 1.7 and 1.8 it follows that in the 1960s and at the beginning of the 1970s productivity per hour worked was the main determinant of the per capita income differential between Europe and Spain,

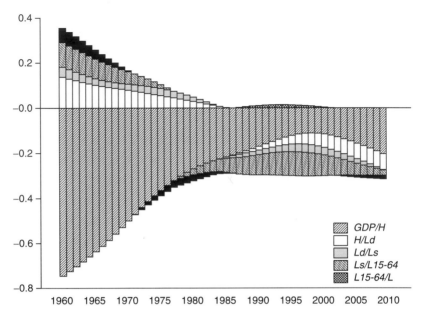

Figure 1.8 Logarithmic differences of determinants of per capita income in the EU-12 compared with the USA, 1960–2009

on the one hand, and the United States, on the other. However, from the mid-1970s onwards gains in productivity per hour were almost off-set by the poor performance of the European labour market (a decline in the activity rate and an increase in the unemployment rate). In the case of Spain, when the labour market began to improve in the mid-1990s, with an important increase in employment and activity rates, relative per capita income barely improved, because of the reduction in the number of hours per worker and, above all, because of the worse relative per-formance of productivity per hour. In the last few years up to 2009, productivity per hour worked in Europe explained half of the gap in per capita income with the United States. The rest of the gap is explained by the lower activity rate and in particular by the lower number of hours worked per employee.

To sum up, the Spanish economy has significantly reduced the per capita income gap with respect to the United States and the European Union over recent decades as a result of a highly significant decrease in the differential of productivity per hour worked, peaking in 1995. The positive trend in productivity in Spain since 1960 was mainly because of sectorial changes that gave rise to a more modern production structure (with agriculture becoming less important), an increase in productive capital and a process of technological diffusion over this period in which other nearby countries were also involved. Nevertheless, since the mid-1990s, productivity per hour in Spain has grown at a much lower rate than in the United States. As a result, the differential as regards the United States has widened again (reaching approximately 24 percentile points in 2009). The scope for improvement in terms of participation and working-age ratios is small (and depends almost entirely on the women's segment) now that European averages have been reached. For this reason the possibility of the Spanish economy continuing to progress in relative prosperity will depend mainly on two aspects. First, raising significantly the growth rates of productivity per hour worked; and, second, in view of the most recent evolution of the data, reducing once and for all its persistently higher unemployment rate.

1.3 The determinants of labour productivity

In this section we carry out an empirical analysis of the relative contribution of the classical determinants of labour productivity. This allows us to explain the importance of each of these factors to the observed productivity wedge with respect to Europe and the United States. As an initial approximation, productivity per hour worked can be decomposed into three elements: (1) the quantity and quality of physical capital; (2) the quantity and quality of human capital; and (3) total factor productivity (TFP), which proxies technological improvements. In order to analyse this new breakdown we shall assume, as is usual in the growth accounting literature, that the technology to produce goods and services in the economy is characterised by the following Cobb–Douglas type of production function:

$$Y_t = A_t \left(K_t\right)^{\alpha} \left(h_t L_t^d\right)^{1-\alpha} \exp\{\beta s_t\} \tag{1.3}$$

where Y_t is GDP, A_t is TFP, K_t is private productive physical capital, h_t is the number of hours worked by employed workers, L^d is the number of employed workers and s_t is human capital per worker, where β stands for the elasticity of output with respect to human capital stock. Assuming constant returns to scale on labour and private productive capital (that is, a 1 per cent increase in these factors increases output by exactly 1 per cent), productivity per hour worked can be written as a function of the private productive capital stock per hour worked and of human capital as follows:

$$\ln\left(\frac{Y_t}{h_t L_{dt}}\right) = \ln A_t + \alpha \ln\left(\frac{K_t}{h_t L_{dt}}\right) + \beta s_t \qquad (1.4)$$

Therefore the evolution of labour productivity analysed in the previous section depends positively on the level of TFP, the ratio of private productive capital to labour and the human capital endowment of workers.[7]

Private productive physical capital has been constructed by employing the method used by de la Fuente and Doménech (2010) and real rates of private productive investment have been taken from the June 2010 update of the OECD's Analytical Database. In the case of the countries for which there are data only from 1970 we have used the shares of private productive investment available in the work by Kamps (2006) for the previous years. The investment rate has been extrapolated backwards to 1950 with information from Penn World Tables 6.2, and the average shares in the 1960s of the three types of gross fixed capital formation (public and private productive and residential). Given that investment rates are used in real terms, changes in the relative prices of these types of goods are being included so that changes in the quality of investment goods are being incorporated at least in part. This is known as incorporated technical progress and so A_t measures technical progress not incorporated in capital goods. Moreover, investment rates (as well as the rest of the variables that are measured in real terms) are corrected for international differences in price levels as they are expressed in Purchasing Power Parity (PPP) terms. Therefore the resulting capital series allow not only an analysis of trends over time but also a comparison of levels across different countries.

Figure 1.9 illustrates the private productive capital per hour worked series for the period 1960–2009. As can be seen, the three economies increased their capital per hour worked considerably, especially up to the mid-1980s, but the process has been stronger in Spain and the European Union, which surpassed the United States from the 1980s–2000s. Blanchard (1997) argues that the different behaviour of the labour market in Europe as regards the United States, having more rigidities and institutions that give rise to a less flexible performance of employment and to more expensive labour costs, might have encouraged the use of more capital-intensive production processes. Figure 1.10, which represents the private productive capital to GDP ratio (K/Y), clearly reveals that both Europe and Spain need to use greater capital stock than the United States to obtain the same level of output. Nevertheless, this gap

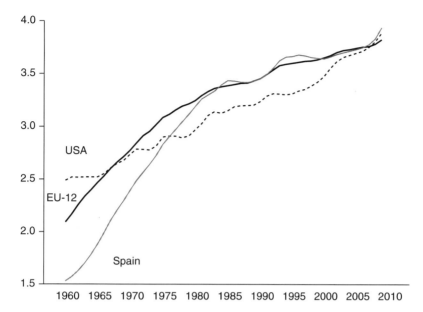

Figure 1.9 Private productive capital per hour worked (in logs), 1960–2009

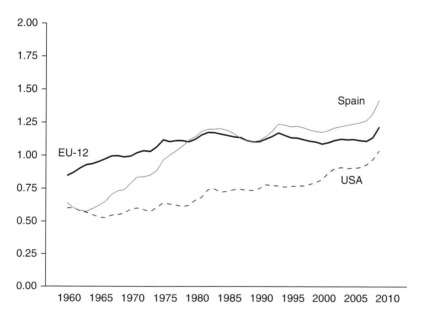

Figure 1.10 Private productive capital over GDP, 1960–2009

has been seen to narrow as a result of the substantial investment made in the United States in order to massively incorporate investment goods related to the new information and communication technologies (ICT) into its productive system. It is interesting to note that, after controlling for its countercyclical behaviour, the capital–output ratio has remained relatively stable since the mid-1980s. As we discuss in the next chapter, this stylised fact is particularly important in the calibration of our model.

Workers' human capital endowment (that is, the level of qualification of these workers) has been proxied by the years of schooling of the over-25 population in OECD countries. As can be seen in Figure 1.11, there has been a sizeable increase in the three areas considered, although the United States clearly ranks first.

However, Figure 1.12 reveals how the improvement in human capital endowment in Europe, and especially in Spain, has been much greater than in the United States. European human capital stands at the time of writing around 15 per cent below that of the United States, whereas at the beginning of the 1960s the gap exceeded 20 per cent. The Spanish case is more outstanding because only from the end of the dictatorship did the distance that existed in terms of education, between Spanish workers and those in the most advanced economies, begin to shorten.

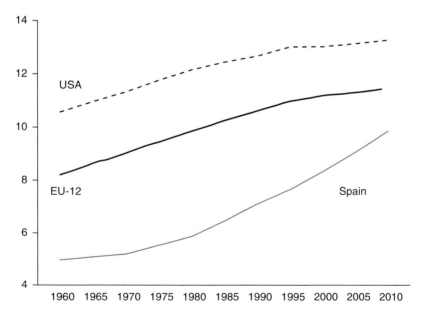

Figure 1.11   Years of schooling per adult (*S*), 1960–2009

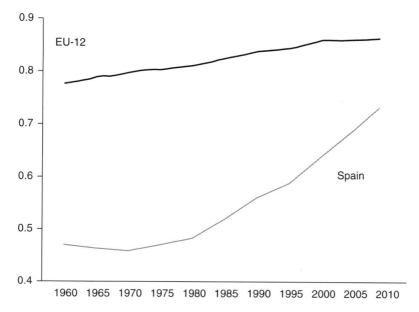

Figure 1.12 Years of schooling of adult population compared with the USA (S_i/S_{USA}), 1960–2009

Since then, convergence has accelerated, going from five years of average schooling at the beginning of the 1970s to more than nine years at the time of writing. Moreover, it can be emphasised that this convergence process has not been slowed by the marked influx of migrants into Spain during the 1990s/2000s. Immigrants went from representing less than 1 per cent of the population at the beginning of the 1990s to 10 per cent in 2006. In fact, statistics show that immigrants in Spain have a similar level of education to the native population. However, when comparing these immigrants with natives of the same age, it turns out that the latter have had more years of schooling. Therefore one of the challenges of Spanish society is to integrate immigrants accordingly and this, without any doubt, requires their level of education to be similar to that of Spaniards.

Once we have constructed these two variables (private productive capital stock and human capital), and bearing in mind productivity per hour as obtained in the previous section, we can now calibrate parameters α and β in Equation (1.4) to be able to calculate TFP as a residual. The first, elasticity of output with respect to private productive physical capital stock, equals the capital share in the economy's value added, assuming perfect competition in goods and factors markets. This ratio ranges between 30 per cent and 40 per cent in all developed countries. Here we make α equal to 0.36, the average of the three economic areas considered. In the case of the second parameter, the elasticity of output with respect to human capital stock, we have taken a value of 0.045 from the research by de la Fuente and Doménech (2006a).

Following this procedure, these three economic areas display trends in TFP. To be more precise, both Europe and Spain have recorded a marked convergence towards the United States, which has traditionally ranked first. However, the convergence process stopped towards the mid-1990s, coinciding with the process of incorporation of the new information and communication technologies into the production process. If we compare the Spanish experience, it has been even more unfavourable since then because, after having virtually converged with the United States, TFP then plummeted.

Empirical analysis initially suggested that the recent difference in the advance of technical progress between the United States and Europe was related to ICT sectors (which are characterised by their spectacular increases in productivity) representing a larger proportion of the productive framework in the United States. However, later studies suggest that the differentials in productivity growth between the two areas are not explained by the sectors producing ICT but rather by those that use these new technologies, in particular trade and financial services. From this perspective, European economies have exhibited some backwardness in incorporating these new technologies into the productive system. This could be a consequence of the greater rigidity shown by the labour market in Europe compared to the United States, and of the lower level of competition in its product markets. In particular, it appears to have been proved that, to maximise the impact on productivity of the incorporation of ICT into the production process in a firm, a profound reorganisation of the firm is needed and this usually requires the hiring and firing of workers. With regard to competitive environment in which businesses operate, different analyses of international organisms (see, for example, Nicoletti and Scarpetta, 2003) show that enterprises have more incentives to introduce product and process innovations the closer the markets where they sell their output are to free competition.

To bring this section to a conclusion, Figures 1.13 and 1.14 show the contributions of each of the determinants of labour productivity to the productivity gap between both Europe and Spain with respect to the United States, according to Equation (1.4). In this way we can identify the areas where there is more scope for improvement and those where more effort has to be made. In the case of the EU-12 approximately

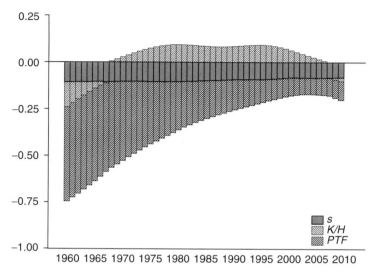

Figure 1.13   Contribution of private productive capital (*K/H*), human capital (*S*) and total factor productivity (*PTF*) to the labour productivity differential (*GDP/H*) of the EU compared with the USA, 1960–2009

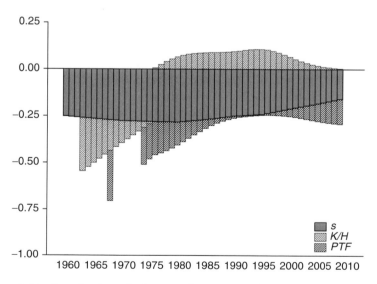

Figure 1.14   Contribution of private productive capital (*K/H*), human capital (*S*) and total factor produtivity (*PTF*) to the labour productivity differential (*GDP/H*) of Spain compared with the USA, 1960–2009

half of the productivity gap with the United States is explained by TFP and the rest by human capital. Regarding physical capital endowment per worker, there are no differences between the geographical areas. Therefore Europe should begin to consider taking the technological lead worldwide and concentrate its efforts in accumulating human capital in order to achieve convergence in living standards with those enjoyed by the citizens of the United States.

Spain appears to be an extreme case in Europe. With regard to TFP, convergence had been achieved in the past but the weak performance in productivity in the fifteen years has resulted in a clear margin for improvement. In the case of physical capital endowment per worker, a very favourable position has also been achieved. Nevertheless the widest gap, despite the improvement observed since the mid-1990s, is in the level of education of the adult population, which should be raised in the next few decades if Spain intends to stand in line with the most advanced countries in terms of productivity and welfare.

1.4   Cyclical regularities of the Spanish economy

The empirical implementation of the model we shall introduce in the next chapter needs to be consistent with the long-run features discussed in the previous sections, along with the cyclical regularities of the Spanish economy. To analyse these regularities, as is usually done in the empirical literature on business cycles, we rely on an extended set of quarterly variables instead of the annual variables previously analysed. Thus we have constructed a quarterly dataset for the Spanish economy from 1980Q1 to 2009Q4, the details of which are explained in Appendix 1. Thus, in this section, we document the cyclical properties of the main macroeconomic aggregates. As a robustness check, the cyclical properties obtained from these variables are compared with previous related contributions in the literature.

An initial and thorough description of the cyclical regularities of the Spanish economy was provided by Dolado *et al.* (1993). Puch and Licandro (1997) later carried out an update of second-moment properties of the data together with a revision of their balanced-growth patterns in a dynamic stochastic general equilibrium setting. Other authors have subsequently produced analyses of the cyclical patterns of Spanish macroeconomic aggregates in a Real Business Cycle framework, as reviewed by Lores (2001). The results presented here are comparable to those reported in this strand of the literature.

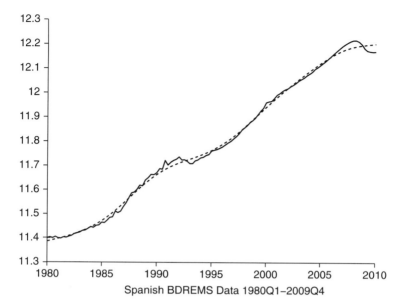

Figure 1.15 HP trend of GDP in logs

Figure 1.15 displays the Hodrick Prescott trend (dashed line) extracted from the logarithm of real GDP per capita over the period 1980–2009. As shown in previous sections, the evolution of this variable shows sustained growth over the whole time span at an average annual growth rate of 1.6 per cent. Three cycles are also detected, with corresponding peaks in 1992, 2001 and 2007. The recessions in 1993 and 2008–9 are also clearly seen in this figure.

Before going into the analysis of the business cycle, we can still obtain some conclusions related to several other features of the Spanish economy that should be taken into account in the calibration and estimation of the model presented in the next chapter. In particular, a refined analysis on the basis of the relevant ratios and growth rates describing the economic system precludes the hypothesis of the Spanish economy moving along its steady-state path before the mid-1980s. Several features observed in the data support this, as we have claimed earlier. First, hours worked per adult exhibit a marked downward trend until the mid-1980s (Figure 1.16). This is explained by an important reduction in the number of hours per worker during the 1970s (see Figure 1.5) that continues moderately at the begining of the 1980s and, to a lesser extent, by a decrease in the employment rate during the 1980s. Secondly, the capital–output

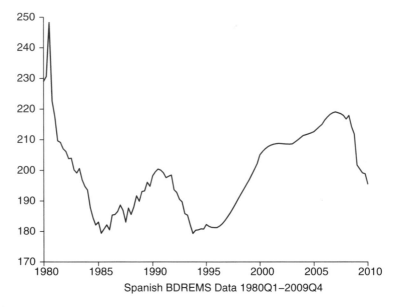

Figure 1.16   Hours per adult

ratio displays a marked upward trend before the 1980s (see Figure 1.10). In the last years of the sample, as shown by Figure 1.17, the increase in the capital–output ratio is explained by the rapid and intense fall of GDP at the end of 2008 and during 2009, whereas the fall in the invest-ment rate (after reaching a peak in 2007 equal to 31 per cent of GDP) translates slowly to the capital stock.[8] Third, the hypothesis that deep changes in the Spanish economy may be underlying heterogeneous pat-terns in the variables describing technology is reinforced by the vacancies series, whose long-run trend (Figure 1.18) parallels that observed in the capital–output ratio. Finally, while private consumption has been grow-ing hand-in-hand with GDP, investment has outpaced GDP, particularly in the years previous to the crisis in 2008–9. This pattern has been accompanied by a sustained increase in imports during this period.

Overall, from the mid-1980s onwards the growth rate of most macroe-conomic aggregates points to a movement of the Spanish economy around its balanced-growth path, were it not for the fact that the impact of increasing external openness since the 1980s has induced remark-able growth in the foreign sector, whereby the average rate of growth of exports and imports has risen to 6 per cent and 7.4 per cent, respectively.

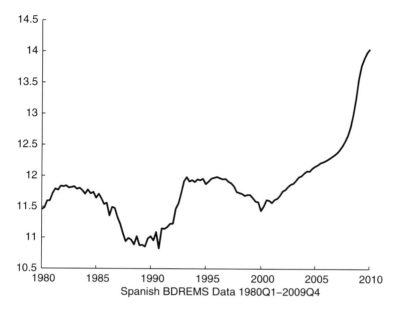

Figure 1.17   Capital–output ratio

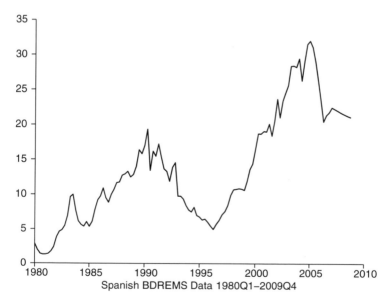

Figure 1.18   Vacancies per adult

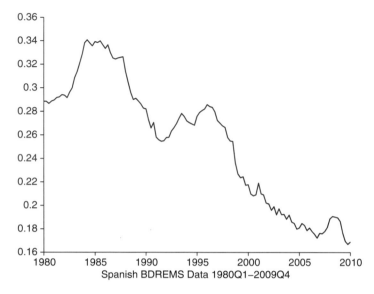
Spanish BDREMS Data 1980Q1–2009Q4

Figure 1.19   Money (M1) velocity

Similarly, a mild expansion has occurred in money aggregates, particularly when measured by means of more liquid assets (see, for example, Figure 1.19, where we represent the ratio of nominal GDP over M1), and less intense in the case of M3 measures.

As shown by Figure 1.20, the unemployment rate has exhibited very important fluctuations, reaching a maximum level close to 21 per cent in 1994. Since that year the Spanish economy reduced the unemployment rate significantly, to as low as 7 per cent in 2007, but the 2008–9 crisis has undone this improvement, with a rapid increase in the unemployment rate that in just two years increased to 20 per cent again. This evidence also corroborates the relevance of changes in the trend component of the unemployment rate, suggesting the need for a detailed and careful specification of the labour market in any model of the Spanish economy. Figure 1.21 confirms that the cyclical fluctuations of the unemployment rate are closely related to the output gap (the contemporaneous correlation between these variables is −0.878, as shown in Table 1.1), a result that is consistent with Okun's Law (see Doménech and Gómez, 2005, 2006, for a thorough analysis of this evidence).

Figures 1.22 to 1.25 plot the trend and the cycle components of GDP, private consumption, investment and public consumption, whereas the statistics describing the cyclical regularities displayed by the main

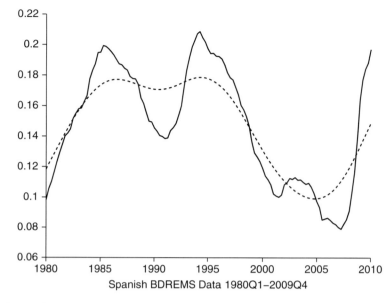

Figure 1.20 Unemployment rate and its trend (dotted line)

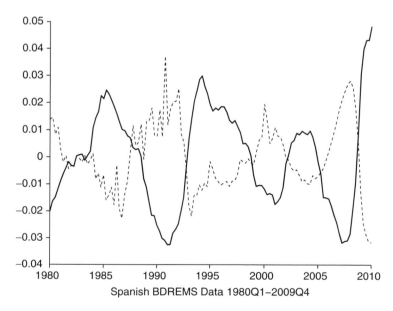

Figure 1.21 Cyclical unemployment (solid line) and output gap (dotted line)

Table 1.1 First and second moments (HP-filtered) properties of main macroeconomic aggregates, 1980–2009

	Levels (over GDP)	Annual rates of growth	Relative volatility (to GDP)	Cross-correlations of GDP in t with key aggregates in t − j					Auto-correlations
				x_{t-2}	x_{t-1}	x_t	x_{t+1}	x_{t+2}	x_{t-1}
GDP	1	0.0260	1*	0.755	0.852	1	0.827	0.703	0.930
Private consumption	0.6044	0.0242	1.1890	0.778	0.867	0.887			0.655
Government consumption	0.1711	0.0435	1.0356	0.253	0.362	0.441	0.398	0.365	0.911
Gross fixed capital formation	0.2353	0.0362	3.5296	0.788	0.852	0.870	0.768	0.661	0.607
Exports	0.2173	0.0604	2.6274	0.347	0.368	0.383	0.259	0.126	0.849
Imports	0.2318	0.0743	4.1420	0.775	0.805	0.787	0.686	0.561	0.991
Net exports	−0.0145	—	3.4429	−0.326	−0.335	−0.325	−0.343	−0.350	0.965
Capital stock	11.8201	0.0333	0.3849	0.098	0.277	0.463	0.577	0.659	0.719
Hours worked/adult	—	−0.0048	1.5809	0.629	0.699	0.754	0.719	0.659	0.789
Vacancies/adult	—	0.1584	16.7959	0.169	0.159	0.209	0.139	0.125	0.969
Unemployment rate	—	—	1.4321	−0.807	−0.869	−0.878	−0.826	−0.724	0.853
GDP deflator	—	0.0524	0.6653	−0.408	−0.289	−0.167	−0.120	−0.046	0.810
Energy price index	—	0.0533	4.6128	−0.089	−0.011	0.086	0.129	0.155	0.885
M1	3.7049	0.1061	2.7088	0.596	0.582	0.544	0.503	0.451	0.836
M1 velocity	—	−0.0165	2.4421	0.422	−0.322	−0.193	−0.207	−0.187	0.892
Debt	1.7982	0.1336	3.4446	−0.472	−0.616	−0.726	−0.758	−0.773	

24

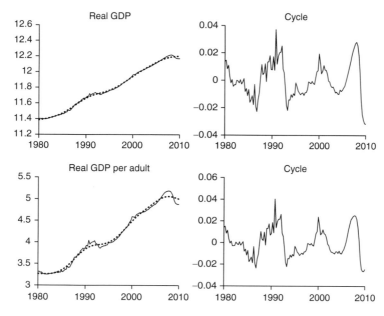

Figure 1.22 Trend and cycle decomposition of GDP and GDP per adult

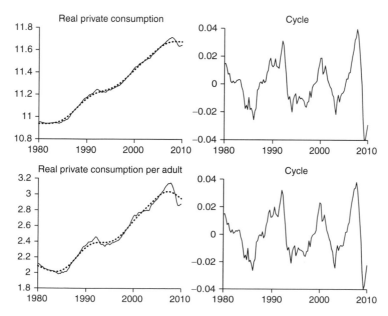

Figure 1.23 Trend and cycle components of private consumption (level and per adult)

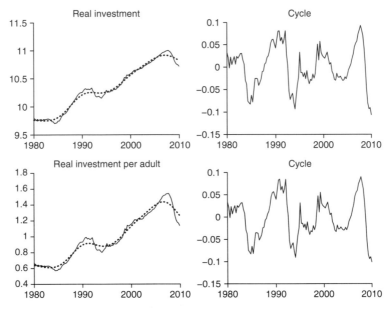

Figure 1.24   Trend and cycle components of investment (level and per adult)

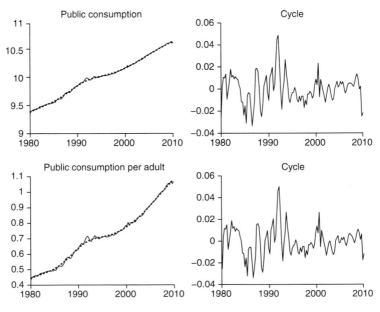

Figure 1.25   Trend and cycle components of public consumption (level and per adult)

macroeconomic variables from 1980 to 2009 are shown in Table 1.1. The regularities we obtain are comparable to other related studies on the short-term performance of the Spanish economy. Such regularities include the low volatility of Spanish GDP (1.29 per cent) compared with other industrialised economies, the relatively high volatility of private consumption – seemingly in contradiction with the life-cycle hypothesis – and the strong countercyclical behaviour of net exports. Also, in line with international evidence, vacancies shows rather volatile and persistent behaviour, whereas M1 and velocity are procyclical and prices appear to be countercyclical with the energy price index leading the cycle slightly. Finally, government debt exhibits a countercyclical pattern lagging behind the cycle. A look at cross-correlations unveils that the autocorrelation structure of the main aggregates is also in line with that reported in previous analyses of the same nature. Similar conclusions apply to the cross-correlations between the main aggregates and GDP.

1.5 Conclusions

In this chapter we have analysed both the long-run and cyclical features of the Spanish economy. With respect to the long run we have studied the main determinants of Spanish economic growth. We have shown that the evolution of per capita GDP depends on the productivity per hour worked, the number of hours worked by an occupied person, the employment rate, the participation rate and the age structure of the population. After studying how each component has evolved over time, the conclusion is that economic growth in Spain could be greatly improved by significantly raising the growth rate of productivity per hour worked and reducing the high unemployment rate reached at the end of 2009. We then turned to the study of the productivity determinants using a classical decomposition by venturing a Cobb–Douglas aggregate production function. The main conclusion is that the level of education of the adult population and total factor productivity are the key factors to be raised in the next few decades if Spain wishes to stand in line with the most advanced countries in terms of productivity and welfare.

The analysis of the main stylised facts of the Spanish business cycle shows characteristics of the cycle that are rather similar to those obtained by other related studies. To sum up the most important ones, we have found a low volatility of Spanish GDP compared with other industrialised economies, a relatively high volatility of private consumption, a strong countercyclical behaviour of net exports, a very high relative volatility of vacancies, and a countercyclical pattern of government debt that lags behind the output cycle.

Because of its descriptive nature in characterising the recent past of key macroeconomic aggregates of the Spanish economy, this chapter can be considered as the touchstone to provide policy guidelines for the near future, both for stabilising the business cycle in the short run and for promoting long-run growth. In this sense, in the following chapters we evaluate the effects of different demand and supply policies with a dynamic general equilibrium model carefully designed to deal with some of the Spanish economy's most important challenges.

Notes

1. In this chapter, data for the EU-12 refer to the EU-15 excluding Spain, Luxembourg and Portugal. The two latter countries, which represented just 2.1 of EU-15 GDP in 2006 purchasing power parities, are excluded from the sample because of the lack of data needed to build the time series of some of the variables used in the following sections. Spain is excluded in order to make more precise comparisons, avoiding the European aggregate being influenced by the performance of the Spanish economy, which accounted for 10.6 per cent of the EU-15 GDP in 2006 purchasing power parities. The database used in this chapter is an extension of the one constructed by de la Fuente and Doménech (2010). See Appendix 1 for further details and sources of the different variables.
2. The relationship between the current account deficit and productivity is conditioned by many factors so it cannot be unambiguously concluded that the external deficit is the result of a poor performance in productivity. For example, since the mid-1990s the United States has been one of the countries where productivity, as well as the current account deficit, increased the most as a consequence of the massive foreign capital inflows that sought the high yields generated by this increase in productivity. As pointed out by Barro *et al.* (1995) among others, the increase in the current account deficit is the logical consequence of a per capita income convergence process. A good example of such a process is the high foreign deficit in the majority of new EU members following the last few enlargements. In the case of Spain, Campa and Gavilán (2006) estimate that future growth expectations of the Spanish economy explained nearly two-thirds of the foreign deficit in 2005.
3. See, for example, the works by Jimeno and Sánchez (2006), Estrada and López Salido (2004b), Hernando and Núñez (2004), de la Fuente (2002), Pérez *et al.* (2006), de la Fuente and Doménech (2010), and Doménech and García (2010), as well as the references included therein.
4. Figure 1.1 also represents the trend component of relative per capita GDP. This variable has been calculated as the ratio of trend components of per capita GDP in each economy using the Hodrick–Prescott filter, with a smoothing parameter equal to 50. It is advisable to use the trend in order to correct the cyclical swings that affect every economy. Even if the different synchronous character of fluctuations is of little relevance when making long-run comparisons, it could be

important when we try to draw conclusions for shorter periods affected by the economic cycle, as, for example, in 2009. A more structural analysis of the effects of the recent economic crisis on potential growth is done by BBVA (2009c).

5. The economic consequences of immigration on the Spanish economy have been studied by the Economic Bureau of the Prime Minister (2006), Izquierdo and Jimeno (2005), Izquierdo *et al.* (2010), and Conde-Ruiz *et al.* (2008) among others.

6. Bentolila and Jimeno (2006) and the references in their paper are an excellent starting point for understanding how unemployment rates have varied over time in Spain.

7. In relation to this expression, Caselli (2005) performs a sensitivity analysis of growth accounting exercises to the measurement of productive factors, the sectorial composition and the neutrality of total factor productivity.

8. It is worth noting that the capital stock in Figure 1.10 refers only to private business capital, therefore excluding public capital and the residential capital stock. These two types of capital are included in Figure 1.17, where the housing boom during the last expansion is also responsible for the huge increase in the capital–output ratio.

2
REMS: A Rational Expectations Model for Simulation and Policy Evaluation of the Spanish Economy

J. E. Boscá, A. Díaz, R. Doménech, J. Ferri, E. Pérez and L. Puch

2.1 Introduction

REMS is a small open economy dynamic general equilibrium (DGE) model that attempts to feature the main characteristics of the Spanish economy. It builds on the existing literature on macroeconomic models.[1] The model is primarily intended to serve as a simulation tool for the Spanish Ministry of Economic and Financial Affairs, with a focus on the economic impact of alternative policy measures over the medium term. The most valuable asset of REMS is the rigour of the analysis of the transmission channels linking policy options to economic outcomes.

The small open economy assumption implies that a number of foreign variables are given from the perspective of the national economy, and that the magnitude of spillover effects is small. This modelling choice seems to us to be a fair compromise between realism and tractability.

REMS is in the tradition of DGE models. As such, it departs from MOISEES[2] in a number of modelling routes. Equations in the model are derived explicitly from intertemporal optimisation by representative households and firms under technological, budgetary and institutional constraints. Thus economic decisions are solidly micro-founded and any ad hoc dynamics have been avoided. Unlike the traditional Keynesian approach adopted in MOISEES, with backward-looking behaviour strongly focused on the demand side of the economy, REMS is a New Neoclassical–Keynesian synthesis model. Behaviour is predominantly forward-looking, and short-term dynamics are embedded in a neoclassical growth model that determines economic developments over the long run. However, as markets do not generally work in a competitive fashion, the levels of employment and economic activity will be lower than those that would prevail in a competitive setting.

In the short run, REMS incorporates nominal, real and financial frictions. Real frictions include adjustment costs in consumption (via the incorporation into the model of consumption habits and rule-of-thumb households) and investment into physical capital. Because of financial frictions, there is no perfect arbitrage between different types of assets. The model also allows for slow adjustment in wages and price rigidities, which are specified through a Calvo-type Phillips curve. All these modelling choices are pretty much in line with other existing models for the Spanish economy. The main contribution of REMS to this renewed vintage of dynamic (stochastic) general equilibrium (D(S)GE) models is the specification of the labour market according to the search paradigm. This approach has proved to be successful in providing micro-foundations for equilibrium unemployment in the long run, and accounting for both the extensive and intensive margins of employment at business-cycle frequencies. It is therefore best suited to the assessment of welfare policies having an impact on the labour market.

The model is parameterised using Spanish data. To this end, a database (REMSDB[3]) has been prepared that satisfies the estimation and calibration requirements of the model and is suitable for generating a baseline scenario for REMS.

The chapter is organised as follows. Section 2.2 details the theoretical model. Section 2.3 discusses the calibration strategy. Section 2.4 shows the properties of the model by analysing the basic transmission channels following standard simulations. Section 2.5 presents the main conclusions.

2.2 Theoretical framework

We model a decentralised, small open economy where households, firms, policy-makers and the external sector actively interact in each period by trading one final good, n differentiated intermediate goods, government bonds, two primary production factors and one intermediate input. Households are the owners of the available production factors and all the firms operating in the economy. Thus households rent physical capital and labour services out to firms, for which they are paid interest, income and wages. In the final goods sector, firms produce goods that are imperfect substitutes for goods produced abroad. The intermediate sector is composed of monopolistically competitive firms that produce intermediate varieties employing capital, labour and energy. Job creation is costly in terms of time and real resources. Thus pure economic rent arises from each job match over which the worker and the firm negotiate in an efficient-bargaining manner.

Each period, the government faces a budget constraint where overall expenditure is financed by debt issuance and various distortionary taxes. Intertemporal sustainability of fiscal balance is ensured by a conventional policy reaction function, whereby a lump-sum transfer accommodates the deviation of the debt-to-GDP ratio from its target level.

Monetary policy is managed by the European Central Bank (ECB) via a Taylor rule, which allows for some smoothing of the interest rate response to the inflation and output gap.

Each household is made up of working-age members who may be either active or inactive. In turn, active workers participating in the labour market may either be employed or unemployed. Unemployed workers are actively searching for a job. Firm investment in vacant posts is endogenously determined and so are job inflows. Finally, job destruction is taken as exogenous.

2.2.1   Consumption behaviour

A large body of empirical literature documents substantial deviations of consumption from the permanent-income hypothesis. To account for this evidence, we incorporate liquidity-constrained consumers into the standard Keynesian model along the lines of Galí et al. (2007). The household sector consists of a continuum of households of size N_t. A number N_t^o of these households have unlimited access to capital markets where they can buy and sell government bonds and accumulate physical capital. These financial transactions enable non-liquidity constrained households to smooth consumption intertemporally in response to changes in the economic environment. The superscript 'o' stands for 'optimising consumers'. The remaining N_t^r households is liquidity constrained. These households cannot trade in financial and physical assets and consume out of their disposable income each period. The superscript 'r' stands for 'rule-of-thumb (RoT) consumers'. The size of the working-age population is given by $N_t = N_t^o + N_t^r$. Let $1 - \lambda^r$ and λ^r denote the shares of optimising and RoT consumers in the working-age population. Working-age population, optimising and RoT consumers all grow at the exogenous (gross) rate of $\gamma_N = N_t/N_{t-1}$, implying that λ^r is constant over time.

Let $\overline{A}_t$ represent the trend component of total factor productivity at time t, which will be assumed to grow at the exogenous rate of $\gamma_A = \overline{A}_t/\overline{A}_{t-1}$. Balanced growth in the model can be ensured by transforming variables in a convenient way. More specifically, any flow or stock variable X_t is made stationary through $x_t \equiv X_t/\overline{A}_t N_t$.

Following Andolfatto (1996) and Merz (1995), we assume that households pool their income and distribute it evenly among its members. This allows household members to fully insure each other against fluctuations in employment.

2.2.2 Optimising households

Ricardian households face the following maximisation programme:

$$
\max_{\substack{c_t, j_t, k_{t+1}, \\ b^o_{t+1}, b^{o,emu}_{t+1}, m^o_t}} E_t \sum_{t=0}^{\infty} \beta^t \left[\begin{array}{l} \ln\left(c^o_t - h^o c^o_{t-1}\right) + n^o_t \phi_1 \frac{(T-l_{1t})^{1-\eta}}{1-\eta} \\ + (1-n^o_t)\phi_2 \frac{(T-l_{2t})^{1-\eta}}{1-\eta} + \chi_m \ln\left(m^o_t\right) \end{array} \right] \tag{2.1}
$$

subject to

$$
\left(r_t(1-\tau^k_t) + \tau^k_t \delta\right) k^o_t + w_t\left(1-\tau^l_t\right)\left(n^o_t l_{1t} + \overline{rr}s(1-n^o_t)l_{2t}\right)
$$

$$
+ \left(\left(1-\tau^l_t\right)g_{st} - trh_t\right) + \frac{m^o_{t-1}}{1+\pi^c_t} + (1+r^n_t)\frac{b^o_t}{1+\pi^c_t} + (1+r^{emu}_t)\frac{b^{o,emu}_t}{1+\pi^c_t}
$$

$$
- (1+\tau^c_t)c^o_t \frac{P^c_t}{P_t} - \frac{P^i_t}{P_t} j^o_t \left(1 + \frac{\phi}{2}\left(\frac{j^o_t}{k^o_t}\right)\right) - \gamma_A \gamma_N \left(m^o_t + b^o_{t+1} + \frac{b^{o,emu}_{t+1}}{\phi_{bt}}\right) = 0 \tag{2.2}
$$

$$
\gamma_A \gamma_N k^o_{t+1} = j^o_t + (1-\delta)k^o_t \tag{2.3}
$$

$$
\gamma_N n^o_{t+1} = (1-\sigma)n^o_t + \rho^w_t s(1-n^o_t) \tag{2.4}
$$

$$
k^o_0, n^o_0, b^o_0, b^{ow}_0, m^o_0 \tag{2.5}
$$

c^o_t, n^o_t and $s(1-n^o_t)$ represent, consumption, the employment rate and the unemployment rate of optimising households; s is the (exogenous) share of the non-employed workers actively searching for jobs;[4] T, l_{1t} and l_{2t} are total endowment of time, hours worked per employee and hours devoted to job search by the unemployed; l_{1t} is determined jointly by the firm and the worker as part of the same Nash bargaining that is used to determine wages (see Section 2.4); l_{2t} is assumed to be a function of overall economic activity, so that individual households take it as given.[5]

There are a number of preference parameters defining the utility function of optimising households. Future utility is discounted at a rate of $\beta \in (0,1)$. The parameter η defines the Frisch elasticity of labour supply, which is equal to $\frac{1}{\eta}$; $h^o > 0$ indicates that consumption is subject to habits. The subjective value imputed to leisure by workers may vary with employment status, and thus $\phi_1 \neq \phi_2$ in general.

For simplicity, we adopt the money-in-the-utility function approach to incorporate money into the model. The timing implicit in this specification assumes that this variable is the household's real money holdings at the beginning of period ($m_t^o = \frac{M_t^o}{P_t A_t N_t^o}$ where P_t is the aggregate price level). Thus, after having purchased consumption goods, this yields utility.[6]

The maximisation of Equation (2.1) is constrained as follows. The budget constraint in Equation (2.2) describes the various sources and uses of income. The term $w_t \left(1 - \tau^l\right) n_t^o l_{1t}$ captures net labour income earned by the fraction of employed workers, where w_t stands for hourly real wages. The product $\bar{\pi} w_t \left(1 - \tau^l\right) s \left(1 - n_t^o\right) l_{2t}$ measures unemployment benefits accruing to the unemployed, where $\bar{\pi}$ denotes the replacement rate of the unemployment subsidy to the market wage. Ricardian households hold four kinds of assets, namely private physical capital (k_t^o), domestic and euro-zone bonds (b_t^o and b_t^{ow}), and money balances (M_t^o). Apart from money, the remaining assets yield some remuneration. As reflected in $r_t k_t^o (1 - \tau^k) + \tau^k \delta k_t^o$, optimising households pay capital income taxes less depreciation allowances after their earnings on physical capital. Interest payments on domestic and foreign debt are captured respectively by $r_t^n \frac{b_t^o}{1+\pi_t^c}$, and $r_t^{emu} \frac{b_t^{ow}}{1+\pi_t^c}$, where r^n and r^{emu} represent the nominal interest rates on domestic and EMU bonds, which differ because of a risk premium (see further below). The remaining two sources of revenues are lump-sum transfers, trh_t, and other government transfers, g_{st}.

Household consumption is given by $(1 + \tau^c) \frac{P_t^c}{P_t} c_t^o$, where τ^c is consumption income tax. Investment into physical capital, which is affected by increasing marginal costs of installation, is captured by $\frac{P_t^i}{P_t} j_t^o \left(1 + \frac{\phi}{2} \left(\frac{j_t}{k_t}\right)\right)$. Note that the presence in the model of the relative prices P_t^c/P_t and P_t^i/P_t implies that a distinction is made between the three deflators of consumption, investment and aggregate output.

The remaining constraints faced by Ricardian households concern the laws of motion for capital and employment. In each period the private capital stock k_t^o depreciates at the exogenous rate δ and is accumulated through investment, j_t^o. Thus it evolves according to Equation (2.3). Employment obeys the law of motion Equation (2.4), where n_t^o and $s(1 - n_t^o)$ respectively denote the share of employed and unemployed optimising workers in the economy at the beginning of period t.

Each period, employment is destroyed at the exogenous rate σ and new employment opportunities appear at the rate ρ_t^w, which represents the probability that one unemployed worker will find a job. While the job-finding rate ρ_t^w is taken as given by individual workers, it is determined endogenously at aggregate level according to the following Cobb–Douglas matching function[7]:

$$\rho_t^w s(1 - n_t) = \vartheta_t \left(v_t, n_t\right) = \chi_1 v_t^{\chi_2} \left[s\left(1 - n_t\right) l_{2t}\right]^{1-\chi_2} \tag{2.6}$$

Finally, $k_0^o, n_0^o, b_0^o, b_0^{o,emu}, m_0^o$ in Equation (2.5) represents the initial conditions for all stock variables entering the maximisation problem.

Given the recursive structure of this problem, it may be rewritten equivalently in terms of a dynamic programme. Thus the value function $W(\Omega_t^o)$ satisfies the following Bellman equation:

$$W(\Omega_t^o) = \max_{\substack{c_t, j_t, k_{t+1}, \\ b_{t+1}^o, b_{t+1}^{o,emu}, m_t^o}} \left\{ \begin{array}{l} \ln\left(c_t^o - h^o c_{t-1}^o\right) + n_t^o \phi_1 \dfrac{(T - l_{1t})^{1-\eta}}{1 - \eta} + (1 - n_t^o)\phi_2 \dfrac{(T - l_{2t})^{1-\eta}}{1 - \eta} \\ + \chi_m \ln\left(m_t^o\right) + \beta E_t W(\Omega_{t+1}^o) \end{array} \right\} \tag{2.7}$$

where maximisation is subject to the constraints in Equations (2.2) to (2.4).

The solution to the optimisation programme above generates the following first-order conditions for consumption, investment, capital stock, government debt foreign debt and money holdings:

$$\lambda_{1t}^o = \frac{1}{(P_t^c/P_t)(1 + \tau_t^c)} \left(\frac{1}{c_t^o - h^o c_{t-1}^o} - \beta \frac{h^o}{c_{t+1}^o - h^o c_t^o} \right) \tag{2.8}$$

$$\gamma_A \gamma_N \frac{\lambda_{2t}^o}{\lambda_{1t}^o} = \beta E_t \frac{\lambda_{1t+1}^o}{\lambda_{1t}^o} \left\{ \left[r_{t+1}(1 - \tau_{t+1}^k) + \tau_{t+1}^k \delta \right] \right. $$
$$\left. + \frac{\phi}{2} \frac{P_{t+1}^i}{P_{t+1}} \frac{j_{t+1}^{o2}}{k_{t+1}^{o2}} + \frac{\lambda_{2t+1}^o}{\lambda_{1t+1}^o}(1 - \delta) \right\} \tag{2.9}$$

$$\lambda_{2t}^o = \lambda_{1t}^o \frac{P_t^i}{P_t} \left[1 + \phi\left(\frac{j_t^o}{k_t^o}\right) \right] \tag{2.10}$$

$$\gamma_A \gamma_N E_t \frac{\lambda_{1t}^o}{\lambda_{1t+1}^o} = \beta E_t \frac{1 + r_t^n}{1 + \pi_{t+1}^c} \tag{2.11}$$

$$\gamma_A \gamma_N \lambda_{1t}^o \frac{1}{\phi_{bt}} = \beta E_t \frac{\lambda_{1t+1}^o (1 + r_t^{emu})}{1 + \pi_{t+1}^c} \tag{2.12}$$

$$\frac{\chi_m}{m_t^o} = \gamma_A \gamma_N \lambda_{1t}^o \frac{r_t^n}{1 + r_t^n} \tag{2.13}$$

as well as the three household restrictions in Equations (2.2), (2.3) and (2.4).

Because of the presence of consumption habits, Equation (2.8) evaluates the current-value shadow price of income in terms of the difference between the marginal utility of consumption in two consecutive periods t and $t + 1$.

Expression (2.9) ensures that the intertemporal reallocation of capital cannot improve household utility. $\frac{\lambda_{2t}^o}{\lambda_{1t}^o}$ denotes the current-value shadow price of capital. This arbitrage condition includes two terms. The first term represents the present discounted value of its cash-flow in $t + 1$, defined as the sum of rental cost net of taxes, depreciation allowances and total adjustment costs evaluated in terms of consumption. The second term represents the present value in $t + 1$ of an additional unit of productive capital corrected for the depreciation rate.

Equation (2.10) states that investment is undertaken until the opportunity cost of a marginal increase in investment in terms of consumption is equal to its marginal expected contribution to household utility.

The marginal utility of consumption evolves according to Equation (2.11), which is obtained by deriving the Lagrangian with respect to domestic government bonds b_{t+1}^o. Equations (2.11) and (2.8) jointly yield the Euler condition for consumption.

Equation (2.12) is obtained by deriving the Lagrangian with respect to foreign debt $b_{t+1}^{o,emu}$. Note that the specification above assumes that there is no perfect arbitrage between domestic and foreign bonds. This line is taken in Turnovsky (1985), Benigno (2001), Schmitt-Grohe and Uribe (2003) or Erceg *et al.* (2005), as a way of ensuring that net foreign assets are stationary. When taking a position in the international bonds market, optimising households face a financial intermediation risk premium (ϕ_{bt}) which depends on net holdings of internationally traded bonds. The risk premium is therefore modelled as follows

$$\ln \phi_{bt} = -\phi_b \left(\exp \left(b_t^{o,emu} \right) - 1 \right) \tag{2.14}$$

The rest of the section simply rearranges first-order conditions to facilitate the economic interpretation of Ricardian household behaviour. To obtain the arbitrage relationship between domestic and foreign bonds we combine Equation (2.12) with Equations (2.11). This algebra yields

$$1 + r_t^n = \phi_{bt}(1 + r_t^{nw}) \tag{2.15}$$

which is the interest parity condition modified to incorporate the effect of the risk premium. Note also that Equation (2.15) differs from the standard uncovered interest parity condition in that there is no risk associated with exchange rate movements, as both domestic and foreign bonds are expressed in the same currency.[8]

To obtain the arbitrage relationship between physical capital and government bonds it is convenient to define $q_t \equiv \lambda_{2t}^o / \lambda_{1t}^o$, which allows us to rewrite Equation (2.9) as

$$q_t = \frac{1 + \pi_{t+1}^c}{1 + r_t^n} \left[r_{t+1}(1 - \tau_{t+1}^k) + \tau_{t+1}^k \delta + \frac{P_{t+1}^i}{P_{t+1}} \frac{\phi}{2} \frac{j_{t+1}^2}{k_{t+1}^2} + q_{t+1}(1 - \delta) \right] \tag{2.16}$$

This is a Fisher-type condition in a context characterised by adjustment costs of installation of physical capital. To see this more clearly let $\phi = 0$, implying that the investment process is not subject to any installation costs. In this case, Equation (2.10) simplifies to $q_t = q_{t+1} = 1$ and Equation (2.16) becomes

$$E_t \left[1 + (r_{t+1} - \delta)\left(1 - \tau^k\right) \right] = E_t \left(\frac{1 + r_{t+1}^n}{1 + \pi_{t+1}^c} \right) \tag{2.17}$$

which is the conventional Fisher parity condition.

Finally, Equation (2.13) can easily be rewritten as a money demand function by using the current-value shadow price of income in Equation (2.8):

$$m_t^o = \frac{1}{\gamma_A \gamma_N} \chi_m \left(1 + \tau_t^c\right) \frac{P_t^c}{P_t} \frac{1 + r_t^n}{r_t^n} \frac{1}{\left(\frac{1}{c_t^o - hc_{t-1}^o} - \beta \frac{h}{c_{t+1}^o - hc_t^o} \right)} \tag{2.18}$$

Now it is convenient to derive the marginal value of employment for a worker $\left(\frac{\partial W_t^o}{\partial n_t^o} \equiv \lambda_{ht}^o \right)$, given that later we shall use it to obtain the wage and hours equation in the bargaining process.

$$\lambda_{ht}^o = \lambda_{1t}^o w_t \left(1 - \tau_l^l\right)(l_{1t} - \overline{rr}sl_{2t}) + \left(\phi_1 \frac{(1 - l_{1t})^{1-\eta}}{1 - \eta} - \phi_2 \frac{(1 - l_{2t})^{1-\eta}}{1 - \eta}\right)$$

$$+ (1 - \sigma - \rho_t^w)\beta E_t \frac{\partial W_{t+1}^o}{\partial n_{t+1}} \tag{2.19}$$

where λ_{ht}^o measures the marginal contribution of a newly created job to household utility. The first term captures the value of the cash-flow generated by the new job in t; that is, labour income measured according to its utility value in terms of consumption (λ_{1t}^o). The second term on the right-hand side of Equation (2.19) represents the net utility arising from the newly created job–that is, the difference between the value imputed to leisure by an employed and an unemployed worker. Finally, the third term represents the 'capital value' of an additional employed worker, given that the employment status will persist into the future, conditional to the probability that the new job will not be destroyed.

Rule-of-thumb households

RoT households do not have access to capital markets, so that they face the following maximisation programme:

$$\max_{c_t^r} E_t \sum_{t=0}^{\infty} \beta^t \left[\ln\left(c_t^r - h^r c_{t-1}^r\right) + n_t^r \phi_1 \frac{(T - l_{1t})^{1-\eta}}{1 - \eta} \right.$$

$$\left. + (1 - n_t^r)\phi_2 \frac{(T - l_{2t})^{1-\eta}}{1 - \eta} \right]$$

subject to the law of motion of employment in Equation (2.21) and the specific liquidity constraint whereby the consumption expenditure in each period must be equal to current labour income and government transfers, as reflected in:

$$w_t \left(1 - \tau_t^l\right)(n_t^r l_{1t} + \overline{rr}s(1 - n_t^r)l_{2t}) + g_{st}\left(1 - \tau_t^l\right) - trh_t - (1 + \tau_t^c)c_t^r \frac{P_t^c}{P_t} = 0 \tag{2.20}$$

$$\gamma_N n_{t+1}^r = (1 - \sigma)n_t^r + \rho_t^w s(1 - n_t^r) \tag{2.21}$$

$$n_0^r \tag{2.22}$$

where n_0^r represents the initial aggregate employment rate, which is the sole stock variable in the above programme. Note that RoT consumers do not save, thus they do not hold any assets.

In this case, the value function $W(\Omega_t^r)$ satisfies the following Bellman equation:

$$
W(\Omega_t^r) = \max_{c_t^r} \left\{ \ln\left(c_t^r - hc_{t-1}^r\right) + n_t^r \phi_1 \frac{(1 - l_{1t})^{1-\eta}}{1 - \eta} \right.
$$

$$
\left. + (1 - n_t^r)\phi_2 \frac{(1 - l_{2t})^{1-\eta}}{1 - \eta} + \beta E_t W(\Omega_{t+1}^r) \right\} \tag{2.23}
$$

where maximisation is subject to the constraints in Equations (2.20) and (2.21).

The solution to the optimisation programme is characterised by the following first-order condition:

$$
\lambda_{1t}^r = \frac{1}{(P_t^c/P_t)c_t^r(1 + \tau_t^c)} \left(\frac{1}{c_t^r - h^r c_{t-1}^r} - \beta \frac{h^r}{c_{t+1}^r - h^r c_t^r} \right) \tag{2.24}
$$

The marginal value of employment for a consumption-restricted worker ($\frac{\partial W_t^r}{\partial n_t^r} \equiv \lambda_{ht}^r$) can be obtained as,

$$
\lambda_{ht}^r = \lambda_{1t}^r w_t \left(1 - \tau_l^l\right)(l_{1t} - \overline{rr}sl_{2t}) + \left(\phi_1 \frac{(1 - l_{1t})^{1-\eta}}{1 - \eta} - \phi_2 \frac{(1 - l_{2t})^{1-\eta}}{1 - \eta} \right)
$$

$$
+ (1 - \sigma - \rho_t^w)\beta E_t \frac{\partial W_{t+1}^r}{\partial n_{t+1}} \tag{2.25}
$$

whose interpretation is analogous to that of optimising households.

It is worth mentioning that the optimising behaviour of RoT households preserves to some extent the dynamic nature of the model, as a result of consumption habits and the dynamic nature of the employment decision.

Aggregation

Aggregate consumption and employment can be defined as a weighted average of the corresponding variables for each household type:

$$
c_t = \left(1 - \lambda^r\right)c_t^o + \lambda^r c_t^r \tag{2.26}
$$

$$
n_t = \left(1 - \lambda^r\right)n_t^o + \lambda^r n_t^r \tag{2.27}
$$

For the variables that concern Ricardian households exclusively, aggregation is performed as:

$$k_t = \left(1 - \lambda^r\right) k_t^o \tag{2.28}$$

$$j_t = \left(1 - \lambda^r\right) j_t^o \tag{2.29}$$

$$b_t = \left(1 - \lambda^r\right) b_t^o \tag{2.30}$$

$$b_t^{emu} = \left(1 - \lambda^r\right) b_t^{oemu} \tag{2.31}$$

$$m_t = \left(1 - \lambda^r\right) m_t^o \tag{2.32}$$

2.2.3   Factor demands

Production in the economy takes place at two different levels. At the lower level, an infinite number of monopolistically competing firms produce differentiated intermediate goods y_i, which imperfectly substitute each other in the production of the final good. These differentiated goods are then aggregated by competitive retailers into a final domestic good (y) using a CES aggregator.

Intermediate producers solve a two-stage problem. In the first stage, each firm faces a cost minimisation problem, which results in optimal demands for production factors. When choosing optimal streams of capital, energy, employment and vacancies, intermediate producers set prices by varying the mark-up according to demand conditions. Variety producer $i \in (0, 1)$ uses three inputs: namely, a CES composite input of private capital and energy, labour and public capital. Technology possibilities are given by:

$$y_{it} = z_{it} \left\{ \left[ak_{it}^{-\rho} + (1-a)e_{it}^{-\rho} \right]^{-\frac{1}{\rho}} \right\}^{1-\alpha} (n_{it}l_{i1t})^{\alpha} \left(k_{it}^p \right)^{\zeta} \tag{2.33}$$

where all variables are scaled by the trend component of total factor productivity and z_t represents a transitory technology shock. Each variety producer rents physical capital, k_t, and labour services, $n_t l_{1t}$, from households, and uses public capital services, k_t^p, provided by the government. Intermediate energy inputs e_t can either be imported from abroad or produced at home. The elasticity of substitution between private capital and energy is given by $\frac{1}{1+\rho}$ where $a \in (0, 1)$ is a distribution parameter which determines relative factor shares in the steady state. For the sake of clarity, let us denote capital services by k_{iet} as:

$$k_{iet} = \left[ak_{it}^{-\rho} + (1-a)e_{it}^{-\rho} \right]^{-\frac{1}{\rho}} \tag{2.34}$$

Note that if $\rho = 0$, Equation (2.34) simplifies to the Cobb–Douglas case. Our specification is more general–that is, private capital and energy can be seen as either complements ($\rho > 0$) or more substitutes than Cobb Douglas ($\rho < 0$), depending on the value of ρ. Our calibration strategy will nevertheless pin down the value of ρ to ensure that the elasticity of substitution between private capital and energy is smaller than the elasticity of substitution between the capital–energy composite and labour.

Factor demands are obtained by solving the cost minimisation problem faced by each variety producer (we drop the industry index i when no confusion arises)

$$\min_{k_t,v_t,e_t} E_t \sum_{t=0}^{\infty} \beta^t \frac{\lambda^0_{1t+1}}{\lambda^0_{1t}} \left(r_t k_t + w_t \left(1 + \tau^{sc}\right) n_t l_{1t} + \kappa_v v_t + \frac{P^e_t}{P_t} e_t \left(1 + \tau^e\right) \right)$$

(2.35)

subject to

$$y_t = z_{it} \left(\left[a k_t^{-\rho} + (1-a) e_t^{-\rho} \right]^{-\frac{1}{\rho}} \right)^{1-\alpha} (n_t l_{1t})^\alpha \left(k_t^p \right)^\zeta$$

(2.36)

$$\gamma_N n_{t+1} = (1-\sigma) n_t + \rho^f_t v_t$$

(2.37)

$$n_0$$

(2.38)

where, in accordance with the ownership structure of the economy, future profits are discounted at the household relevant rate $\beta \frac{\lambda^0_{1t+1}}{\lambda^0_{1t}}$, κ_v captures recruiting costs per vacancy, τ^{sc} is the social security tax rate levied on gross wages, and ρ^f_t is the probability that a vacancy will be filled in any given period t. It is worth noting that the probability of filling a vacant post ρ^f_t is taken exogenously by the firm. However, from the perspective of the overall economy, this probability is determined endogenously according to the following Cobb–Douglas matching function:

$$\rho^w_t s(1 - n_{t-1}) = \rho^f_t v_t = \chi_1 v_t^{\chi_2} \left[s(1 - n_t) l_{2t} \right]^{1-\chi_2}$$

(2.39)

Proceeding as we did with workers, we can express the maximum expected value of the firm in state Ω^f_t as a function $V(\Omega^f_t)$ that satisfies the following Bellman equation:

$$V(\Omega_t^f) = \max_{k_t, v_t, e_t} \left\{ y_t - r_t k_t - w_t \left(1 + \tau^{sc}\right) n_t l_{1t} - \kappa_v v_t + \beta E_t \frac{\lambda_{1t+1}^o}{\lambda_{1t}^o} V(\Omega_{t+1}^f) \right\}$$

(2.40)

Under the assumption of symmetry, the solution to the optimisation programme above generates the following first-order conditions for private capital, energy and number of vacancies

$$r_t = (1 - \alpha) mc_t \frac{y_t}{ke_t} a \left(\frac{ke_t}{k_t} \right)^{1+\rho}$$

(2.41)

$$(1 - \alpha)(1 - a) mc_t \frac{y_t}{ke_t} \left(\frac{ke_t}{e_t} \right)^{1+\rho} = \frac{P_t^e}{P_t} (1 + \tau_t^e)$$

(2.42)

$$\frac{\kappa_v}{\rho_t^f} = \beta E_t \frac{\lambda_{1t+1}^o}{\lambda_{1t}^o} \frac{\partial V_{t+1}}{\partial n_{t+1}}$$

(2.43)

where the real marginal cost (mc_t) corresponds to the Lagrange multiplier associated with the first restriction in Equation (2.36), whereas λ_t^{nd} denotes the Lagrange multiplier associated with the second restriction in Equation (2.37).

The demand for private capital is determined by Equation (2.41). It is related positively to the marginal productivity of capital $(1 - \alpha)$ $\frac{y_{t+1}}{ke_{t+1}} a \left(\frac{ke_{t+1}}{k_{t+1}} \right)^{1+\rho}$ times the firm's marginal cost, mc_{t+1},[9] which, in equilibrium, must equate to the gross return on physical capital.

Energy demand is defined by Equation (2.42). It is related positively to the marginal productivity of energy $(1 - \alpha)(1 - a) \frac{y_t}{ke_t} \left(\frac{ke_t}{e_t} \right)^{1+\rho}$ times the marginal cost mc_t which, in equilibrium, must equate the real price of energy including energy taxes.

Equation (2.43) reflects that firms choose the number of vacancies in such a way that the marginal recruiting cost per vacancy, κ_v, is equal to its expected present value, $\lambda_t^{nd} \frac{\chi_1 v_t^{\chi_2} (s(1-n_t)l_{2t})^{1-\chi_2}}{v_t}$, where λ_t^{nd} denotes the shadow price of an additional worker, and $\frac{\chi_1 v_t^{\chi_2} (s(1-n_t)l_{2t})^{1-\chi_2}}{v_t}$ is the transition probability from an unfilled to a filled vacancy.

Using the Bellman equation, the marginal value of an additional employment in t for a firm $\left(\lambda_{ft} \equiv \frac{\partial V_t}{\partial n_t} \right)$ is,

$$\lambda_{ft} = \alpha mc_t \frac{y_t}{n_t} - w_t (1 + \tau_t^{sc}) l_{1t} + (1 - \sigma) \beta E_t \frac{\lambda_{1t+1}^o}{\lambda_{1t}^o} \frac{\partial V_{t+1}}{\partial n_{t+1}}$$

(2.44)

where the marginal contribution of a new job to profits equals the marginal product net of the wage rate, plus the capital value of the new job in t, corrected for the probability that the job will continue in the future.

Now using Equation (2.44) one period ahead, we can rewrite the condition in Equation (2.43) as:

$$\frac{\kappa_v}{\rho_t^f} = \beta E_t \left[\frac{\lambda_{1t+1}^0}{\lambda_{1t}^0} \left(\alpha mc_{t+1} \frac{y_{t+1}}{n_{t+1}} - w_{t+1}(1+\tau_{t+1}^{sc})l_{1t+1} + (1-\sigma)\frac{\kappa_v}{\rho_{t+1}^f} \right) \right]$$

(2.45)

2.2.4 Pricing behaviour of intermediate firms: the New Phillips curve

Since each firm produces a variety of domestic good that is an imperfect substitute for the varieties produced by other firms, it acts as a monopolistic competitor facing a downward-sloping demand curve of the form:

$$y_{it} = y_t \left(\frac{P_{it}}{P_t} \right)^{-\varepsilon}$$

(2.46)

where $\left(\frac{P_{it}}{P_t} \right)$ is the relative price of variety y_i, $\varepsilon = (1+\varsigma)/\varsigma$, where $\varsigma \geq 0$ is the elasticity of substitution between intermediate goods, and y_t represents the production of the final good which combines varieties of differentiated intermediate inputs as follows

$$y_t = \left(\int_0^1 y_{it}^{1/1+\varsigma} \, di \right)^{1+\varsigma} \quad \text{and} \quad P_t = \left(\int_0^1 P_{it}^{-\frac{1}{\varsigma}} \, di \right)^{-\varsigma}$$

(2.47)

Variety producers act as monopolists and set prices when allowed. As in the Calvo hypothesis (Calvo, 1983), we assume overlapping price adjustment. Each period, a proportion θ of non-optimising firms index prices to lagged inflation, according to the rule $P_{it} = (1+\pi_{t-1})^{\varkappa} P_{it-1}$ (with $\varkappa$ representing the degree of indexation); a measure $1-\theta$ of firms set their prices $\widetilde{P}_{it}$ optimally; that is, to maximise the present value of expected profits. Consequently, $1-\theta$ represents the probability of adjusting prices each period, whereas θ can be interpreted as a measure of price rigidity. Thus the maximisation problem of the representative variety producer can be written as:

$$\max_{\widetilde{P}_{it}} E_t \sum_{j=0}^{\infty} \rho_{it,t+j}(\beta\theta)^j \left[\widetilde{P}_{it}\overline{\pi}_{t+j}y_{it+j} - P_{t+j}mc_{it,t+j}y_{it+j} \right]$$

(2.48)

subject to

$$y_{it+j} = \left(\widetilde{P}_{it}\overline{\pi}_{t+j}\right)^{-\varepsilon} P_{t+j}^{\varepsilon} y_{t+j} \tag{2.49}$$

where $\widetilde{P}_{it}$ is the price set by the optimising firm at time t, β is the discount factor, $mc_{t,t+j}$ represents the marginal cost at $t+j$ of the firm that last set its price in period t, $\overline{\pi}_{t+j} = \prod_{h=1}^{j}\left(1+\pi_{t+h-1}\right)^{\varkappa}$. $\rho_{t,t+j}$, a price kernel which captures the marginal utility of an additional unit of profits accruing to Ricardian households at $t+j$, is given by

$$\frac{E_t\rho_{t,t+j}}{E_t\rho_{t,t+j-1}} = \frac{E_t(\lambda_{1t+j}^0/P_{t+j})}{E_t(\lambda_{1t+j-1}^0/P_{t+j-1})} \tag{2.50}$$

The first-order condition of the optimisation problem above is

$$\widetilde{P}_{it} = \frac{\varepsilon}{\varepsilon-1}\frac{\sum_{j=0}^{\infty}(\beta\theta)^j E_t\left[\rho_{it,t+j}P_{t+j}^{\varepsilon+1}mc_{it+j}y_{t+j}\overline{\pi}_{t+j}^{-\varepsilon}\right]}{\sum_{j=0}^{\infty}(\beta\theta)^j E_t\left[\rho_{it,t+j}P_{t+j}^{\varepsilon}y_{t+j}\overline{\pi}_{t+j}^{(1-\varepsilon)}\right]} \tag{2.51}$$

and the corresponding aggregate price index is equal to

$$P_t = \left[\theta\left(\pi_{t-1}^{\varkappa}P_{t-1}\right)^{1-\varepsilon} + (1-\theta)\widetilde{P}_t^{1-\varepsilon}\right]^{\frac{1}{1-\varepsilon}} \tag{2.52}$$

As standard in the literature (see, for example, Galí et al., 2001), Equation (2.52) can be used to obtain an expression for aggregate inflation of the form:

$$\pi_t = \frac{\beta}{1+\varkappa\beta}E_t\pi_{t+1} + \frac{(1-\beta\theta)(1-\theta)}{\theta(1+\varkappa\beta)}\widehat{mc}_t + \frac{\varkappa}{1+\varkappa\beta}\pi_{t-1} \tag{2.53}$$

where $\widehat{mc}_t$ in $mc_t = \frac{\varepsilon-1}{\varepsilon}(1+\widehat{mc}_t)$ measures the deviation of the firm's marginal cost from the steady state. Equation (2.53) is known in the literature as the New Phillips curve. It participates in the conventional Phillips-curve philosophy that inflation is influenced by activity in the short run. However, the New Phillips curve emphasises real marginal costs as the relevant variable to the inflation process, which in turn is seen as a forward-looking phenomenon. This is so because, when opportunities to adjust prices arrive infrequently, a firm will be concerned about future inflation. A second departure of the New Phillips curve from the traditional one is that it is derived from the optimising behaviour of firms. This makes it possible to define the marginal cost elasticity of inflation, λ, as a function of the structural parameters in the model, β and θ :

$$\lambda = \frac{(1-\beta\theta)(1-\theta)}{\theta(1+\varkappa\beta)} \tag{2.54}$$

Equation (2.54) shows that an increase in the average time span between price changes, θ, makes current inflation less responsive to $\widehat{mc}_t$. Output movements will therefore have a smaller impact on current inflation, holding expected future inflation constant. The reduced form of the New Phillips curve can be written as:

$$\pi_t = \beta^f E_t \pi_{t+1} + \lambda \widehat{mc}_t + \beta^b \pi_{t-1} \tag{2.55}$$

Notice that, for the sake of simplicity, the model neglects the influence of the distribution of prices (implicit in the Calvo hypothesis) in equilibrium. However, as shown by Burriel *et al.* (2010) in a DGE setting with nominal rigidities, such a simplifying assumption does not affect the explanatory power of the model either dynamically or in the steady state.

2.2.5 Trade in the labour market: the labour contract

The key departure of search models from the competitive paradigm is that trading in the labour market is subject to transaction costs. In each period, the unemployed engage in search activities to find vacant posts spread throughout the economy. Costly search in the labour market implies that there are simultaneous flows into and out of the state of employment, thus an increase (reduction) in the stock of unemployment takes place whenever job destruction (creation) predominates over job creation (destruction). Therefore unemployment stabilises if inflows and outflows cancel one another out; that is,

$$\rho_t^f v_t = \rho_t^w s(1 - n_{t-1}) = \chi_1 v_t^{\chi_2} \left[(1 - n_{t-1}) l_{2t} \right]^{1-\chi_2} = (1 - \sigma) n_{t-1} \tag{2.56}$$

Because it takes time (for households) and real resources (for firms) to make profitable contacts, some pure economic rent emerges with each new job, which is equal to the sum of the expected search costs that the firm and the worker will further incur if they refuse to match. The presence of such rents gives rise to a bilateral monopoly framework, whereby both parties co-operate for a win–win job match, but compete for the share of the overall surplus.

Several wages and hours determination schemes can be applied to a bilateral monopoly framework. In particular, we shall assume that firms and workers negotiate a labour contract in hours and wages in an efficient-bargaining manner. As discussed by Pissarides (2000, ch.7: 176), hours of work may be determined either by the worker in such a way as to maximise his or her utility, or by a bargain between the firm and the worker. The efficient number of hours is nevertheless determined by a Nash bargain. If workers choose their own hours of work, they will choose to work too few. The reason for this inefficiency is related to the existence of search costs.[10]

Note that, because homogeneity holds across all job–worker pairs in the economy, the outcome of this negotiation will be the same every-where. However, an individual firm and worker are too small to influence the market. As a result, when they meet they negotiate the terms of the contract by taking the behaviour in the rest of the market as given. Once a representative job-seeking worker and vacancy-offering firm match, they negotiate a labour contract in hours and wages. There is risk-sharing at household level but not between households. Although optimising and RoT households have different reservation wages, they pool together in the labour market and bargain with firms to distribute employment according to their share in the working-age population. The implication of this assumption is that all workers receive the same wages, work the same number of hours and suffer the same unemployment rates.

Following standard practice, the Nash bargain process maximises the weighted product of the parties' surpluses from employment.

$$
\max_{w_t, l_{1t}} \left((1 - \lambda^r) \frac{\lambda^o_{ht}}{\lambda^o_{1t}} + \lambda^r \frac{\lambda^r_{ht}}{\lambda^r_{1t}} \right)^{\lambda^w} \left(\lambda_{ft} \right)^{1 - \lambda^w} = \max_{w_t, l_{1t}} \left(\lambda_{ht} \right)^{\lambda^w} \left(\lambda_{ft} \right)^{1 - \lambda^w}
$$

(2.57)

where $\lambda^w \in [0, 1]$ reflects workers' bargaining power. The first term in brackets represents the worker surplus (as a weighted average of RoT and Ricardian workers' surpluses), while the second is the firm surplus. More specifically, $\lambda^o_{ht}/\lambda^o_{1t}$ and $\lambda^r_{ht}/\lambda^r_{1t}$, respectively, denote the earning pre-mium (in terms of consumption) of employment over unemployment for a Ricardian and an RoT worker. Notice that both earning premia are weighted according to the share of RoT consumers in the population (λ^r).

The solution of the Nash maximisation problem gives the optimal real wage and hours worked (see Appendix 1 for further details):

$$
w_t\left(1-\tau^l\right)l_{1t} = \lambda^w\left[\frac{\left(1-\tau^l\right)}{\left(1+\tau^{sc}\right)}\alpha mc_t\frac{y_t}{n_t}+\frac{\left(1-\tau^l\right)}{\left(1+\tau^{sc}\right)}\frac{\kappa_V v_t}{\left(1-n_t\right)}\right]
$$

$$
+(1-\lambda^w)\left[\left(\frac{(1-\lambda^r)}{\lambda_{1t}^o}+\frac{\lambda^r}{\lambda_{1t}^r}\right)\left(\phi_2\frac{(1-l_{2t})^{1-\eta}}{1-\eta}-\phi_1\frac{(1-l_{1t})^{1-\eta}}{1-\eta}\right)\right.
$$

$$
\left.+\left(1-\tau^l\right)g_{ut}\right]+(1-\lambda^w)(1-\sigma-\rho_t^w)\lambda^r\beta E_t\frac{\lambda_{3t+1}^r}{\lambda_{1t+1}^r}\left(\frac{\lambda_{1t+1}^o}{\lambda_{1t}^o}-\frac{\lambda_{1t+1}^r}{\lambda_{1t}^r}\right)
$$

$$
(2.58)
$$

$$
\frac{\left(1-\tau^l\right)}{\left(1+\tau^{sc}\right)}\alpha mc_t\frac{y_t}{n_t l_{1t}}=\phi_1(T-l_{1t})^{-\eta}\left[\frac{1-\lambda^r}{\lambda_{1t}^o}+\frac{\lambda^r}{\lambda_{1t}^r}\right] \qquad (2.59)
$$

where we see that the equilibrium wage in a search framework is a weighted average between the highest feasible wage (that is, the marginal productivity of labour augmented by the expected hiring cost per unemployed worker) and the lowest acceptable wage (that is, the reservation wage, as given by the second and third terms on the right-hand side of Equation (2.58)). Weights are given by the parties' bargaining power in the negotiation, λ^w and $(1-\lambda^w)$. Notice that when $\lambda^r=0$, all consumers are Ricardian and therefore the solutions for the wage rate and hours simplify to the standard ones (see Andolfatto, 1996).

Putting aside the last term on the right-hand side of Equation (2.58) for the moment, the outside option (that is, the reservation wage) is given first by the gap between the value imputed to leisure by an unemployed worker and by an employed worker. This gap is, in turn, a weighted average of the valuation of leisure by Ricardian and RoT workers, which differ in their marginal utilities of consumption (λ_{1t}^o and λ_{1t}^r). Notice that the higher the marginal utility of consumption, the more willing workers are to accept relatively lower wages. Second, the reservation wage also depends on unemployment benefits (g_{ut}). An increase in the replacement rate improves the worker's threat point in the bargain process and exerts upward pressure on the bargained wage.

The third term on the right-hand side of Equation (2.58) is a part of the reservation wage that depends only on the existence of RoT workers (if

$\lambda^r > 0$ this term is different from zero). It can be interpreted as an inequality term in utility. The economic intuition is as follows: RoT consumers are not allowed to use their wealth to smooth consumption over time, but they can take advantage of the fact that a match today continues with some probability $(1 - \sigma)$ into the future, yielding a labour income that, in turn, will be used to consume tomorrow. Therefore, they use the margin that hours and wage negotiation gives them to improve their lifetime utility, by narrowing the gap in utility with respect to Ricardian consumers. In this sense, they compare the intertemporal marginal rate of substitution had they not been income constrained $\left(\frac{\lambda_{1t+1}^0}{\lambda_{1t}^0} \right)$ with the expected rate given their present rationing situation $\left(\frac{\lambda_{1t+1}^r}{\lambda_{1t}^r} \right)$. For example if, *ceteris paribus*, $\frac{\lambda_{1t+1}^0}{\lambda_{1t}^0} > \frac{\lambda_{1t+1}^r}{\lambda_{1t}^r}$ the whole third term in Equation (2.58) is positive, indicating that RoT individuals put additional pressure on the average reservation wage, as a way of easing their period-by-period constraint on consumption. The importance of this inequality term is positively related to the earning premium of being matched in the next period $\left(\frac{\lambda_{ht+1}^r}{\lambda_{1t+1}^r} \right)$, because it increases the value of a matching to continue in the future and is negatively related to the job-finding probability $\left(\rho_t^w \right)$, which reduces the loss of breaking up the match.

Finally, fiscal variables also influence the division of the surplus rather than the definition of the worker's and firm's threat points in the bargain. As noted earlier, the replacement rate increases the bargained wage because it raises income from unemployment. Both consumption and labour marginal taxes influence equilibrium wages because the imputed value of leisure is not taxed. An increase in either τ_t^c or τ^l make leisure more attractive in relation to work and, by doing so, increase wages in equilibrium. By contrast, an increase in social security contributions reduces wages by making recruiting an additional worker more expensive.

2.2.6 Government

Each period, the government decides the size and composition of public expenditure and the mix of taxes and new debt holdings required to finance total expenditure. It is assumed that government purchases of goods and services (g_t^c) and public investment (g_t^i) follow an exogenously given pattern, while interest payments on government bonds $(1 + r_t)b_t$ are model-determined, as well as unemployment benefits $g_{ut}(1 - n_t)$ and government social transfers g_{st} which are given by

$$g_{ut} = \overline{rr} w_t \tag{2.60}$$

$$g_{st} = \overline{tr} g d p_t \tag{2.61}$$

whereby g_{ut} and g_{st} are indexed to the level of real wages, w_t, and activity, $g d p_t$, through $\overline{rr}$ and $\overline{tr}$.

Government revenues are made up of direct taxation on labour income (personal labour income tax, τ_t^l, and social security contributions, τ_t^{sc}) and capital income (τ_t^k), as well as indirect taxation, including a consumption tax at the rate τ_t^c, and an energy tax at the rate τ_t^e. Government revenues are therefore given by

$$t_t = (\tau_t^l + \tau_t^{sc}) w_t (n_t l_{1t}) + \tau_t^k (r_t - \delta) k_t \tag{2.62}$$

$$+ \tau_t^c \frac{P_t^c}{P_t} c_t + \tau_t^e \frac{P_t^e}{P_t} e_t + trh_t + \tau_t^l \overline{rr} w_t s (1 - n_t) l_{2t} + \tau_t^l g_{st}$$

where trh_t stands for lump-sum transfers as defined further below.

Government revenues and expenditures in each period are made consistent by means of the intertemporal budget constraint

$$\gamma_A \gamma_N b_{t+1} = g_t^c + g_t^i + g_{ut} s (1 - n_t) l_{2t} + g_{st} - t_t + \frac{(1 + r_t^n)}{1 + \pi_t} b_t \tag{2.63}$$

Equation (2.63) reflects that the gap between overall receipts and outlays is financed by variations in lump-sum transfers to households, trh_t (which enter the fiscal budget rule through the term t_t), and/or debt issuance. Note that government cannot raise income from seigniorage.

Dynamic sustainability of public debt requires the introduction of a debt rule that makes one or several fiscal categories an instrument for debt stabilisation. To enforce the government's intertemporal budget constraint, the following fiscal policy reaction function is imposed

$$trh_t = trh_{t-1} + \psi_1 \left[\frac{b_t}{g d p_t} - \overline{\left(\frac{b}{g d p} \right)} \right] + \psi_2 \left[\frac{b_t}{g d p_t} - \frac{b_{t-1}}{g d p_{t-1}} \right] \tag{2.64}$$

where $\psi_1 > 0$ captures the speed of adjustment from the current ratio towards the desired target $\left(\frac{b}{g d p} \right)$. The value of $\psi_2 > 0$ is chosen to ensure a smooth adjustment of current debt towards its steady-state level. Note that while, in the baseline specification, debt stabilisation is achieved through variations in lump-sum transfers, other receipt and spending categories could also take this role.

Government investment (exogenous in the model) augments public capital, which, given the depreciation δ^p, follows the law of motion:

$$\gamma_A \gamma_N k_{t+1}^p = g_t^i + (1 - \delta^p) k_t^p \tag{2.65}$$

2.2.7 Monetary policy

Monetary policy is managed by the European Central Bank (ECB) using the following Taylor rule, which allows for some smoothing of the interest rate response to inflation and the output gap

$$\ln \frac{1 + r_t^{emu}}{1 + \overline{r^{emu}}} = \rho^r \ln \frac{1 + r_{t-1}^{emu}}{1 + \overline{r^{emu}}} + \rho^\pi (1 - \rho^r) \ln \frac{1 + \pi_t^{emu}}{1 + \overline{\pi^{emu}}}$$
$$+ \rho^y (1 - \rho^r) \ln \Delta \ln y_t^{emu}$$

where all the variables with the superscript 'mu' refer to EMU aggregates Thus, r_t^{emu} and π_t^{emu} are the euro-zone (nominal) short-term interest rate and inflation as measured in terms of the consumption price deflator, and $\Delta \ln y_t^{emu}$ measures the relative deviation of GDP growth from its trend. There is also some inertia in nominal interest-rate setting. As discussed by Woodford (2003), Equation (2.62) is the optimal outcome of a rational central bank facing an objective function, with output and inflation as arguments, in a general equilibrium setting.

The Spanish economy contributes to EMU inflation according to its economic size in the euro-zone, ω_{Sp}:

$$\pi_t^{emu} = (1 - \omega_{Sp}) \overline{\pi_t^{remu}} + \omega_{Sp} \pi_t \tag{2.66}$$

where $\overline{\pi_t^{remu}}$ is average inflation in the rest of the euro-zone.

The disappearance of national currencies since the inception of the monetary union means that the intra-euro-area real exchange rate is given by the ratio of relative prices between the domestic economy and the remaining EMU members, so real appreciation depreciation developments are driven by the inflation differential of the Spanish economy vis-à-vis the euro area:

$$\frac{rer_{t+1}}{rer_t} = \frac{1 + \pi_{t+1}^{emu}}{1 + \pi_{t+1}} \tag{2.67}$$

2.2.8 The external sector

The small open economy assumption implies that world prices and world demand are given from the perspective of the national economy. It also means that feedback linkages between the Spanish economy, EMU and the rest of the world are ignored. Another simplifying assumption concerns the nature of final and intermediate goods produced at home, which are all regarded as tradable.

The allocation of consumption and investment between domestic and foreign produced goods

Aggregate consumption and investment are constant elasticity of substitution (CES) composite baskets of home- and foreign-produced goods. Consumption and investment distributors determine the share of aggregate consumption (investment) to be satisfied with home-produced goods c_h and i_h, and foreign-imported goods c_f and i_f. The aggregation technology is expressed by the following CES functions:

$$c_t = \left((1-\omega_{ct})^{\frac{1}{\sigma_c}} c_{ht}^{\frac{\sigma_c-1}{\sigma_c}} + \omega_{ct}^{\frac{1}{\sigma_c}} \left(c_{ft} \right)^{\frac{\sigma_c-1}{\sigma_c}} \right)^{\frac{\sigma_c}{\sigma_c-1}} \tag{2.68}$$

$$i_t = \left((1-\omega_{it})^{\frac{1}{\sigma_i}} i_{ht}^{\frac{\sigma_i-1}{\sigma_i}} + \omega_{it}^{\frac{1}{\sigma_i}} \left(i_{ft} \right)^{\frac{\sigma_i-1}{\sigma_i}} \right)^{\frac{\sigma_i}{\sigma_i-1}} \tag{2.69}$$

where σ_c and σ_i are the consumption and investment elasticities of substitution between domestic and foreign goods.

In each period, the representative consumption distributor chooses c_{ht} and c_{ft} so as to minimise production costs subject to the technological constraint given by Equation (2.68). The Lagrangian of this problem can be written as:

$$\min_{c_{ht}, c_{ft}} \left\{ \left(P_t c_{ht} + P_t^m c_{ft} \right) \right.$$

$$\left. + P_t^c \left[c_t - \left((1-\omega_c)^{\frac{1}{\sigma_c}} c_{ht}^{\frac{\sigma_c-1}{\sigma_c}} + \omega_c^{\frac{1}{\sigma_c}} \left(c_{ft} \right)^{\frac{\sigma_c-1}{\sigma_c}} \right)^{\frac{\sigma_c}{\sigma_c-1}} \right] \right\} \tag{2.70}$$

where P_t and P_t^m are, respectively, the prices of home- and foreign- produced goods. Note that P_t^c represents both the price of the consumption good for households and the shadow cost of production faced by the aggregator.

The optimal allocation of aggregate consumption between domestic and foreign goods, c_{ht} and c_{ft}, satisfies the following conditions:

$$c_{ht} = (1 - \omega_c) \left(\frac{P_t}{P_t^c} \right)^{-\sigma_c} c_t \tag{2.71}$$

$$c_{ft} = \omega_c \left(\frac{P_t^m}{P_t^c} \right)^{-\sigma_c} c_t \tag{2.72}$$

Proceeding in the same manner as with the investment distributor problem, similar expressions can be obtained regarding the optimal allocation of aggregate investment between domestic and foreign goods, i_{ht} and i_{ft}

$$i_{ht} = (1 - \omega_i) \left(\frac{P_t}{P_t^i} \right)^{-\sigma_i} i_t \tag{2.73}$$

$$i_{ft} = \omega_i \left(\frac{P_t^m}{P_t^i} \right)^{-\sigma_i} i_t \tag{2.74}$$

Price formation

The price of domestically produced consumption and investment goods is the GDP deflator, P_t. To obtain the consumption price deflator, the demands for home and foreign consumption goods in Equations (2.71) and (2.72) need to be incorporated into the cost of producing one unit of aggregate consumption goods ($P_t c_{ht} + P_t^m c_{ft}$). Bearing in mind that the unitary production cost is equal to the price of production, one can express the consumption and investment price deflators as a function of the GDP and import deflators

$$P_t^c = \left((1 - \omega_{ct}) P_t^{1-\sigma_c} + \omega_{ct} P_t^{m 1-\sigma_c} \right)^{\frac{1}{1-\sigma_c}} \tag{2.75}$$

$$P_t^i = \left((1 - \omega_{it}) P_t^{1-\sigma_i} + \omega_{it} P_t^{m 1-\sigma_i} \right)^{\frac{1}{1-\sigma_i}} \tag{2.76}$$

The exogenous world price is a weighted average of the final and intermediate goods prices, $\overline{PFM}$ and $\overline{P}^e$, both expressed in terms of the domestic currency. Given the small open economy assumption, the relevant foreign price is defined as:

$$P_t^m = \left(\tilde{\alpha}_e P_t^e + (1 - \tilde{\alpha}_e) \overline{PFM}_t \right) \tag{2.77}$$

where $\tilde{\alpha}_e$ stands for the ratio of energy imports to overall imports.

We assume that export prices set by Spanish firms deviate from competitors' prices in foreign markets, at least temporarily. This is known in the literature as the 'pricing-to-market hypothesis' and is consistent with a model of monopolistic competition among firms where each firm regards its influence on other firms as being negligible. To make this assumption operational, we consider a fraction of $(1 - ptm)$ firms whose prices at home and abroad differ. The remaining ptm goods can be freely traded by consumers, so firms set a unified price across countries (that is, the law of one price holds). In light of the arguments above, the Spanish export price deflator is defined as

$$P_t^x = P_t^{(1-ptm)} \left(\overline{PFM_t} \right)^{ptm} \tag{2.78}$$

where P_t^x is the export price deflator, $\overline{PFM_t}$ is the competitors' price index expressed in euros and the parameter ptm determines the extent to which there is pricing-to-market.

Exports and imports

The national economy imports two final goods, consumption and investment, and one intermediate commodity, energy:

$$im_t = c_{ft} + i_{ft} + \alpha_e e_t \tag{2.79}$$

where α_e represents the ratio of energy imports over total energy consumption.

Exports are a function of aggregate consumption and investment abroad, $\bar{y}_t^w$, and the ratio of the export price deflator to the competitors price index (expressed in euros), $P_t^x / \overline{PFM_t}$:

$$ex_t = s_t^x \left(\frac{P_t^x}{\overline{PFM_t}} \right)^{-\sigma_x} \bar{y}_t^w \tag{2.80}$$

where σ_x is the long-run price elasticity of exports. Plugging Equation (2.78) into Equation (2.80) yields the exports demand for a small open economy under the pricing-to-market hypothesis:

$$ex_t = s_t^x \left(\frac{\overline{PFM_t}}{P_t} \right)^{(1-ptm)\sigma_x} \bar{y}_t^w \tag{2.81}$$

Note that with full pricing-to-market $ptm = 0$, $P_t^x = P_t$ and expression (2.80) simplifies to

$$ex_t = s_t^x \left(\frac{P_t}{P_t^m} \right)^{-\sigma_x} \bar{y}_t^w = s_t^x \left(\frac{P_t}{\overline{PFM_t}} \right)^{-\sigma_x} \bar{y}_t^w \tag{2.82}$$

Conversely, if the law of one price holds for all consumption and investment goods, then $ptm = 1$, $P_t^x = P_t^m = \overline{PFM}_t$ and expression (2.80) simplifies to

$$ex_t = s_t^x \overline{y}_t^w \tag{2.83}$$

Thus if the law of one price holds, exports are a sole function of total aggregate consumption and investment from abroad. Under full pricing-to-market ($ptm = 0$), exports are also a function of relative prices with elasticity σ_x. Under the more general case of partial pricing-to-market ($0 < ptm < 1$), the price elasticity of exports is given as $(1 - ptm)\sigma_x$.

Stock-flow interaction between the current account balance and the accumulation of foreign assets

In the model, the current account balance is defined as the trade balance plus net factor income from abroad (that is, interest rate receipts/payments from net foreign assets):

$$ca_t = \frac{P_t^x}{P_t} ex_t - \frac{P_t^m}{P_t} im_t + \left(r_t^{emu} - \pi_t\right) b_t^{oemu} \tag{2.84}$$

Following standard practice in the literature (see, for example, Obstfeld and Rogoff, 1995, 1996), net foreign assets are regarded as a stock variable resulting from the accumulation of current account flows. This is illustrated by the following dynamic expression:

$$\frac{\gamma_A \gamma_N b_{t+1}^{oemu}}{\phi_{bt}} = \frac{\left(1 + r_t^{emu}\right)}{1 + \pi_t^c} b_t^{oemu} + \frac{P_t^x}{P_t} ex_t - \frac{P_t^m}{P_t} im_t \tag{2.85}$$

Equation (2.85) is obtained by combining the Ricardian households' budget constraint (assuming a zero net supply for domestic bonds and money), the government's budget constraint and the economy's aggregate resource constraint (see Appendix 2 for details).

2.2.9   Accounting identities in the economy

Gross output can be defined as the sum of (final) demand components and the (intermediate) consumption of energy:

$$y_t = c_{ht} + i_{ht} + g_t^i + g_t^c + \frac{P_t^x}{P_t} ex_t + \kappa_v v_t + \frac{P_t^e}{P_t}(1 - \alpha_e)e_t + \kappa_f \tag{2.86}$$

where κ_f is an entry cost which ensures that extraordinary profits vanish in imperfectly competitive equilibrium in the long run. Value added generated in the economy (that is, GDP in efficiency units, denoted by y_t^n) is given by:

$$y_t^n = gdp_t = y_t - \frac{P_t^e}{P_t} e_t - \kappa_f - \kappa_v v_t \tag{2.87}$$

where, in line with definitions above in Equations (2.71) and (2.73), c_{ht} and i_{ht} are equal to overall domestic consumption and investment minus consumption and investment goods imported from abroad.

2.3 Model solution method and parameterisation

2.3.1 Model solution method

The number of equations involved in the model and the presence of non-linearities do not allow for a closed-form solution for the dynamic stable path. To provide a solution for dynamic systems of this nature it has become common practice in the literature to use a numerical method. There are several ways of solving forward-looking models with rational expectations. Most of them rely on algorithms that are applied to the linearised version of the system around the steady state. This approach, which is very popular in the literature, was first introduced by Blanchard and Kahn (1980).

To solve the model, we follow the method developed by Laffarque (1990), Boucekkine (1995) and Juillard (1996). As various endogenous variables in the model have leads, representing expectations of these variables in future time periods, an assumption has to be made regarding the formation of expectations. In REMS, expectations are rational and therefore model-consistent. This means that each period's future expectations coincide with the model's solution for the future. In simulations this implies that the leads in the model equations are equal to the solution values for future periods. This rational expectations solution is implemented by applying a stacked-time algorithm that solves for multiple time periods simultaneously–that is, it stacks the time periods into one large system of equations and solves them simultaneously using Newton–Raphson iterations. The method is robust because the number of iterations is scarcely affected by convergence criteria, the number of time periods or the size of the shock. The model is simulated using the Dynare software system.

REMS obeys the necessary local condition for the uniqueness of a stable equilibrium in the neighbourhood of the steady state–that is, there are as many eigenvalues larger than one in modulus as there are forward-looking variables in the system.

2.3.2   Model parameterisation

Model parameters have been fixed using a hybrid approach of calibration and estimation. Some parameter values are taken from QUEST II and other related DGE models. Several other parameters are obtained from steady-state conditions. The remaining parameters have been estimated on the basis of selected models equations. Together, these parameters produce a baseline solution that accurately resembles the behaviour of the Spanish economy since the mid-1980s.

The data used for calibration purposes come from the REMSDB database and cover the period 1985:3 to 2009:4, during which the behaviour of endogenous variables complies with cyclical empirical regularities (see Puch and Licandro, 1997, and Boscá *et al.*, 2007). The group of variables without statistical counterparts in official sources include consumption and employment of RoT and optimising consumers, Lagrange multipliers, Tobin's q, the composite of private physical capital and energy, marginal cost and total factor productivity. These variables are computed using their corresponding behavioural equations in the model (see Appendix 3 for further details).

Table 2.1 lists the values of parameters and exogenous variables. The implied steady-state values of the endogenous variables are given in Table 2.2.[11] Broadly speaking, the calibration strategy follows a sequence which we start by setting the value of a number of parameters that are

Table 2.1   Parameter values

θ	0.0092	γ	1.75	κ_f	0.129148	ρ^w	0.75
α	0.59387	ρ^r	0.75	$\overline{PFM}$	1.002991	ϕ_e	25
ζ	0.06	$\left(\frac{b}{gdp}\right)$	2.40	$\bar{y}^w$	7.306437	ρ_e	0.85
δ	0.01587	$\bar{\pi}$	0.20225	T	1.369	s	0.269341
δ^p	0.01058	τ^l	0.110766	χ_m	0.20347	ϕ_b	0.006
κ_v	0.18414	τ^k	0.208272	s^x	0.021345	ptm	0.57675
σ	0.08625	τ^c	0.106985	ω_c	0.1395	λ^w	0.42743
χ_1	0.61158	τ^{sc}	0.221531	ω_i	0.423765	$\overline{mc}$	0.840691
χ_2	0.57257	τ^e	0.20	λ^r	0.5	σ_c	1.20548
$\overline{l_2}$	0.21828	ψ_1	0.01	h^o	0.6	σ_x	1.3
ϕ_1	3.23775	ψ_2	0.2	h^r	0.0	σ_i	0.93043
ϕ_2	2.59905	η	2.0	α_e	0.498	λ	0.2006
ρ	0.99776	γ_A	1.00170	$\tilde{\alpha}_e$	0.10489	β^f	0.4965
a	0.99888	γ_N	1.00325	$\overline{tr}$	0.138154	β^b	0.5035
ϕ	5.50	r^{nw}	0.0142	$\overline{trh}$	0.0259859	ω_{Sp}	0.1000

Table 2.2 Steady state

b_t	1.4207	i_{ht}	0.0787	λ^r_{3t}	1.5633	g_{st}	0.0818
b^o_t	1.4207	im_t	0.1542	λ^{nd}_t	0.5119	trh_t	0.0326
c_t	0.3618	j_t	0.1408	λ^o_{1t}	2.2221	t_t	0.2104
c_{ft}	0.0633	j^o_t	0.2816	λ^r_{1t}	3.1218	g_{ut}	0.2724
c_{ht}	0.2999	ρ^w_t	0.0732	$\frac{p^c_t}{p_t}$	0.9694	v_t	0.1120
c^o_t	0.4251	k_t	6.7604	π_t	0.0000	w_t	1.5147
c^r_t	0.2985	ke_t	5.7032	gdp_t	0.5920	$\tilde{w}_t$	1.5147
e_t	0.0402	k^o_t	13.521	π^c_t	0.0000	y_t	0.7764
rer_t	0.8157	k^p_t	1.1028	$\frac{p^i_t}{p_t}$	0.9119	z_t	0.0000
ex_t	0.1394	m_t	3.2536	$\frac{p_t}{p^m_t}$	0.8037	g^i_t	0.0171
b^w_t	0.0000	$\widehat{mc}_t$	0.0000	$\frac{p_t}{p^x_t}$	0.8892		
b^{ow}_t	0.0000	m^o_t	6.5072	q_t	1.0164		
g^c_t	0.0895	n_t	0.4499	r_t	0.0331		
l_{1t}	0.4369	n^o_t	0.4499	r^n_t	0.0142		
i_t	0.1489	n^r_t	0.4499	ϕ_{bt}	1.0000		
i_{ft}	0.0709	λ^o_{3t}	0.1560	l_{2t}	0.2183		

subsequently used to obtain a measure of the level of total factor productivity. This makes it possible to express all variables in the model in terms of efficiency units. The remaining parameters are then fixed on the basis of the model's equations with variables measured in efficiency units.

The Cobb–Douglas parameter α matches the average value of the labour share in the data, as measured by the ratio of compensation of employees to GDP. The public capital elasticity of output, ζ, has been set at 0.06, which falls within the range of the estimated values reported by Gramlich (1994). Given the values of α and ζ it is straightforward to obtain the level of technological efficiency, A_t, using Equation (2.33). HP-filtered total factor productivity is then used to rescale all variables with respect to efficiency. Technical progress, γ_A, is given by the growth rate of trend productivity.

The calibrated values of a number of parameters are taken from QUEST II. This is the case of the subjective discount rate, β, the parameter of adjustment costs in the investment function, ϕ, the long-run price elasticity of exports, σ_x, and fiscal rule parameters, ψ_1 and ψ_2.

Following Andolfatto (1996), we choose a value of 2 for the parameter defining the degree of intertemporal labour substitution, η, whereas the amount of time devoted to looking for a job, $\overline{l_2}$, is estimated as half the quarterly average of working time. Parameter κ_v is calibrated to match an overall cost of vacant posts equal to 0.5 percentage points of GDP. As in Burnside *et al.* (1993), we fix total productive time endowment T at 1.369 (thousand) hours per quarter. The exogenous job destruction rate, σ, is calibrated from the law of motion of employment – Equation (2.4). The share of non-employed workers actively searching for a job, s, is obtained from the ratio between the unemployment rate and one minus the employment rate $(1 - n)$.

We follow Doménech *et al.* (2002) in calibrating the parameters that enter the monetary policy reaction function γ_{EMU} and ρ_{EMU}^r . The weight of the Spanish economy in euro-zone inflation, ω_{Sp}, is set at 10 per cent. The public debt-to-GDP target ratio has been set at 2.4. This corresponds to a 60 per cent value on an annual basis, which is equal to the limit established in the Stability and Growth Pact. Tax rates on labour and capital income and consumption expenditure $(\tau^l, \tau^k, \tau^{sc}, \tau^c)$ have been constructed following the methodology developed by Boscá *et al.* (2005). The tax rate on energy, τ_t^e, has been set at 0.20. The growth rate of population, γ_N, has been computed on the basis of working-age population data. We use the ratio of unemployment benefits to labour compensation to calibrate the replacement rate, $\overline{rr}$.

The value of 0.6 for h^0, the parameter that captures habits in consumption of Ricardian households, has been taken from Smets and Wouters (2003). The fraction of RoT consumers in the Spanish economy, λ^r, is assumed to be 0.5, quite a standard value. The risk premium parameter, ϕ_b, is fixed at 0.006. This is somewhat higher than the value given in Erceg *et al.* (2005), implying faster convergence of the foreign asset position to the steady state. The scale parameter of the matching function, χ_1, and the elasticity of matchings with respect to vacant posts, χ_2, have been estimated at, respectively, 0.61 and 0.57. In line with the efficiency condition in Hosios (1990), workers' bargaining power is set at $1 - \chi_2$.

The entry cost, κ_f, is calculated at 0.13 from a mark-up of 20 per cent. Using data on the weight of intermediate inputs in gross output from the Input–Output tables, the distributional parameter in the energy–capital composite, a, has been set to 0.99. The estimated value of ρ is 0.99, which corresponds to an elasticity of substitution $1/(1+\rho)$ of 0.50, implying that private capital and energy are complements in production. Value added is then computed using the accounting identity given in Equation (2.87). The ratio of energy imports to total energy consumption, α_e, is taken from the Input–Output Tables (year 2000). Private and public capital depreciation δ and δ^p are the rates implicit in the capital series in BDREMS, respectively around 6 per cent and 4 per cent per year.

With respect to the preference parameters in the household utility function, ϕ_1 has been estimated from the hours schedule equation (2.59), whereas ϕ_2, has been computed as a weighted average (with weights λ^r and $(1 - \lambda^r)$) of the estimates arising from the two labour supply conditions in Equations (2.19) and (2.25). Overall, our values for ϕ_1 and ϕ_2 resemble those obtained by Andolfatto (1996) and other related research in the literature, implying that the imputed value of leisure of an employed worker is situated well above the imputed value of leisure of an unemployed person.

We use the employment demand to obtain a series for the firm's marginal cost, mc_t. The steady-state value, $\overline{mc}$, is set at the sample mean. We choose the degree of price indexation $\varkappa$ at 1 (hypothesis testing of an estimated value of 1 for $\varkappa$ results in no rejection), and use Equation (2.53) to obtain a GMM estimation of the fraction of non-optimising firms, θ. The estimated value is equal to 0.54. Together with the subjective discount rate, these two parameters imply a value of 0.20 for the marginal cost elasticity of inflation λ,[12] and 0.50 for the weights attached to the forward and backward components of inflation, β^f and β^b. Values of these parameters close to 0.5 are a key feature of the hybrid Phillips curve with full indexation, as evidenced by the empirical literature.[13]

In the external sector we have used Equations (2.78) and (2.77) to obtain estimations of the pricing-to-market parameter, ptm, and the ratio of energy imports to overall imports, $\tilde{\alpha}_e$. Our estimate for $\tilde{\alpha}_e$ suggests that energy represents around 10 per cent of total imports. The estimated value of the ptm parameter (0.58) is of the same order of magnitude as in QUEST II (0.61). The weight of domestic consumption goods in the CES aggregator, ω_c, and the consumption elasticity of substitution between domestic and foreign goods, σ_c, are estimated simultaneously using the conditions in Equations (2.71) and (2.72). Similarly, in the case of investment goods, ω_i and σ_i are estimated simultaneously using Equations (2.73) and (2.74). The estimated elasticities suggest a slightly higher elasticity of substitution between domestic and foreign goods for consumption goods compared to investment goods. We use the export Equation (2.80) to calibrate the scale parameter s^x. The energy price index, P^e, and the world price index, $\overline{PFM}$, match sample averages calculated over the calibration period.

The value of two parameters has been accommodated to ensure the desirable long-run properties of the model. The world interest rate, $\overline{r^{emu}}$, is set to satisfy the static version of Equation (2.11), so that the current account is balanced in the steady state. Second, foreign output, $\bar{y}^w$, is adjusted to obtain a steady-state value of the real exchange rate close to the observed rate.

Finally, the value of a number of parameters has been chosen for labour market variables to display plausible dynamic patterns. Namely, we assume partial inertia in the search effort, ρ_e. As in Blanchard and Galí (2006), we allow for slow adjustment in wages, which evolve according to the expression $w_t = w_{t-1}^{\rho^w} \tilde{w}_t^{(1-\rho^w)}$, with $\tilde{w}_t$ being the Nash-bargained wage. This hypothesis is introduced in the model in an ad hoc manner, with an estimated value of $\rho^w = 0.75$.

2.4   Simulations

This section shows the properties of the model and examines the basic transmission channels at work by presenting standard simulations. Simulated scenarios include a technology shock and a public consumption shock. The two shocks are of a temporary nature and fully anticipated by economic agents.

2.4.1   A transitory technology shock

In this section an exogenous productivity improvement is implemented as a 1 per cent increase of z_i. The technology shock is modelled as a first-order autoregressive process with a persistence parameter of 0.9, implying that the level of total factor productivity after five years is situated 0.2 percentage points above the steady-state level.

Figure 2.1 displays the (quarterly) dynamic responses of selected macroeconomic variables in the model. Simulation results are percentage deviations from the baseline, except for the trade surplus and GDP deflator inflation, which are absolute deviations.

Figure 2.1 shows that the multiplier on GDP on impact is close to one third. The GDP effect is quite persistent, reaching a peak after four quarters. There are also positive and long-lasting effects on consumption, investment and wages. Slow adjustment in Nash-bargained wages is reflected in a positive, albeit muted, effect on wages, which generates a marked response in employment. The shock also leads to an increase in consumption, which peaks after five quarters. Hump-shaped consumption dynamics are explained by the presence of RoT households, which display relatively more volatile and less persistent consumption compared with Ricardians. It is worth mentioning that our impulse-response functions closely resemble those presented in Andrés *et al.* (2008) who, extending the research of Andrés and Domenech (2006), also find small

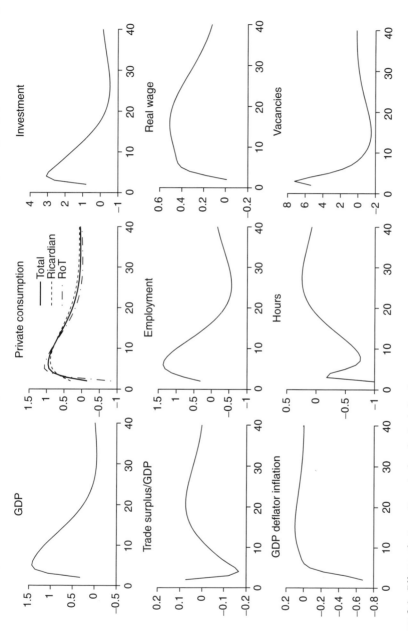

Figure 2.1 Effects of a transitory technological shock

61

effects in the very short run following a technology shock in the context of a model with price rigidities and RoT consumers.

As expected, the technology shock has a sizeable effect on marginal costs (not shown in Figure 2.1), which fall on impact, thereby increasing Tobin's q and stimulating capital accumulation through investment. Also, the fall in marginal costs moderates inflation, improves price competitiveness and encourages export demand. However, the boom in domestic absorption accelerates imports and more than offsets the positive effect of real depreciation on the trade balance in the short run.

The effect on vacancies is quite pronounced. To give an order of magnitude, note that the response of vacancies on impact is more than 10 times as large as that of GDP. This result is explained by the positive impact that enhanced GDP growth has on search effort. Moreover, our model can account for the evidence documented by Fujita (2004) and Ravn and Simonelli (2007), whereby vacancies display a hump-shaped pattern and peak around three quarters after the shock. In our model, following the initial positive response, vacancies register an increase, only to decline later as the labour market becomes tighter. Though short-lived, the increase in vacancies encourages job creation and employment, the effects of which are more persistent, as explained further below.

The behaviour of (full-time-equivalent) employment is plotted in Figure 2.2. The dynamics of this variable are in sharp contrast to the pattern implied by a standard RBC model with flexible prices. In the presence of price rigidities, responses in both the intensive and extensive margins of labour differ in direction and size. While the employment rate rises over time, hours per worker fall sharply on impact. Overall, (full-time equivalent) employment falls over the first four quarters and only attains pre-shock levels after one year. These predictions match the empirical findings of a growing literature beginning with Galí (1999) (see, for example, section 2 in Galí and Rabanal, 2004, and Andrés *et al.* 2008, for an overview of research that has reached similar conclusions).

2.4.2   A transitory public consumption shock

With a view to illustrating further transmission channels in REMS, this section discusses an exogenous transitory shock affecting the steady-state level of public consumption. The fiscal impulse amounts to 1 per cent of baseline GDP (or 6.5 per cent of g^c) and is assumed to follow a first-order autoregressive process with a persistence parameter of 0.9. Figure 2.3 displays the quarterly dynamic responses of the main macroeconomic variables in the model.

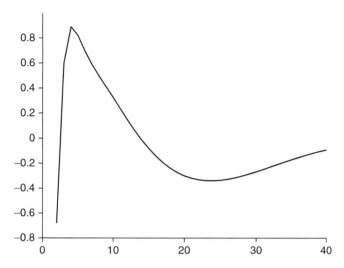

Figure 2.2   Effects of a technology shock on full-time equivalent employment

The multiplier on GDP ($\Delta GDP/\Delta g^c$) on impact is equal to 1. A transitory impulse to public consumption leads to a significant increase in consumption (of around 0.5 percentile points on impact) that lasts for about two quarters. This is confirmed by existing evidence of models allowing for liquidity-constrained (see Blanchard and Galí, 2006, and Galí *et al.*, 2007). As suggested by the second panel in Figure 2.3, the dynamics of overall consumption are largely driven by the behaviour of RoT households, whose consumption increases on impact by more than one percentile point. In contrast, optimising households, which are fully aware of the transitory nature of the shock, revise their current consumption downwards to offset the negative effect of the fiscal stimulus on government savings.

Private investment falls immediately after the shock and continues to drop by up to 1.5 per cent after three or four quarters, suggesting a sizeable crowding-out effect. The trough in investment can be rationalised in terms of a decline in Tobin's q, a slightly higher euro-zone nominal interest rate (as higher inflation and output gaps in the Spanish economy affect the corresponding euro-zone variables in a proportion determined by the weight of the domestic economy in the euro area) and a higher risk premium. The latter results in a lower level of external debt held by domestic households.

Figure 2.3 shows that employment, hours, real wages and vacancies increase on impact and then gradually return to normal. The jump

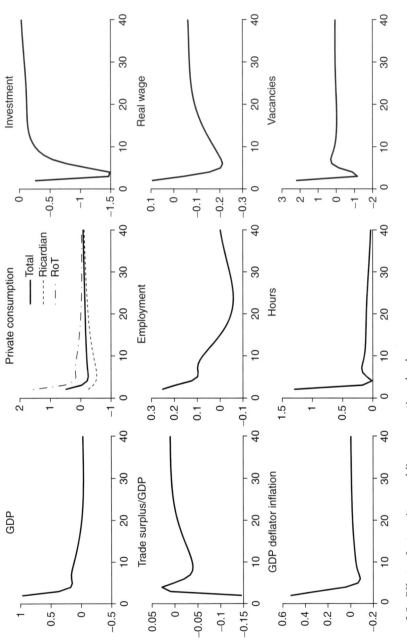

Figure 2.3 Effects of a transitory public consumption shock

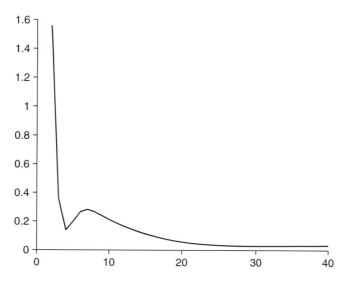

Figure 2.4 Effects of a public consumption shock on full-time equivalent employment

in vacant posts is explained by improved search effort and a higher shadow price of employment, λ^{nd}. Full-time-equivalent employment (see Figure 2.4) is enhanced by the positive response of employment both in terms of headcounts and hours worked.

2.5 Conclusions

This chapter presented a rational expectations model for simulation and policy evaluation of the Spanish economy (REMS). REMS is a dynamic general equilibrium model for a small open economy. It is primarily constructed to serve as a tool for simulation and policy evaluation of alternative scenarios. This means that REMS is not used for forecasting, but rather to analyse how the effects of policy shocks are transmitted over the medium term. It also means that the emphasis of the model is on the transmission channels through which policy action affects the domestic economy.

As far as economic theory is concerned, REMS can be characterised as a New Keynesian model with the optimising behaviour of households and firms being deeply rooted in the rational expectations hypothesis. The supply side of the economy is modelled through a neoclassical production function, implying that the long-term behaviour of the model closely reproduces the Solow growth model; that is, the economy reaches a steady-state path with a growth rate determined by the rate of exogenous technical progress plus the growth rate of the population. However, some prominent features differentiate this model from the neoclassical paradigm in the long term. First, trading both in the goods and the labour market is not achieved under Walrasian conditions. Firms in goods markets operate under monopolistic competition, setting prices sluggishly. In the labour market, firms and workers negotiate how to distribute the rents generated in the matching process. Consequently, in our model equilibrium unemployment will persist in the long term. Second, a share of households behave as myopic consumers that do not optimise intertemporally. Additionally, consumers take into account past consumption (habits) in their decisions. As a result, the behaviour of aggregate consumption after a fiscal shock deviates considerably from what could be expected in a neoclassical setting. In the short term, REMS is also influenced by the New Keynesian literature, allowing for a stabilising role of demand-based policies.

Nevertheless, the model still lacks sufficient detail to make a direct link between some specific reform efforts and economic performance. Several ways of improving the model are open for the future. For example, one weak point of the existing version of the model is that it is not detailed enough to differentiate across skill groups of the labour force. Also, REMS sticks to the exogenous nature of technical progress, whereas it is widely recognised today that knowledge investment is a key to economic growth and there is a link between the growth rate of technical progress and R&D spending. Moreover, as the financial crisis of 2008–09 has clearly demonstrated, a better understanding of the linkages between the financial sector and the real sector is needed. Finally, the estimation techniques used by this model could also be improved. Forthcoming versions of REMS should estimate the model using Bayesian estimation techniques.

Notes

1. Many central banks and international institutions have elaborated D(S)GE models. These include, *inter alia,* SIGMA for the US (Erceg *et al.*, 2006); the NAWM for the EMU (Christoffel *et al.*, 2008, and Smets *et al.* 2010); the BEQM for the UK (Harrison *et al.*, 2005); the TOTEM for Canada (Murchison *et al.*, 2004); AINO for Finland (Kilponen *et al.*, 2004); or the models devised by Smets and Wouters (2003) for the EMU; Lindé *et al.* (2004) for Sweden; and Cadiou *et al.* (2001) for 14 OECD countries. Two alternative models of the

Spanish economy are BEMOD and MEDEA, developed respectively by Andrés *et al.* (2006, 2010) and Burriel *et al.* (2010).

2. MOISEES (Modelo de Investigacion y Simulacion de la Economia Española) is the preceding simulation tool available at the Spanish Ministry of Economic and Financial Affairs. See Molinas *et al.* (1990).

3. See Boscá *et al.* (2007) for further details.

4. For the sake of simplicity, we assume that the leisure utility of the unemployed searching for a job is the same as for the non-active:

$$s(1 - n_t^o)\phi_2 \frac{(T - l_{2t})^{1-\eta}}{1-\eta} = (1-s)(1 - n_t^o)\phi_3 \frac{(T - l_{3t})^{1-\eta}}{1-\eta}.$$

5. More specifically, we assume that the search effort made by unemployed people increases during expansions, depending positively on the GDP growth rate:

$$l_{2t} = \left(\overline{l_2} \left(\frac{gdp_t}{gdp_{t-1}} \right)^{\phi_e} \right)^{(1-\rho_e)} l_{2t-1}^{\rho_e}$$

where ϕ_e is the elasticity of search effort with respect to the rate of growth of GDP and ρ_e captures the strength of inertia in the search effort. The reason for endogenising search effort in this way is an empirical one, making it possible to obtain a reasonable volatility of vacancies.

6. Carlstrom and Fuerst (2001) have criticised this timing assumption on the grounds that the appropriate way to model the utility from money is to assume that money balances available before going to purchase goods yield utility. However, we follow the standard approach in the literature whereby the end-of-period money holdings yield utility.

7. Note that this specification presumes that all workers are identical to the firm.

8. For simplicity, it is assumed that foreign bonds are expressed in euros. We could assume instead that some bonds could be from the rest of the world, expressed in a foreign currency. In this case, the uncovered interest rate parity for the euro area ensures that

$$1 + r_t^{emu} = E_t \frac{er_{t+1}}{er_t}(1 + r_t^w) \tag{2.88}$$

where *er* is the nominal exchange rate. Given the relative small size of Spain in the EMU, we assume that the euro exchange rate with the rest of the world is unaffected by Spanish variables, even though Spanish inflation has a small influence on ECB interest rates. This assumption is additionally supported by the empirical evidence since, as documented by many authors (see, for example, Adolfson *et al.*, 2007, and the references therein), the uncovered interest parity condition cannot account for the forward premium puzzle shown by the data. For these reasons, all foreign prices, including those of foreign bonds, are taken to be exogenous and are expressed in euros.

9. Under imperfect competition conditions, cost minimisation implies that production factors are remunerated by the marginal revenue times their marginal productivity. In our specification for factor demands, the marginal revenue has been replaced by the corresponding marginal costs. We are legitimated to

proceed in this manner because in equilibrium these two marginal concepts are made equal by the imperfectly competitive firm.

10. See also Trigari (2006) for further details about the implications of using alternatively the so-called right-to-manage hypothesis.

11. The model has been programmed in relative prices. This means that nominal variables are normalised with, P_t, the price deflator of domestic final goods.

12. This value is significantly higher than that obtained by Galí and López-Salido (2001).

13. Bils and Klenow (2004) find that the average duration between price adjustments is more than six months. The evidence on price setting in the euro area at individual level by Álvarez *et al.* (2006) shows that prices in the euro area are stickier than in the United States.

3
Job Creation in Spain: Productivity Growth, Labour Market Reforms or Both?

J. Andrés, J. E. Boscá, R. Doménech and J. Ferri

3.1 Introduction

The Spanish economy enjoyed a prolonged period of high growth between 1994 and 2007, characterised by extensive job creation. From the 1960s to the early 1990s the number of jobs in the Spanish economy had fluctuated around a steady level of some 13 million. This led many people to support the idea that the Spanish economy could never break through this ceiling. However, between 1994 and 2007 the labour market saw an increase in employment from 13.3 to 20.6 million workers. This great modernation period brought the Spanish economy historically low interest rates and an expansion of credit facilities, which helped to sustain a vigorous and prolonged path of both private consumption and investment growth. Spain also managed to reduce public debt to a previously unknown level of around 30 per cent, and turned endemic public deficits into surpluses, reaching 2 percentage points of GDP in 2007. Throughout this expansionary process the labour force increased considerably as a result of sustained immigration flows; nevertheless, the unemployment rate converged to average European levels. In this sense, the rate of unemployment fell from around 20 per cent in the mid-1990s to a level of 8 per cent in 2007. For the first time since the first big oil price shock in the 1970s, Spanish unemployment was similar to the average in the European Union.

This rapid growth has been far from healthy, however, and throughout this period the Spanish economy accentuated some imbalances that help to explain the differential effect of the late-2000s recession as far as unemployment is concerned. First and foremost, while the Spanish economy was growing faster than most countries in Europe, productivity growth was almost zero. Also, the sector composition of production was heavily biased towards relatively low productivity sectors (mainly real estate construction and services), which had experienced the bulk of employment creation. From the beginning of the twenty-first century, Spanish real estate prices increased enormously (multiplying by about 2.5 from 2000 to 2007), contributing heavily to an increase in the levels of indebtedness among many households financing mortgages and consumption credit. The specialisation in goods with low value-added per worker, the limits to competition and the pressure of domestic demand drove prices upwards, generating persistent positive inflation differentials that deteriorated competitiveness *vis-à-vis* Spain's trade partners. In fact, the Spanish economy accumulated an impressive current account deficit that reached 10 per cent of GDP in 2007, and whose quantitative amount was the second largest in the world (after the United States). Finally, while the process of job creation has been very successful since the mid-1990s, the functioning of the Spanish labour market has been far from perfect. Unemployment has never fallen below the EU average, and the market is characterised by a strong degree of duality, with some highly protected workers and high dismissal costs, along side other workers with very low protection and low or nil dismissal costs.[1]

As a result of these imbalances, the Spanish economy has suffered the effects of the world recession far more intensively than have most advanced countries. The poor performance of its economy is particularly noticeable in the labour market. Since the beginning of the recession the rate of unemployment has more than doubled, reaching 18 per cent in 2010, and is expected to increase further. Thus, while the fall in economic activity has been more moderate than in other countries, job destruction has been much more intense. The collapse of real estate construction impacted heavily on employment, but other sectors in the economy (namely, industry and services) also reduced employment at a fast rate.

Why has the labour market performed so poorly in Spain? Some analysts argue that labour market institutions function reasonably well, and that the main cause of disproportionate job losses (relative to a fall in GDP) is the low productivity of many firms, in particular those in building and tourism-related activities. The job creation boom from the mid-1990s to 2007 was based on low-productivity sectors, mainly building and services, generally employing low-skilled workers. As a result, the downturn has mainly destroyed lower-level jobs and firms that are unlikely to show any real signs of recovery in the foreseeable future, as neither the building sector nor the service sector are destined to become once more the growth engine of the Spanish economy. Thus, the proponents of this view argue, the reallocation of resources towards industries with higher value-added and an intensive use of technology (or 'a change in the growth model', as it has been termed) is a sufficient condition to achieve significant and permanent reductions in the unemployment rate.

Many economists view this approach to the causes of unemployment in Spain as inadequate. Major changes in the allocation of resources are complex and lengthy processes. Besides, such a change can hardly be conceived without wise and profound reforms of labour market institutions in an economy that has been characterised by high and persistent unemployment, even in the years of extraordinary employment growth (see Romero-Ávila and Usabiaga, 2007, for a recent study). In a wide study using 21-OECD economies since 1980, Garibaldi and Mauro (2002) found evidence that labour market institutions such as unemployment benefits, trade union coverage, level of taxation, and employment protection influence the rate of growth of employment. These authors also found that the sector composition of employment plays only a minor part.

In this chapter, we argue that, whereas steps towards productivity-based growth are key for a strategy of high and stable employment, this does not make the need for labour reforms any less pressing. On the contrary, the end of the low-interest, high-demand years is likely to imply slower job creation. If the government manages to find the right incentives to promote investment in high-value-added sectors to bring Spain's economy closer to the European average, the rate of job creation is bound to be far more modest than the one that has been witnessed since the mid-1990s. We shall show that, in that scenario, the application of suitable reforms in labour contracts, collective bargaining, and active and passive labour policies can help to speed up the reduction of the unemployment rate.

Section 3.2 summarises some stylised facts about the growth model in Spain. In particular, we provide evidence of how the relationship between production growth and change in unemployment (Okun's law) has changed over time. In section 3.3 we construct a European average benchmark for a new growth model and perform an accounting exercise to analyse the effects of changing the growth model in Spain. In section 3.4 we discuss a framework for reforming the labour market in Spain, and use REMS to evaluate the benefits of the labour market reform, and in section 3.5 we draw our conclusions.

3.2 The Spanish growth model

In this section we compare some of the characteristics of the Spanish production structure with that of other developed countries. In particular, we document medium-run differences in aggregate employment and productivity growth, taking sector composition into account. We shall also explore the relationship between output growth and unemployment changes (Okun's law), in both Spain and the European Union (EU).

The Spanish economy has been a reference in employment creation across Europe from the second half of the 1990s onwards, as shown in Figure 3.1. During the period 1994–2007, annual rates of growth in employment have been consistently well above those of the United States, Germany, or an aggregate of ten European countries.[2] Annual employment growth in Spain averaged 3.15 percentage points from 1994 to 2007, while this figure was only 0.41 per cent, 0.80 per cent and 1.33 per cent in the cases of Germany, EU-10 and the United States, respectively. This had a striking effect on Spanish unemployment rates (see Figure 3.2) which fell from almost 20 per cent in 1994 to average European levels of around 8 per cent in 2007.

These large swings in Spanish unemployment figures are not a novel feature. During the 1985–91 boom the unemployment rate fell from 18 per cent to 13 per cent. However, during the ensuing recession this rate jumped to almost 20 per cent in 1994. What the 1992–4 and the 2008–9

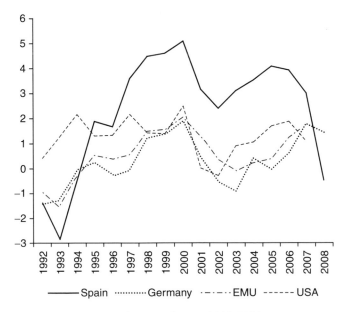

Figure 3.1 Employment growth, annual rates, 1992–2008
Source: Annual macro-economic database of the DG ECFIN (AMECO).

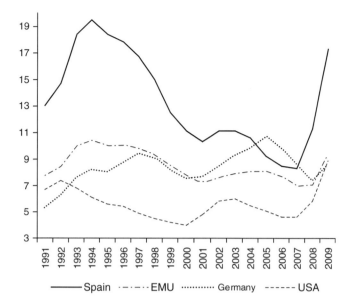

Figure 3.2   Unemployment rate, 1991–2009
Source: Annual macro-economic database of the DG ECFIN (AMECO).

episodes teach us is that both employment and unemployment levels have been much more volatile in Spain than in other developed countries. Beneath these quantitative features, a much more worrying picture emerges with regard to quality, in terms of wages and productivity, for jobs created in boom periods. Figures 3.3 and 3.4 show how the years of high employment creation have been characterised by productivity stagnation. Productivity growth averaged an annual rate of 0.2 per cent in Spain between 1994 and 2007, against 1.4 per cent in Germany (1.8 and 1.2 points in the United States and EU-10, respectively). This generated a sharp divergence from the rest of the EU-10. While productivity (in purchasing power standards) was almost identical in Spain and the EU-10 in 1991, in 2007 it was 15 per cent lower in Spain (see Figure 3.3).

Several authors have documented the negative (positive) trade-off between employment (unemployment) and productivity growth that has occurred in Western Europe since the 1970s (see Rezai and Semmler, 2007; Dew-Becker and Gordon, 2008; and Enflo, 2009, for some recent references). One simple explanation for this negative relationship between productivity and employment can be attributed to positive shocks in labour force participation. However, as stated by Gordon (1995), this is a short-run implication, since other shocks may drive

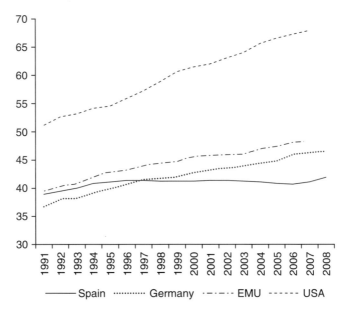

Figure 3.3   Evolution of productivity per worker, 1991–2008
Source: Annual macro-economic database of the DG ECFIN (AMECO).

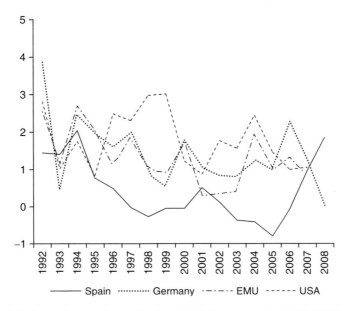

Figure 3.4   Annual rates of growth of productivity per worker, 1992–2008
Source: Annual macro-economic database of the DG ECFIN (AMECO).

both employment and productivity upwards. Thus, in the medium run, capital accumulation may increase productivity and eliminate the negative trade-off. In fact, Ball and Mankiw (2002) uncovered a positive correlation between productivity growth and structural employment in the United States. Thus understanding the factors that cause this trade-off to persist in Spain over time is crucial in order to assess the effectiveness of alternative policies designed to reduce unemployment (or increase employment).[3]

The nexus of productivity and unemployment (or employment) can be established through the lenses of Okun's law. Given that the growth rate of output is the sum of productivity growth and employment growth, we can start from an aggregate production function to obtain Okun's relationship[4] and analyse the possible sources of variations in the trade-off between unemployment changes and production growth. More specifically, let us consider the following production function with disembodied technology in per capita terms:

$$Y = A\left(\frac{cK}{L}\right)^{1-\alpha}\left(\frac{N}{L}H\right)^{\alpha} L$$

where Y stands for production, K for the capital stock, c for the capital capacity utilisation rate, N for employed workers, H for hours per worker, A for total factor productivity and L for total population in the economy. This expression can be written in terms of the per capita capital stock, k, the labour force, S, and the level of unemployment, U, as

$$Y = A\left(ck\right)^{1-\alpha}\left(\frac{S-U}{L}H\right)^{\alpha} L$$

or,

$$Y = A\left(ck\right)^{1-\alpha}\left(\frac{S}{L} - \frac{U}{L}\right)^{\alpha} H^{\alpha} L = A\left(ck\right)^{1-\alpha}\left(\frac{S}{L} - \frac{U}{S}\frac{S}{L}\right)^{\alpha} H^{\alpha} L$$

$$= A\left(ck\right)^{1-\alpha} \left(s(1-u)\right)^{\alpha} H^{\alpha} L$$

where s is the participation rate and u the unemployment rate. Taking logs and first differences we can obtain the equivalent expression in terms of the rate of growth of the variables,[5]

$$\frac{\Delta Y}{Y} = \frac{\Delta A}{A} + \frac{\Delta L}{L} + (1-\alpha)\left(\frac{\Delta k}{k} + \frac{\Delta c}{c}\right) + \alpha\frac{\Delta s}{s} + \alpha\frac{\Delta H}{H} - \frac{\alpha}{e}\Delta u$$

or,

$$\Delta u = \frac{e}{\alpha}\left[\frac{\Delta A}{A} + \frac{\Delta L}{L} + (1-\alpha)\left(\frac{\Delta k}{k} + \frac{\Delta c}{c}\right) + \alpha\frac{\Delta s}{s} + \alpha\frac{\Delta H}{H}\right] - \frac{e}{\alpha}\frac{\Delta Y}{Y} \quad (3.1)$$

where e stands for the employment rate and $\dot{u}$ is the change in the unemployment rate.

Let us now assume that total factor productivity, population (through higher immigration), capital utilisation, labour force participation and average working hours are pro-cyclical. Then we may establish the following structural linear relationships:

$$\frac{\Delta A}{A} = \beta_1 \frac{\Delta Y}{Y}, \quad \frac{\Delta L}{L} = \beta_2 \frac{\Delta Y}{Y}, \quad \frac{\Delta c}{c} = \beta_3 \frac{\Delta Y}{Y}, \quad \frac{\Delta s}{s} = \theta_4 + \beta_4 \frac{\Delta Y}{Y}, \quad \frac{\Delta H}{H}$$

$$= \theta_5 + \beta_5 \frac{\Delta Y}{Y}.$$

where all βs are positive and the θs represent shocks which stand for different institutional and economic factors that may influence some labour market variables irrespective of the business cycle. For example, a positive (negative) shock to θ_5 causes the relationship between hours and output to become less (more) than proportional. Also θ_4 can be seen as a shock to labour supply.

Plugging these relationships into Equation (3.1) allows us to obtain the following reduced form for Okun's law

$$\Delta u = \delta_t - \beta_t \frac{\Delta Y}{Y} \tag{3.2}$$

where

$$\delta_t = \frac{e_t}{\alpha} \left((1 - \alpha) \frac{\Delta k}{k}(t) + \theta_4(t) + \theta_5(t) \right)$$

and

$$\beta_t = \frac{e_t}{\alpha} \left(\begin{array}{c} 1 - \beta_{1t} - \beta_{2t} - (1 - \alpha)\beta_{3t} \\ -\alpha\beta_{4t} - \alpha\beta_{5t} \end{array} \right)$$

We have included time dependence in the parameters to account for the fact that the unemployment–growth link is time-varying (see Huang and Lin, 2008, for econometric evidence).

Notice that any shock affecting the parameters in the intercept positively (or negatively) moves Okun's curve outwards (or inwards), implying that a higher (or lower) variation in unemployment will be associated with a similiar rate of growth of output. Accordingly, a negative shock affecting labour force or hours per employee growth will shift the Okun's curve inwards. A set of labour market policies and institutional changes affect hours or labour force and move Okun's curve downwards. For example, with respect to working hours, any measure that induces a decrease in market tightness will reduce the implicit cost of hiring, increasing the willingness of firms to substitute employment for hours, thus pulling θ_5 down. An even more direct effect occurs with a decrease in the cost of posting vacancies, or when there is an improvement of efficiency in the way vacancies and unemployed workers are matched to each other. Also, a reduction in labour hoarding causes working hours per employee to shrink, thus reducing unemployment for a given growth of output. Finally, any measure aimed at reducing the marginal cost of firms also tends to reduce working hours per employee and moves Okun's curve in the right direction. Regarding θ_4, any shock in the activity rate will affect the position of Okun's curve. For example, the incorporation of immigrants and other specific population groups, such as women and young people, into the labour force may be processes behind shifts in Okun's law. Also, a reduction in any of the betas, which will indicate a lower degree of covariance between the variable and output, makes the slope of Okun's curve steeper.

Thus we have seen that changes in technology, including skill-biased technological change, government regulations in the labour market, immigration policies, taxes, sector distribution, labour market tightness, input prices and so on, would all contribute to modifying the Okun schedule over time, by changing the structural relations behind the reduced-form parameters in Equation (3.2).

To illustrate these effects, Figure 3.5 represents three different Okun's curves – that is, three negative linear relationships between the rates of growth of production and variations in the unemployment rate.[6] To simplify the interpretation, we focus only on the region where the growth rate of production is positive. Consider first the continuous line passing through points A and B. For this economy, when output growth is zero, the unemployment rate is changing at a rate $A = \delta_t$. On the other hand, $B = \frac{\delta_t}{\beta_t}$ is the rate of GDP growth necessary to maintain a constant unemployment rate over time. Obviously, in order to see a reduction in the unemployment rate, output should grow at a higher rate than B.

Upward shifts of this schedule can be considered as short-run 'unfavourable shifts' for unemployment. Conversely, any change moving Okun's curve downwards is a short-run 'favourable shift' for unemployment. Therefore the schedule represented in the figure by the dashed line DE is more favourable to employment creation and to unemployment reduction than the initial curve. This means that, for a given rate of production growth, the performance of the labour market is better if the economy is located in this second schedule. Coming back to Equation (3.2), a reduction (increase) in $\delta(t)$ related to less (more) hours

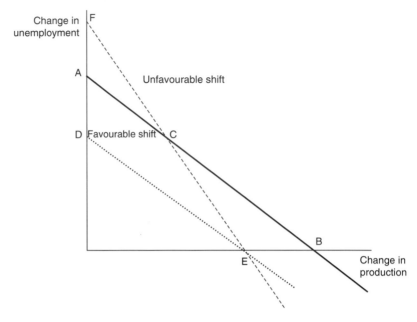

Figure 3.5   Okun's law

worked per employee, to a reduction (increase) in the activity rate, or
to an unskilled-biased (skilled-biased) technological change that leads to
lower (higher) capital growth will change the Okun schedule to the left
(right), improving (worsening) the capability of the economy to reduce
the unemployment rate for a given growth rate of production. Notice
that this shift in the Okun's curve will be more important the higher the
employment rate.

    Think now of the dotted line FE that crosses the initial AB line at point
C. The different location of this Okun's curve with respect to the initial
one is a consequence of two factors: an increase in δ_t, which produces an
unfavourable shift that pushes the schedule to the right, and an increase
in the slope captured by the term β_t. This change in the slope turns the
curve towards the right over point E. With respect to the initial schedule
AB, the new schedule FE has a better (worse) performance of the unemployment rate for any growth rate of production higher (lower) than C.
That is, an economy characterised by the curve FE reduces the unemployment rate more quickly than an economy represented by the curve
AB, when the rate of production growth is strong, but it destroys more
jobs and increases the unemployment rate faster when the rate of growth

of production is weak. In other words, the economy with Okun's law FE has a more volatile labour market than the economy characterised by the AB schedule.

Looking at the previous analysis regarding Okun's relationship, how can we interpret the high volatility of the Spanish labour market as documented in previous paragraphs? This high volatility may result from structural characteristics of the economy not associated with the business cycle which are, in turn, a combination of different drivers. With respect to parameter δ_t, possible explanations are related to high investment levels that have caused capital accumulation to take place at higher rates. In fact, Spain sustained high investment rates in the years up to the crisis of 2008–9, given that it was able to attract foreign savings quite easily. Also, increases in the labour force as a consequence of massive immigration and a rise in the number of women in the workplace are well-documented phenomena. Regarding the slope β_t, in addition to the factors mentioned for the intercept, another candidate to explain the high volatility of unemployment in Spain is a weakening of the relationship between total factor productivity and output (β_1) caused, for example, by unskilled-biased technological change as the building and tourism sectors expanded.

What do the observed data tell us about Okun's curve for Spain? To answer this question we adjust linearly the percentage point variation in the unemployment rate and the growth rate of output in two different periods. Figure 3.6 represents the shift in Okun's curve for Spain between the periods 1961–83 and 1984–2008, along with Okun's law for the aggregate EU-15 in the first period. Figure 3.7 displays the same information for Spain, but using the EU-15 Okun's law for the period 1984–2008 as the basis for comparison. We use as a threshold the year 1984, when Spain undertook deep labour market reforms, which allowed for a widespread use of fixed-term contracts and significantly reduced the dismissal costs of temporary workers.

Some conclusions arise from the study of both figures. First, the Spanish Okun's curve has been located in what we defined previously as an 'unfavourable region' with respect to the European curve, in both the first and second periods. Before 1984 it took much stronger economic growth in Spain than in the rest of European countries to reduce the unemployment rate by the same amount. From 1984 onwards things have changed substantially, however: whereas the EU-15 curve has moved in the right direction over time (a roughly parallel inward shift), the Spanish schedule has experienced a pronounced change in the slope that has very much increased the volatility of the labour market with respect to the first

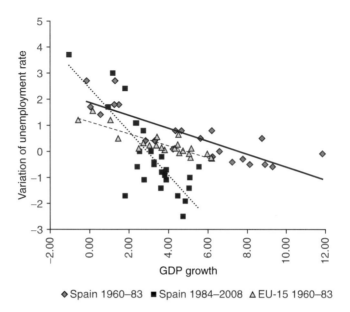

Figure 3.6 Okun's law in Spain in 1960—83 and 1984–2008, and in EU-15 1960–83.

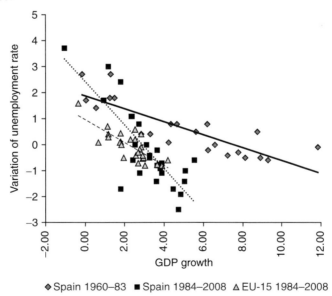

Figure 3.7 Okun's law in Spain in 1960–83 and 1984–2008, and in EU-15 1984–2008

period, and also with respect to the average EU-15. On the positive side, the steeper slope means that the unemployment rate in Spain decreased much faster than in the EU-15 in years of vigorous GDP growth (3.5 per cent). The opposite happens in a downturn, in which a steeper Okun's law implies faster job destruction. For example, according to the most recent Okun's curves, a 2 per cent growth rate in GDP leaves unemployment rates unchanged in Europe, whereas in Spain the unemployment figure increases by around 1 point.[7]

The analysis so far has been conducted at an aggregate level. However, given that productivity is distributed unevenly across sectors, one may think that production composition can play a part in explaining employment or unemployment links with production growth. Figures 3.8 and 3.9 offer a glimpse of sectoral productivity distribution[8] and employment in Spain and in the EU-10. With the exception of the agricultural sector, where productivity is almost the same in both economies, Spain displays lower labour productivity levels at the end of the sample period (average of 2003–7 period) in all sectors. Productivity differentials are especially pronounced in the case of industry. Furthermore, according to Figure 3.9, Spain is an economy with high specialisation (relative

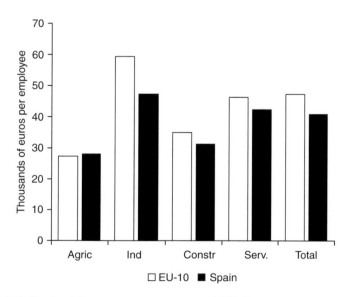

Figure 3.8 Productivity across sectors, averages 2003–7
Source: Annual macro-economic database of the DG ECFIN (AMECO).

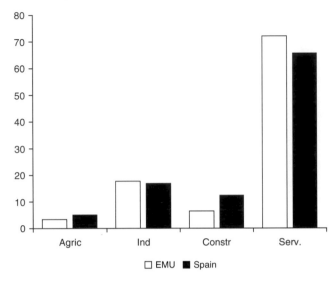

Figure 3.9   Distribution of employment across sectors, averages 2003–7
Source: Annual macro-economic database of the DG ECFIN (AMECO).

abundance of employment) in sectors of relatively low productivity, such as building or agriculture.[9] One of the claims of proponents of change in the growth model in Spain is the creation of necessary incentives to shift the sector distribution of production and employment, and to increase the similarity of the Spanish economy to those countries with better performance in terms of unemployment variations. The ongoing debate places an emphasis on how effective the change in production composition will be in terms of, first, reducing unemployment rapidly and, second, making it less volatile in the future. There is evidence in the literature which challenges the view that making Spain's economic structure more like the EU average will lead to a positive answer to these two questions. In this vein, the work of Groshen and Potter (2003) on the 2001 recession in the United States suggests that such a change in the growth model does not come without costs. The reallocation of workers and capital among industries leads to permanent job losses. So Spain could expect a long lag before employment rebounds. In addition, the effects that a sector shift can induce on Okun's curve, and its consequences for unemployment in a foreseeable context of weaker aggregate demand should be taken into account. The next two sections of this chapter look more deeply into these issues.

3.3 Growth model and job creation: the example of EU-10

In this section we shall perform some simple counterfactual exercises to evaluate the capacity of the so-called new growth model in creating new employment possibilities. We shall take as a benchmark of the so-called new growth model the aggregate of European countries we have used in the descriptive analysis performed in previous sections: EU-10. As Figures 3.8 and 3.9 show, this EU-10 aggregate was 14.9 per cent more productive (in PPSs) than the Spanish economy in 2007; it also displayed higher productivity levels in the industry, building and services sectors. In addition, the EU-10 presents lower rates of employment in low-productivity sectors (the weight of the building sector in employment was 6.6 per cent in EU-10 versus 13.1 per cent in Spain) and a higher weight in high-productivity sectors (services, which include financial institutions, represent 72.7 per cent of employment in the EU-10 versus 66.8 per cent in Spain, whereas industry represented 17.3 per cent of total employment in the EU-10 and 15.6 per cent in Spain).

As a first approach to investigating the employment effects of a more productivity-based growth model, let us consider three simple counterfactual exercises that represent how the Spanish economic structure could perform if it approached the EU-10 average.

1. In the first we assume that Spain preserves its present sector productivity levels but shifts sector employment distribution towards convergence with EU-10 employment weights. This change in the composition would imply a 2.4 per cent increase in aggregate labour productivity in Spain.
2. In the second scenario we assume that Spain keeps its current sector employment weights, but the level of productivity in each sector equals the one in the equivalent sector in EU-10. In this case, Spanish labour productivity would increase by 12.5 points.
3. The final scenario combines the previous two, whereby Spain would converge to both the sectoral employment distribution and productivity level in each sector observed in EU-10. This overall effect would close the productivity gap of the Spanish economy, increasing productivity by 14.9 points.

Our purpose in doing these counterfactual exercises is to answer the following question: how much employment would the Spanish economy have required to generate observed output with employment distribution and productivity levels matching the EU-10 aggregate? To this end, we start by decomposing the observed total labour productivity of the Spanish economy $\left(\frac{Y_t}{N_t}\right)_S$, into the sum of each sector's observed labour productivity $\left(\frac{Y_{jt}}{N_{jt}}\right)_S$ weighted by its employment share $\left(\frac{N_{jt}}{N_t}\right)_S$

$$\underset{\substack{\text{output tot}\\(Y_t)_S}}{} = \left(\overset{\substack{\text{product sect 1}}}{\left(\frac{Y_{1t}}{N_{1t}}\right)_S} \overset{\substack{\text{weight empl sect 1}}}{\left(\frac{N_{1t}}{N_t}\right)_S} + \cdots \overset{\substack{\text{product sect j}}}{\left(\frac{Y_{jt}}{N_{jt}}\right)_S} \overset{\substack{\text{weight empl sect j}}}{\left(\frac{N_{jt}}{N_t}\right)_S} \right) \underset{\substack{\text{empl tot}\\(N_t)_{S0}}}{}$$

(3.3)

Our first exercise consists in changing $\left(\frac{N_{jt}}{N_t}\right)_S$ by the equivalent ratios for the EU-10 $\left(\frac{N_{jt}}{N_t}\right)_E$

$$\underset{\substack{\text{output tot}\\(Y_t)_S}}{} = \left(\overset{\substack{\text{product sect 1}}}{\left(\frac{Y_{1t}}{N_{1t}}\right)_S} \overset{\substack{\text{weight empl sect 1}}}{\left(\frac{N_{1t}}{N_t}\right)_E} + \cdots \overset{\substack{\text{product sect j}}}{\left(\frac{Y_{jt}}{N_{jt}}\right)_S} \overset{\substack{\text{weight empl sect j}}}{\left(\frac{N_{jt}}{N_t}\right)_E} \right) \underset{\substack{\text{empl tot}\\(N_t)_{S1}}}{}$$

(3.4)

where $(N_t)_{S1}$ represents the employment required to generate the observed production in the past, had Spain had the same sector productivity but the employment shares of the EU-10.

In the same way, to establish the effects on aggregate employment in exercise 2, we use the following expression

$$\underset{\substack{\text{output tot}\\(Y_t)_S}}{} = \left(\overset{\substack{\text{product sect 1}}}{\left(\frac{Y_{1t}}{N_{1t}}\right)_E} \overset{\substack{\text{weight empl sect 1}}}{\left(\frac{N_{1t}}{N_t}\right)_S} + \cdots \overset{\substack{\text{product sect j}}}{\left(\frac{Y_{jt}}{N_{jt}}\right)_E} \overset{\substack{\text{weight empl sect j}}}{\left(\frac{N_{jt}}{N_t}\right)_S} \right) \underset{\substack{\text{empl tot}\\(N_t)_{S2}}}{}$$

(3.5)

where we substitute $\left(\frac{Y_{jt}}{N_{jt}}\right)_S$ for the equivalent ratios for the EU-10 $\left(\frac{Y_{jt}}{N_{jt}}\right)_E$. Thus, $(N_t)_{S2}$ stands for the simulated employment in Spain under the second scenario.

Finally, exercise 3 mixes the two previous hypotheses in the following equation

$$\underset{\substack{\text{output tot}\\(Y_t)_S}}{} = \left(\overset{\substack{\text{product sect 1}}}{\left(\frac{Y_{1t}}{N_{1t}}\right)_E} \overset{\substack{\text{weight empl sect 1}}}{\left(\frac{N_{1t}}{N_t}\right)_E} + \cdots \overset{\substack{\text{product sect j}}}{\left(\frac{Y_{jt}}{N_{jt}}\right)_E} \overset{\substack{\text{weight empl sect j}}}{\left(\frac{N_{jt}}{N_t}\right)_E} \right) \underset{\substack{\text{empl tot}\\(N_t)_{S3}}}{}$$

(3.6)

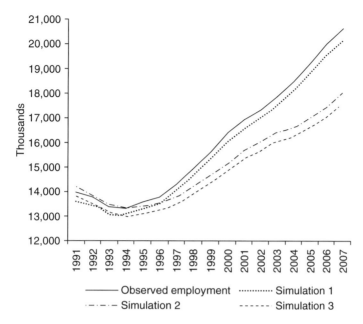

Figure 3.10 Simulated employment (levels) versus observed employment, 1991–2007

where $(N_t)_{S3}$ represents simulated employment had Spain had the employment distribution and the productivity levels of the EU-10 aggregate.

Figure 3.10 displays the evolution in thousands of workers of observed employment in Spain (continuous line) and simulated employment under each of the three scenarios. Figure 3.11 reproduces similar information, but fixing an index 100 for the level of employment in 1991. Two clear messages emerge from these graphs.

First, the composite or reallocation effect is very small. In fact, had Spain had the same employment distribution as the EU-10, but preserved sector productivity, employment growth would have been almost identical to that actually observed: 148 jobs in 2007 for each 100 jobs existing in 1991 (Figure 3.11).

The second counterfactual exercise, also displayed in these Figures, shows that a transition towards sector productivity equivalent to that in the EU-10 would have greatly slowed the rate of job creation, even for the remarkable GDP growth rates of the Spanish economy during the period. More specifically, under this scenario Spain would have seen

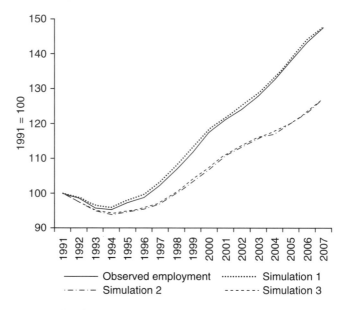

Figure 3.11   Simulated employment, index 1991 = 100

employment figures of 18.0 million in 2007, instead of the actual 20.1 million (in index numbers, employment would have increased from 100 to 127). These exercises must be read cautiously since they are mere counterfactual exercises and do not take into account other effects resulting from changes in productivity levels. Still, they give us a broad picture as to the job creation capacity of a more technology-intensive growth. They indicate that a more balanced growth strategy in favour of higher productivity activities, however convenient in terms of stable employment, is unlikely to result in the kind of fast job creation that the Spanish economy might need to reduce high unemployment rates.

These counterfactuals are carried out assuming that GDP grows at the rate actually observed in Spain since the mid-1990s. It could legitimately be argued that higher productivity might also result in faster growth over and above the observed rates. To account for this, we look at the previous exercises from a different perspective. We assume that the drivers of Spain's GDP growth since the mid-1990s are augmented by the impact of higher productivity and ask what rate of GDP growth would have been required to make EU-10 productivity levels compatible with Spain's job creation rate. To answer this, we reverse the endogenous variable in Equations (3.4) to (3.6) and the answer is an implausibly

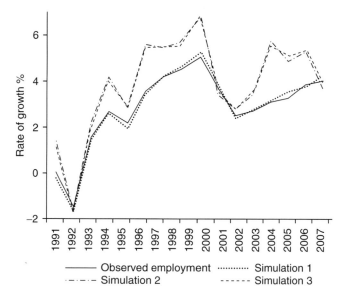

Figure 3.12   Simulated growth of value added, 1991–2007

sustained 3.8 per cent annual rate of GDP growth from 1991 to 2007 (see Figure 3.12).

3.4   General equilibrium evaluation of job creation with the new growth model

In the previous section we carried out a partial equilibrium analysis, similar in spirit to the shift–share analysis of Garibaldi and Mauro (2002), to establish the sector contribution to employment growth, taking output growth and other relevant macroeconomic variables as given. In this section, we switch our focus to a general equilibrium analysis to evaluate the effects of a change in the growth model, characterised here by a change in the determinants of economic growth from demand (interest rate) shocks to productivity growth. We use the REMS model (see Chapter 2), taking into account endogenous relations among the basic macroeconomic aggregates, including key labour market variables such as wages or hours worked.

In this vein, we initially calibrate REMS to reproduce the following stylised facts observed in the Spanish economy in the period between the first half of the 1990s and 2007:

1. A yearly GDP growth rate of 3 per cent reduces the unemployment rate by 1 percentage point (this means that it takes 10 years growing at that rate to reduce the unemployment rate by 10 points).
2. Labour productivity is basically stagnant during these years.

Economic growth in this economy is generated by introducing a positive preference shock on consumption. Notice that this is an indirect way of capturing what has occurred in Spain in the years before the 2007 financial crisis, where households experienced a sharp increase in credit facilities, motivated by the historically low interest rates and the easy access of the economy to international indebtedness. In technical terms, our approach consists in introducing a shock, η_t, into the utility function of households (see Chapter 2):

$$E_t \sum_{t=0}^{\infty} \beta^t \left[\eta_t \ln \left(c_t^o - h^o c_{t-1}^o \right) + n_t^o \phi_1 \frac{(T - l_{1t})^{1-\eta}}{1 - \eta} \right.$$

$$\left. + (1 - n_t^o)\phi_2 \frac{(T - l_{2t})^{1-\eta}}{1 - \eta} + \chi_m \ln \left(m_t^o \right) \right]$$

The alternative scenario (which we shall call the *new growth model* in contrast to the previous *old growth model*) consists of making the Spanish economy more productive by means of a positive shift, μ_t, on labour-augmenting technological progress which increases labour productivity at a 1 per cent rate during the same period. This shock enters the production function as follows (see Chapter 2):

$$y_{it} = z_{it} \left\{ \left[a k_{it}^{-\rho} + (1 - a)e_{it}^{-\rho} \right]^{-\frac{1}{\rho}} \right\}^{1-\alpha} (\mu_t n_{it} l_{i1t})^{\alpha} \left(k_{it}^p \right)^{\zeta}$$

The main objective of this section is to compare the speed with which the economy is capable of reducing the unemployment rate from its initial value (20 per cent) in these two alternative scenarios. The results corresponding to low-productivity demand-driven growth are summarised in row 1 of Table 3.1. As regards the productivity-growth based case we consider that the demand driver loses strength and that the 3 per cent growth rate can be sustained by a favourable technology shock which raises productivity at an annual rate of 1 per cent. The results are shown in row 2.

High demand and low productivity growth combined to facilitate high employment growth and reduce the unemployment rate by 1 point per year. These results brought with them important changes in the labour force, which grew at an average annual rate of 2 per cent between 1990

Table 3.1 Evaluation of the new growth model

	GDP growth	U change	GDP/N	w	l_1	Years to $U = 10\%$
			Growth gap			
Growth model:						
Old model (1984–2008)	3.00	−1.00	–	–	–	10.00
New model (scenario 1)	3.00	−0.49	1.07	0.18	−0.47	20.45
New model (scenario 2)	3.71	−0.72	1.00	0	−0.25	13.88

Notes: U = unemployment rate, w = real wage, N = employment, l_1 = hours per worker. The growth gap is the growth differential with respect to the old model.

and 2007, mainly driven by immigration (the number of immigrants quadrupled between 2000 and 2008). We do not intend to capture such a demographic change in our model. Thus, we assume that the first row in Table 3.1 is a stylised representation of the main medium-run trend of the Spanish economy over the last 15 years, in which productivity has been roughly stagnant. Against this background a switch in the engines of growth towards productivity does not necessarily imply faster job creation. As the results in row 2 show, in this alternative scenario the time span needed to bring the unemployment rate down to half of its initial value actually increases to 20 years.[10] Does this imply that productivity-based growth is an undesirable strategy? Far from it. For one thing, the years of rapid demand growth could not have lasted for very long, and the imbalances accumulated in the Spanish economy, especially in foreign indebtedness, would sooner or later have led to slower growth and perhaps a recession. Thus a repetition of the past is not likely but it is not desirable either. Productivity-based growth can act as a remedy to many of these imbalances; but it will not suffice to create jobs at the pace that would be required to absorb current unemployment within a few years. An analysis of the observed and counterfactual Okun's law helps to come to terms with this apparent paradox.

What our results suggest is that the change in the growth model makes the slope of Okun's curve flatter, because it probably tends to increase the structural parameter β_1 and, to a lesser extent, β_3. This flattens Okun's curve, which is good news as far as unemployment stability is concerned, but bad news if we start from a situation of high unemployment and low output growth, as point F in Figure 3.5, and look for quick-fix solutions to unemployment woes. Figure 3.13, where we present simulations of unemployment changes for different GDP

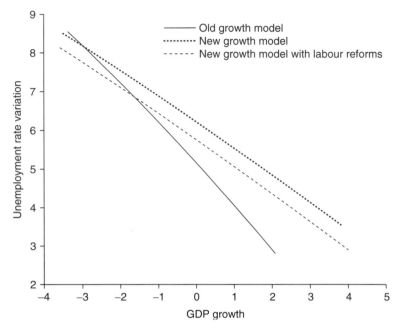

Figure 3.13 Simulation of Okun's curves under different scenarios

growth rates (Okun's laws) under the 'old' and the 'new' growth models' assumptions, confirms our suggestion. The change towards a more productivity-oriented growth strategy does indeed rotate Okun's law around the current GDP growth–unemployment change pair, making eventual reductions in employment slower as the economy recovers. Faster unemployment reduction requires accompanying measures that change the structural unemployment rate to shift this relationship downwards, favouring both stable and rapidly falling unemployment. With regard to Figure 3.5, what we need is not a move from the solid line to the dotted one, but rather one that shifts Okun's law down to the dashed line.

3.4.1 A proposal for reforming the labour market in Spain

Many studies have addressed the incidence of labour market institutions and reforms on unemployment (Blanchard and Wolfers, 2000).[11] For the Spanish case, Aguirregabiria and Alonso-Borrego (2009) evaluate the last sound labour market reform carried out in Spain in 1984. They conclude that the introduction of temporary contracts in 1984 had important effects on employment and job turnover, but very modest effects on productivity. The objective of the simulations we shall present next in this section is to throw light on the foreseeable consequences, in terms of unemployment, of a reform that takes into account the main problems of the Spanish labour market. We shall do so in a scenario where productivity will be growing in accordance with the expected change in the growth model for the economy.

The specific aspects of the reform we shall simulate are in the spirit of a recent proposal put forward by a large number of academics in Spain and other institutions (see FEDEA, 2009; BBVA, 2009a; Costain *et al.*, 2010). To summarise the main aspects of the proposed reform, we shall concentrate on the four basic aspects of the proposal:

1. A *single* permanent labour contract should be introduced for all new employees, with severance payments increasing with seniority.
2. Protection of the unemployed should be designed in a way that it does not discourage job seeking. This can best be achieved by raising benefits in the first months of unemployment, rather than by increasing benefit duration.
3. Firm-level agreements, reached by workers and employers, should have priority over higher-level agreements.
4. Reform in the design and implementation of active labour market policies, including: routine rigorous evaluation of these policies; participation of appropriately licensed labour intermediation companies and private agencies, in co-operation with public agencies in the provision and management of these policies.

Before proceeding with the presentation of the simulation results, we need to establish a link between the theoretical premises of the proposal and the empirical exogenous variables or parameters of REMS. This is done in Table 3.2. The different degrees of employment protection between temporary and regular workers creates a segmentation in the market: separation rates for temporary workers are much higher than for permanent workers. In fact, Sala and Silva (2009), in a dynamic stochastic general equilibrium (DSGE) model with heterogeneous workers, calibrate the job tenure of temporary and permanent workers at 6 months and 10 years, respectively. These numbers imply separation rates of 0.5 and 0.025, respectively. Regarding the first point of the proposal, we consider that the establishment of a single permanent labour contract

Table 3.2   Correspondence between reforms and REMS

Proposal of labour market reforms	Related REMS parameter
A single permanent labour contract	A 5% reduction in σ
Raise U benefits at the beginning and reduce duration	A 1% increase in $\bar{I_2}$
Modernize collective bargaining	A 5% reduction of the Nash parameter, λ^W
Increase the efficiency of *ALMP*	A 10% reduction in the cost of vacancies, κ_v
	A 5% increase in the efficiency of matching, χ_1

might reduce the separation rate, σ. In particular, we simulate a 5 per cent reduction in the separation rate.[12] With respect to the second objective we simulate a 1 per cent increase in job search intensity, which in the REMS model is captured by the parameter $\bar{I_2}$. Regarding the proposal of decentralising bargaining at the enterprise level, we translate this proposal into a 5 per cent reduction of the Nash bargaining parameter, λ^W, in the efficient wage bargaining equation of the model that tightens the link between wages and firms' productivity. The fourth point of the proposal, which aims at improving the design of active labour market policies, is intended to facilitate a better match between unemployed people and vacancies. Better policy implementation is also crucial to enhance the human capital endowments of the unemployed through tight monitoring, thus increasing competition in the labour market and decreasing the degree of market tightness to avoid bottlenecks. We translate this proposal to parameters through a 10 per cent reduction in the cost of vacancies, κ_v, and a 5 per cent increase in the efficiency parameter of the matching function, χ_1.

Table 3.3 summarises the effects of the different proposals of labour market reform. For the sake of comparison, in the first row we reproduce the results in Table 3.1 for the bare change of the growth model. Then, assuming that productivity is the main driver of economic growth, we repeat the simulation, imposing the previously mentioned labour market reforms one at a time. In the last row we present the results under the assumption of a fully fledged labour market reform that changes all labour market parameters $(\sigma, \bar{I_2}, \lambda^W, \kappa_v, \chi_1)$ simultaneously.

In all cases, the speed of unemployment reduction increases substantially. The precise numbers are of little relevance, but by a way of

Table 3.3 Evaluation of labour market reforms

	GDP growth	U change	GDP/N	w	l_1	Years to U = 10%
			growth gap			
Growth model:						
Old model (1984–2008)	3.00	−1.00	–	–	–	10.00
New model (scenario 1)	3.00	−0.49	1.07	0.18	−0.47	20.45
New model (scenario 2)	3.71	−0.72	1.00	0	−0.25	13.88
Labour market reforms:						
5% reduction in Nash parameter	3.00	−0.66	1.06	0.16	−0.87	15.06
5% reduction in separation rate	3.00	−0.68	1.11	0.25	−0.95	14.73
5% increase in matching efficiency	3.00	−0.70	1.11	0.27	−1.01	14.27
10% reduction cost of vacancies	3.00	−0.75	1.11	0.29	−1.13	13.33
1% increase in search intensity	3.00	−0.72	1.07	0.17	−1.00	13.96
All reforms	3.00	−1.54	1.17	0.40	−2.97	6.50

Notes: U = unemployment rate, w = real wage, N = employment, l_1 = hours per worker. The growth gap is the growth differential with respect to the old model.

illustration it is worth noting that each of these measures tends to reduce the number of years needed to cut the unemployment rate by 10 percentage points by one third. In fact, the joint effect of all these measures summarised in Table 3.2 is quite impressive, implying a very significant shortening of this time span to 6.5 years. These changes in labour market regulations not only favour faster employment growth but also higher productivity and wages. In particular, across the board, labour reform triggers an annual increase of real wages of 0.4 per cent.

To understand this pattern, it is important to bear in mind the complex set of events that changes in the labour market parameters unchain. Total employment in this model is the product of the number of job matches multiplied by the number of working hours of each match. Total matches are decided by firms through the process of posting vacancies, whereas optimal hours are the result of an efficient bargaining process between employed workers and firms. With stagnant productivity the 'old growth model' (row 1) requires a substantial increase in labour input that results in a (moderately) rapid unemployment reduction. The productivity-based growth process (row 2) is less labour intensive and thus unemployment is observed to decrease more slowly. Interestingly, this is so, even though job creation is strengthened by a fall in total hours. Firms and workers find it optimal to increase the number of jobs (matching) and reduce hours per worker (the intensive margin) since the productivity gain sharply reduces the costs of vacancy posting. In the bargaining process it turns out to be optimal for firms to rely on new job openings (now relatively cheaper) than on longer hours; workers also find it optimal to increase the demand for leisure as a result of the wealth effect generated by the shock.

When productivity growth is accompanied by labour reforms, the latter effect is further reinforced (rows 4–9). All five parameter changes discussed above increase the incentive to post more vacancies that now become less costly (lower κ_v) or carry a higher expected profit (lower σ, λ^w and higher $\overline{l_2}, \chi_1$). This again shifts the balance towards more vacancy posting and job creation, partly compensated by lower hours. For example, the reduction of 10 points in the unemployment rate would imply, after the 6.5 years needed, a fall of approximately 19.3 per cent in the intensive margin. That is, *ex post*, the reform acts as a *worksharing* mechanism. This work-sharing device not only reduces the parameter θ_5, pulling Okun's curve towards the origin, but probably weakens the pro-cyclicality of hours, reducing the parameter β_5 of the Okun's curve slope, thus making the curve steeper, which is the right movement for reducing unemployment more quickly, when the unemployment rate is high.

3.5   Concluding remarks

The Spanish economy has experienced a trade-off between job creation and stable employment since the late 1980s. From 1997 onwards, Spain greatly championed employment growth in Europe; however, since 2008 this has led to job destruction. The specialisation in low-productivity activities and the availability of unskilled workers explain this pattern to a great extent in an economy in which growth was fuelled by unprecedentedly low real interest rates. But the inadequate legal framework of labour relations should also be blamed for the extraordinary increase in unemployment. Low investment in active labour market policies, the unfriendly design of passive policies and collective bargaining and, above all, the extraordinarily high number of temporary workers are some examples of this ill-designed normative.

The chances of easy and cheap access to external financing are very thin for the foreseeable future, so Spain must seek to promote alternative incentives to growth, mainly by investing in activities with higher value-added and a more intensive use of skilled workers. Politicians and many commentators advocate a change in the growth model, and rightly so. What this chapter shows is that, whatever the benefits that this change might bring to the Spanish economy, its effectiveness in terms of a speedy reduction in unemployment is unclear.

An adequate reform that actually deals with the main inadequacies of our labour regulations is called for in order to ease the employment growth–stability trade-off. Our simulations show that such reforms might speed up the process of unemployment reduction significantly, while also fostering productivity and real wage growth in line with what has been seen in Europe. These reforms act as a powerful tool to increase the extensive margin (job creation) while reducing the intensive margin (hours per worker). That is, *ex-post*, the reform acts as a *work-sharing* mechanism even though the legal changes we have simulated do not include the direct incentive for part-time contracts.

In more formal terms, what we have argued here is that while a change in the growth model is needed to shift the slope of Okun's law, only labour market reforms can help to shift it towards the origin, making GDP growth more efficient in terms of unemployment reduction. We conclude that changes in the economic structure do not make labour reforms any less necessary, but rather the opposite if we want to shorten employment recovery significantly.

Notes

1. Since the reform of 1984, job creation has relied mainly on temporary contracts (see Aguirregabiria and Alonso-Borrego, 2009), and the rate of fixed-term jobs in Spain is the highest in the OECD.
2. Countries included in the aggregate of ten European countries (EU-10) are: Germany, Belgium, Denmark, France, Austria, Italy, The Netherlands, Norway, Portugal and Sweden. These are the only EU countries with available data (for a sufficient time span) on sectoral production and employment.
3. Or, in Gordon's words, 'we should be able to identify the policies that shift the unemployment–productivity tradeoff in the right direction'.
4. See Courtney (1985) for a similar approach.
5. Okun (1962) suggested two alternative approaches for estimating the trade-off between unemployment and production: a 'first difference' and a 'gap' model (output as deviations from the potential level). Here we follow Knoester (1986), Lee (2000) and Huang and Lin (2008) in using the first difference approximation.
6. Notice that the linear schedule is a simplification, because Equation (3.2) shows that the relationship is in fact non-linear.
7. This phenomenon is known as jobless growth (see Khemraj *et al.*, 2006 for a recent study).
8. Levels of productivity are again measured in purchasing power standards (international euro).

9. Spain also specialises in other relatively low-productivity activities such as commerce and hospitality inside the services sector (not shown in the figure).

10. For completeness, we also consider (row 3) the case in which, over and above the demand shock responsible for most of the observed GDP 3 per cent growth rate in the past, there is an additional annual 1 per cent productivity growth. The combination of these two favourable sources of growth raises the average GDP growth rate to 3.71 per cent. In this scenario it takes about fourteen years to reduce the unemployment rate by 10 percentage points. We consider this counterfactual as highly improbable given that the main stimuli that have driven aggregate demand in the past (low interest rates, easy access to international financial markets, high rate of growth of residential investment) are not expected to operate in the future.

11. See also Arpaia and Mourre (2005) and Eichhorst *et al.* (2008), for two recent surveys.

12. The exact variation in the parameters of the model is set more or less arbitrarily, as we are mainly interested in the direction of the results. In any case, we keep the changes in the parameters to modest figures.

4
Productivity and Competitiveness: The Economic Impact of the Services Directive

C. Cuerpo, R. Doménech and L. González-Calbet

4.1 Introduction

Spain became a member of the Economic and Monetary Union (EMU) in 1998 and, up to the international crisis of 2008–9, there were three indications of what most economists agree is a lack of competitiveness on the part of the Spanish economy. The first is the positive inflation differential with the EMU; the second a persistent and growing external deficit; and the third a poor trend in labour productivity, in relation to the United States, but also to other European countries.

There are several ways of illustrating the evidence on the lack of competitiveness. One relatively common approach, particularly among the general public and the media, is to refer to this problem using the inflation differential with other countries. While this approach is not completely appropriate, it is the most popular or common. The idea is relatively simple: within the EMU, with a fixed nominal exchange rate, a positive inflation differential implies an appreciation of the real exchange rate and therefore the country in question loses competitiveness. This approach is correct when all goods are tradable. However, headline inflation measures price changes in tradable and non-tradable goods. Figure 4.1 displays the inflation rate in both Spain and the euro-zone. The shaded area represents the inflation differential, which has averaged nearly one percentage point since Spain became a member of the EMU. Because the inflation differential occurs in aggregate and core inflation, the most volatile elements of inflation, such as energy, are not the causes of this gap. It does not matter whether we measure the inflation differential with total aggregate inflation or just take the core component into account.

One possible explanation is that the inflation differential could be the natural result of a convergence process; that is, the Balassa–Samuelson

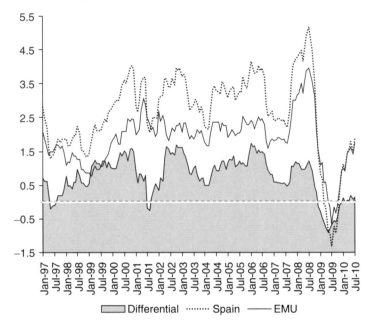

Figure 4.1   Inflation in Spain and the EMU, 1997–2010
Source: Eurostat.

hypothesis. We have known for a long time that countries with lower levels of income per capita also have lower prices (see, Summers and Heston, 1991), and that economies with a higher level of income per capita have higher prices. Figure 4.2 illustrates this evidence: income per capita (in relative terms to the average for the European Union) (EU) is positively correlated with relative prices. The Balassa–Samuelson hypothesis states that if per capita income converge, then prices should also converge, in a process in which inflation and growth differentials are positively related. The mechanism driving price convergence is that, in countries and periods where productivity growth in tradable goods is greater than in non-tradable goods, there should be an above-average increase in prices.

How much does this evidence explain the inflation differentials across European countries? If we analyse the period from 1998 to 2008, the correlation between the average growth rate of income per capita and the inflation rate is positive, but low: the process of real convergence explains less than 25 per cent of the inflation differentials. Furthermore, in the specific case of Spain, the evidence is not favourable to the

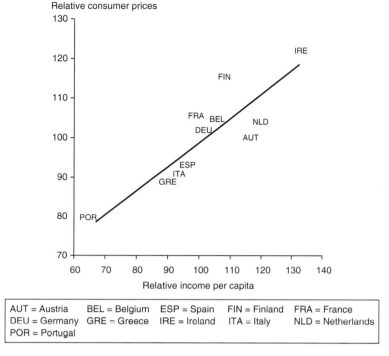

Figure 4.2 Per capita income and consumer price levels in the EMU, 2007 (EMU = 100)
Source: AMECO and Eurostat.

Balassa–Samuelson hypothesis, as Estrada and Lopez-Salido (2004a) conclude. Thus, the correlation between the inflation differential and the productivity growth gap between tradables and non-tradables in Spain is negative, as well as the cross-sectional evidence for the sample of EMU countries. As shown by Figure 4.3, if we exclude Ireland from the sample, which is the only country that clearly confirms the Balassa–Samuelson hypothesis, the relationship is negative and statistically significant.

Therefore, Spanish inflation differentials between 1998 and 2008 has encouraged the appreciation of the real exchange rate not only in the case of non-tradable goods but also in tradable ones. Related to this inflation differential in tradable goods, the external deficit increased until it reached 10 per cent of GDP in 2007 and 2008.

To some extent, external deficits are a consequence of economic integration. For example, following the 2004 enlargement, all the new

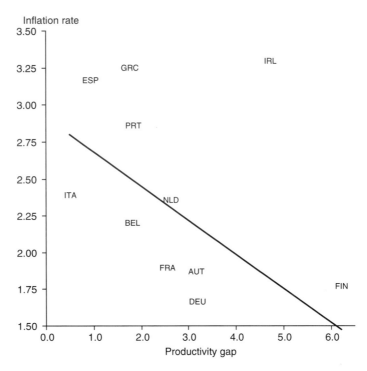

Figure 4.3 Inflation and the productivity growth gap between tradable and non-tradable goods, 1999–2008 averages

members of the European Union displayed deficits, some of which were particularly large. Surpluses were generally registered by countries with the highest levels of income per capita. Figure 4.4 represents precisely the relationship between GDP per capita and the current account balance. While a high degree of volatility is observed, the correlation between income per capita and the current account balance is quite significant, and Spain is one of the countries that bucks this trend. However, bearing in mind its level of income per capita, the external deficit in Spain was far from what could be expected according to the whole sample.

Nonetheless, the large and persistent external deficit of the Spanish economy was the result of two opposing forces. On the one hand, Spanish exports did relatively well in world markets, while on the other, foreign imports penetrated intensively into Spanish domestic markets. Indeed, from Figure 4.5 we can see that external deficit has mainly been related not to a decrease in exports, which remained relatively stable

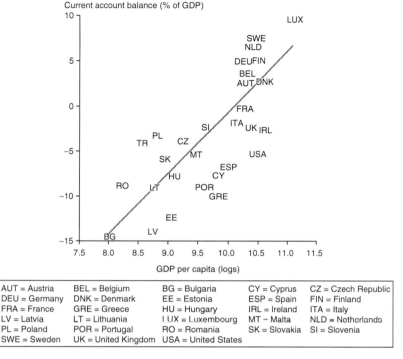

Figure 4.4 Current account balance and GDP per capita, 2002–8 averages

in average terms, but to a marked increase in imports. In fact, when we analyse Spanish exports in relation to worldwide international trade, we find that shares have remained surprisingly constant since the late 1990s, when exports from other countries such as France, the United Kingdom and the United States have been decreasing. The latter is not that surprising, bearing in mind that one of the most noteworthy events in the decade since the end of the 1990s has been the spectacular arrival of China on to the trade scene. However, what is surprising is that Spain and Germany have been the two main economies in the euro-zone that have managed to maintain their export shares. Therefore, the problem with competitiveness and that of the external deficit in the Spanish economy is not so much the performance of exporters, but the fact that the companies aiming to satisfy domestic demand have lost ground in favour of imports from the rest of the world.

Exporting companies in Spain are mainly large enterprises. In addition, they invest a large proportion of their resources in R&D and human

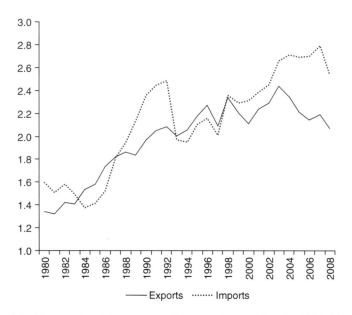

Figure 4.5   Share of Spanish exports and imports in world trade, 1980–2008
Source: World Trade Organization.

capital. And, not surprisingly, their labour productivity is larger. Therefore the external deficit can be understood, at least partially, as a manifestation of the duality problem of the Spanish economy regarding the size of their firms, and its effects on productivity and competitiveness.

In Chapter 1 we offered a detailed analysis of the labour productivity gap, at aggregate level, of Spain with respect to the United States and the main countries in the EU, which we are not going to repeat here. Also, in Chapter 3 we analysed the implications of inefficiencies in the Spanish labour market on its economic performance. Therefore, in this chapter we shall rely only on additional empirical evidence about the relative low labour productivity.

As can be seen from Table 4.1, the issue of relative productivity is related to the size of Spanish companies. The largest Spanish companies are as productive as those in the United States, but the Spanish economy suffers from a composition problem compared with the United States: small and medium-sized enterprises have lower productivity and represent a larger share in terms of production and employment.

Among other factors, such as access to financial resources, capital-intensity or the efficiency of the judicial system (see, for example, Kumar

Table 4.1 Labour productivity and firm size, 2005

	Number of employees				
	1–9	10–19	20–49	50–249	+250
Industry (% of the sector average)					
Spain	53.4	67.7	77.6	101.4	165.5
United States	54.1	46.8	53.8	68.3	129.8
Whole economy (% to the US average)					
Spain	40.6	51.4	58.9	77.0	125.7
United States	54.1	46.8	53.8	68.3	129.8

Source: OECD (2008) and author's own elaboration.

et al., 1999), firm size is also related to regulations in product markets. In economies where regulations create artificial barriers to product competition, less efficient firms are protected from competition. As long as small firms cannot benefit from the economies of scale, better human capital or R&D investment as do larger enterprises, their efficiency levels are almost bound to be lower. Nicoletti and Scarpetta (2003) presented and reviewed all the empirical evidence on product market regulation (PMR) and economic performance. They observed that, generally speaking, production resources were better allocated among sectors and firms, and there were greater incentives for companies to innovate and invest, together with less unemployment, in countries where product markets were better regulated, creating incentives to increase the average size of firms close to the minimum efficient scale of operation.

Figures 4.6 and 4.7 illustrate some of this evidence. As shown by de la Fuente and Doménech (2010), in Figure 4.6 we can see that there is a positive and significant correlation (0.57) between the structural unemployment rate in 2005 and the indicator for goods market regulations in 2003, constructed by the OECD (see Conway *et al.*, 2006, for details about the latter variable). As can be seen, those countries in which this indicator is highest (the least competition in goods markets) have a higher structural unemployment rate. This evidence is consistent with the theoretical (see Andrés, 1993; Blanchard and Giavazzi, 2003; and Layard *et al.*, 2005) and empirical literature (Gianella et al. 2008) that proposes reforms in the goods and services markets as well as in the labour market (such as those described in Chapter 3) to reduce structural unemployment.

Figure 4.7 shows the correlation between the indicator for goods market regulations and the share of employment in firms with fewer than 20 employees in 2006. In this case the correlation is even higher (0.68),

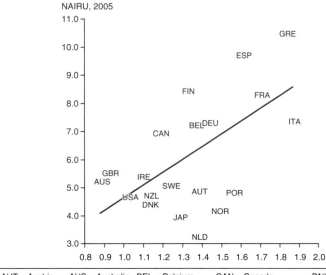

NAIRU, 2005

Figure 4.6 Product market regulations in 2003 and structural unemployment (NAIRU) in 2005

showing that countries where product markets were better regulated (therefore having a lower index in the horizontal axis) were also the countries with a lower share of employment in small firms. Interestingly, in Figure 4.7 Spain and the United States show very different shares of employment in small firms, confirming that the composition effects suggested by Table 4.1 are relevant to explain aggregate productivity differentials.

While Spain improved substantially between 2003 and 2008 in the indicator of product market regulations (PMR) published by the OECD (see Wölfl *et al.*, 2009), is still lagging far behind the countries with the best regulatory environments. In fact, this conclusion is corroborated by other recent indicators published by the IMD World Competitiveness Indicator or the World Bank (Doing Business). For example, Figure 4.8 shows that the correlation between the OECD indicator of PMR and the index elaborated using Doing Business is very high (0.75).[1]

Not surprisingly, and closing the circle of the empirical evidence presented in this section, product market regulations are very much related to inflation differentials in the EMU. As shown by BBVA (2009b), a large

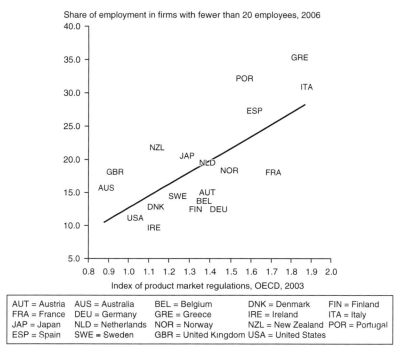

Figure 4.7 Product market regulations in 2003 and share of employment in firms with fewer than 20 employees in 2006

proportion of the inflation differentials in the euro area is explained by profit margins, a result consistent with Przybyla and Roma (2005). The contribution of profit margins to inflation differentials is related to economic growth differentials, and the relation between both variables is intensified by product market regulations. Thus, from 1999 to 2007 the contribution of profit margins to inflation differentials had a higher correlation (0.92) with the interaction of GDP growth and the Doing Business indicator than with economic growth alone (0.84). In fact, this interaction explains almost perfectly the average contribution of profit margins to inflation differentials, as shown in Figure 4.9. While GDP growth in Spain and Greece was lower than in Ireland, the contribution of marginal profit to inflation was higher because of their poorer levels of PMR.

Probably because of this interaction between economic growth and PMR improvements in inflation in the service sector have not been apparent either. As we can see from Figure 4.10, the inflation differential

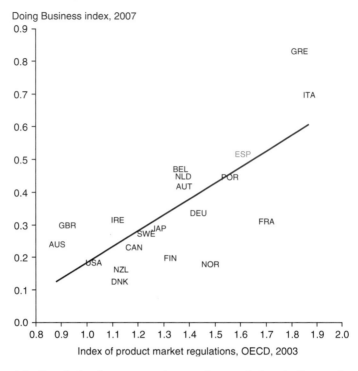

Figure 4.8 Correlation between product market regulations indicators from the OECD and the World Bank (Doing Business)

in services has been large and relatively stable from the Spanish joining the EMU until the crisis of 2008–9. This evidence is worrying for two reasons: first, because the Balassa-Samuelson hypothesis cannot explain this inflation differential, as shown before; and second, because services are by far the largest sector in the economy.

Summarising the empirical evidence of this section, 1999–2007, Spain showed a persistent inflation differential, a growing external deficit and low relative productivity. While many Spanish firms and sectors are highly competitive in international markets, these three problems are closely related and are an indication of the lack of overall competitiveness of the Spanish economy. Since the current crisis began in 2008–9 some of these problems have been tempered significantly, but the cost has been dramatic, with an increase in the unemployment rate unheard of in other European countries. Therefore the challenge should be to reduce unemployment levels over the next few years and do so while improving

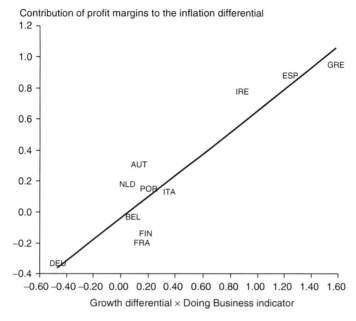

Figure 4.9 Contribution of profit margins to inflation differentials and the interaction of GDP growth and the Doing Business indicator of product market regulations, averages 1999–2007

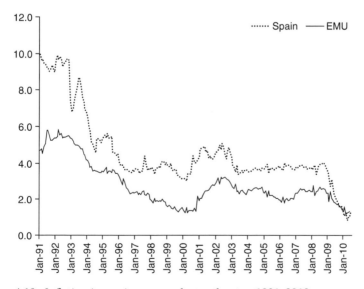

Figure 4.10 Inflation in services, annual growth rates, 1991–2010

competitiveness. In order to succeed, structural reforms can simultaneously reduce unemployment and increase productivity. Among these structural reforms, improvements in the regulations of product markets may play a very important role. For this reason, since the Spanish economy is currently in the process of incorporating the Services Directive, it is particularly interesting to evaluate its effects in terms of GDP, productivity, consumption, investment and real wages, as we shall do in the following sections.

4.2   International evidence on the effects of the Services Directive

The Services Directive (SD) came into force at the end of 2006 in the EU. Three years later, at the end of 2009, the really complex process of its transposition to the Spanish legal system ended with the endorsement of two national laws (known as 'Paraguas' and 'Omnibus'). This approval meant only the beginning of a long road towards the liberalisation of sectors that traditionally present high barriers to competition.

Services represent about two-thirds of the EU economy. However, the weight of services in intra-EU trade is minor. Certainly, the main explanation for this apparent dilemma is the very nature of most services. Production and consumption take place both at the same time and in the same place. Moreover, at the beginning of the twenty-first century many impediments to the free movement of services still remained within the EU. The existing fragmentation in the internal market for services had a negative impact on growth, while at the same time preventing consumers from accessing a greater variety of services at lower prices. It therefore, became essential to make the largest economic sector in the EU more dynamic. In this context, a true internal market for services needed to be configured by adopting a global approach. The SD represents the pillar of a global strategy oriented towards eliminating consistently and effectively the barriers and obstacles that restricted the access of services providers in every country of the EU.

The European Commission's first draft of the SD, also known as the Bolkenstein Directive, published on 13 January 2004, was amended by the European Parliament and the European Council over several readings. At the same time an agreement was reached with the agents involved. The Directive was finally approved by the Council on 12 December 2006.

There is an abundant literature on the economic effects of unnecessary and discriminatory regulation (see OECD, 2003, for a discussion about this). Noteworthy are numerous studies reviewing the economic benefits of a reduction in excessive regulation in manufacturing; see, for example, Buigues *et al.* (1990). However, little research has been devoted to liberalisation policies for services. The launch of the SD meant a turning point as it inspired in-depth studies and discussions about the impact of removing barriers on trade and investment in services.[2] This recent research activity began by focusing on barriers to services provision, their identification and measurement, to further evaluate the economic impact of dropping these obstacles.

The OECD empirical studies measuring national regulation levels are the statistical base for most of these approaches. As discussed in the previous section, one of the main databases allowing international comparison of the level of regulation is the OECD Indicators of Product Market Regulation database, made up of a set of indicators measuring the extent to which policies promote or inhibit competition in areas where competition is viable. They measure the economy-wide regulatory and market environments in OECD countries. The idea of this database is to offer quantitative indicators about regulation based on qualitative information included in laws and ruling. So it is a bottom up approach that makes it possible to trace the indicator scores back to individual policies (see Conway *et al.*, 2006). The analysis is conducted at three different points in time – 1998, 2003 and 2008 – and the indicators cover formal regulations in state control of business enterprises, legal and administrative barriers to entrepreneurship, and barriers to international trade and investment.

In order to estimate the dynamic benefits for Spain of applying the SD, we shall use REMS. First, we will take advantage of some of the recent literature, beginning with Kox *et al.* (2004, 2005). They refined the various OECD empirical studies analysing the relationship between national regulation intensity and trade patterns by focusing on the impact of domestic product-market national regulation on trade and foreign direct investment (FDI) in services. They paid more attention to bilateral differences on product-market regulation than to regulation as such, by establishing bilateral policy heterogeneity indicators, controlling for differences in regulations. By aggregating and averaging about 200 items they built a bilateral heterogeneity index in five domains (barriers to competition, start-up administrative burdens, regulatory opacity, explicit barriers to trade and investment, and state control). They subsequently used a gravity model to explain intra-EU flows as a consequence of a subset of regressors such as, *inter alia*, regulatory indices, distance and language differences. Their results concluded that two of these – barriers to competition and explicit barriers to trade and investment – have had a significant negative impact on bilateral trade in services. Specifically, the easing of barriers to services provision would boost intra-regional trade of a magnitude ranging from 30 per cent to 60 per cent. Later, these results were revised (see De Bruijn *et al.*, 2006) to remove the effect of the 'Country of Origin Principle', absent in the final version of SD, reducing by one third the increase of intra-EU services trade related to the SD.

This is a complementary result to that of Nicoletti *et al.* (2003), who estimate the impact of policies on bilateral trade and bilateral and multilateral FDI. Their conclusion highlights that, despite extensive liberalisation since the 1980s, there is scope for further improvement by reducing policy barriers to the integration of OECD markets. Remaining barriers still have a significant impact on trade and FDI, with anti-competitive domestic regulations estimated to curb integration as much as explicit trade and FDI restrictions. The simulation of the removal of such barriers suggests that the quantitative effects of further liberalisation of trade, FDI and domestic product on global integration could be substantial. They show an inverse relation between national regulation intensity and trade. When they estimate a similar relation referred specifically to services they obtain a more intense effect, showing that removing barriers to competition on national regulation may have a positive and strong effect on bilateral services trade.

Copenhagen Economics (2005) is also based on an index methodology, constructing indices for barriers in service industries. It estimates the effects of these barriers on rents and price–cost margins of firms through a regression among firms' profitability, considering as regressors existing barriers and their heterogeneity level. The combination of factor analysis and estimation techniques yields an insightful result: cost-creating barriers, which have a negative influence on productivity, tend to be at the top of the value-added chain, while rent-creating hurdles, which have a negative impact on competition, lie at the bottom of it. These effects are transformed into tariff equivalents.

Breuss and Badinger (2005) complement Kox *et al.* (2004, 2005) results. They regress competition and productivity using the same variables – the domestic market size and trade. In a second step, they measure the effects of changes in competition and productivity over employment, investment and production. It is interesting to point out that, according to these results, productivity is apparently not affected by the Directive. However, they find significant effects on competition. Market competition would therefore be the main transmission channel, and, through this, they find indirect effects on employment, investment and productivity. They get a statistically significant effect of a 0.127 percentage point reduction in mark-up for every 1 per cent increase in imports. Taking this result together with the central estimate in De Bruijn *et al.* (2006) (an increase of 30 per cent in intra-EU services trade, which represents nearly half of the total trade) the Directive's impact on firms' mark-up represents a reduction of about 3.75 per cent at the EU level. Individual pro-competition effects are constructed taking into account the initial level of national regulation (that is, the level of heterogeneity). Following this methodology, competitive gains in the services sector in Spain would lead to a 3.84 per cent reduction of firms' margins. Second-round effects of greater competition among firms on productivity, employment and investment are found to be significant and positive.

All these papers agree on significant and positive macroeconomic effects of the Services Directive via increased competition. Based on these facts, some authors use computable general equilibrium (CGE) models to simulate macroeconomic effects. These applied Walrasian, multicountry and multisector models are suited to integration policies, such as the liberalisation of the internal services market.

Simulation results are generally positive at the macro level (value added and employment), regardless of the starting point in terms of regulation. Additionally, the authors generally find *ex-post* specialisation. Older member states would take advantage of their first-mover position to reinforce their services sector, while the new EU countries would increase their specialisation in manufacturing. These findings challenge two well-known theoretical propositions: the Polish plumber syndrome and the alleged endogeneity of optimal currency areas (OCAs). Indeed, following Eichengreen (1992) and Krugman (1993), these results could indicate that a monetary union might fail to fulfil OCA criteria *ex post*, even if it did so *ex ante*.

If CGE models are well suited to the analysis of comparative statics, they cannot reflect the dynamics of an economy over time. The development of dynamic general equilibrium (DGE) models attempts to fill this gap. In order to study the impact over the medium term, these models highlight the actual evolution of an economy (usually with a quarterly frequency).

Some of the studies we have mentioned above offer results about the macroeconomic effects of the Service Directive. REMS offers the possibility of analysing these effects on the Spanish economy, by using a similar initial approach, but trying to adapt the shock to the Spanish economy and using a dynamic model specifically designed and calibrated for its salient features.

4.3   Economic impact of the Services Directive in Spain

The recent financial crisis has to some extent corrected Spanish external imbalances. However, competitiveness has improved at the cost of a higher unemployment rate. To ensure a stronger and more competitive economy, Spain needs to focus on structural, long-lasting policies such as the SD. As discussed in the previous section, following Breuss and Badinger (2005), allocative efficiency improvements related to the Services Directive appear as a drop in firms' margins, driving prices closer to marginal costs. We shall therefore simulate a permanent mark-up contraction of 3.84 per cent in line with the above-mentioned analysis. However, some qualifications are needed.

First, we re-estimated Breuss and Badinger's (2005) results on the basis of the latest version of the Services Directive, in which the country of origin principle (CoOP) no longer exists. For this reason we use De Bruijn *et al.*'s (2006) new results. These authors found a new central estimate of a 28 per cent increase in intra-EU trade as a result of the smoothed legal text. Second, as REMS does not distinguish between services and manufactures, we adjust the decrease in the mark-up by the weight of the services subsectors that are actually affected by the final text, which is approximately 43 per cent of GDP. Finally, in order to ensure a stable equilibrium in this set-up of imperfect competition, we adjust firms' fixed costs, κ_f, so that no extraordinary profits exist.[3] The effects on competitiveness are twofold. On the one hand, lower prices will not only benefit consumers but will also reduce Spanish inflation differential with the rest of the EMU and therefore improve short-term competitiveness. On the other hand, a new growth pattern will emerge, oriented towards main driver of competitiveness in the long run: namely, productivity. The simulated results capture the intuition that a reduction in market power increases output, employment and the remuneration of productive factors. The aggregate effects are positive and quantitatively significant.

4.3.1   Long-run effects

The unexpected and permanent reduction in the margin with which firms operate would effectively shift the steady state of our economy. Long-term effects are reported in Table 4.2.[4] Spanish GDP would increase by 1.21 per cent, as a result of both demand and supply factors. We also

Table 4.2 Long-run effects of the Services Directive

Variable	Percentage deviations from initial steady state
GDP	1.21
Inflation	0.02
Consumption	1.19
Investment	0.82
Exports	0.80
Imports	0.09
Terms of trade	−0.62
Real Exchange Rate	1.46
Tot. hours per adult	0.14
Hours per employed	−0.10
Employment rate	0.24
Vacancies	0.70
Real wage	1.33
Return on capital	0.82
Public debt (% of GDP)	−0.02

observe a qualitative change, as growth is no longer labour intensive and the economy is becoming more productive. In fact, total hours per adult scarcely increased – by 0.1 per cent, but allowed labour productivity to go up by more than 1 per cent.

The increase in GDP is explained by both demand and supply factors. On the demand side, a surge in its main components, consumption and investment, can be seen. Consumption is fostered both by an increase in net wealth (as the return on capital increases) and in disposable income, following higher levels of employment and real wages. Because of the neo-Keynesian modelling of the labour market, there is rivalry between employers and workers to increase their own share of national income. A reduction in the mark-up causes an increase in the real product wage, which results in a higher labour share, as can be observed from the comparison between real wages and productivity. A noteworthy result is that productivity increases as well as employment. This is explained by the improvement in the price system as an allocation mechanism related to the decrease in the mark-up, which enhances allocative efficiency.

Investment rises because of several factors. On the one hand, the increase in consumption stimulates production and thus investment, and on the other hand, the return on capital becomes more attractive. This is not only because cross-marginal productivities are positive (that is, the increase in employment pushes up the return on capital), but also because there is a cost reduction caused by more competition, leading to a greater incentive to reduce costs and increase quality.

If we consider productivity as the key determinant of competitiveness in the long run, the SD would effectively put Spain on the road towards closing the labour productivity gap *vis-à-vis* the rest of the EMU and the United States, and becoming a more competitive player. This statement is backed by an improvement in the external sector results following a drop in the terms of trade (p^x/p^m).

4.3.2 Transitional dynamics

Firms will set optimal prices to equate, on average, the desired or friction-less mark-up on top of their marginal costs. The final price is therefore set above a weighted average of present and discounted future marginal costs, introducing a forward-looking component in firms behaviour. This behaviour was embedded in our expression for aggregate inflation, or New Phillips curve, developed in the Chapter 2:

$$\pi_t = \beta^f E_t \pi_{t+1} + \lambda \widehat{mc}_t + \beta^b \pi_{t-1} \tag{4.1}$$

The dynamic effects on the supply side confirm the theoretical prescriptions, as we observe in Figure 4.11. The Directive generates a reduction in the price level as the entry of new competitors in the market increases substitutability between goods and thus reduces the optimal mark-up for companies. The drop in inflation takes place immediately and fades out after five years, as the gap between the desired and the existing mark-up for firms disappears. The decrease in inflation in the services sector entails lower wage demands and lower prices for the rest of the economy, mit-igating the persistent loss of price competitiveness that has contributed to Spain having the biggest current account deficit, in terms in GDP, in the developed world.

The effect on productivity is permanent and builds up progressively, overcoming the employment rate effect after 16 quarters and reaching its new steady-state level around year 10. The transition of the labour market variables confirm the structural features of the regulatory reform taking place. Initially, the employment rate leads the way, as new firms enter the market. This effect is partially compensated by a drop in the number of hours per employee, possibly following a negative Frisch elas-ticity at the intensive margin.[5] As usual, vacancies act as a jumping

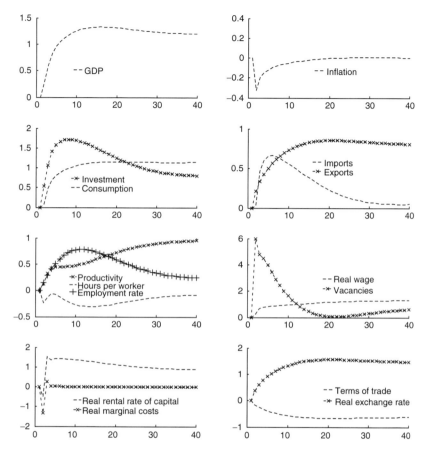

Figure 4.11 Transitional dynamics after permanent reduction in intermediate sector's mark-up

variable, reflecting the entry of new firms which find it more profitable to enter the market. Higher efficiency reached through greater competition allows for a new growth pattern, based on the virtuous circle of higher productivity followed by higher competitiveness which determine a more sustainable external position. A real exchange depreciation accompanied by a deterioration in the terms of trade fosters a permanent increase in exports. The initial increase in imports reflects an income effect related to higher GDP, but it washes out as the relative import prices keep pushing in the opposite direction.

Investment responds in a hump-shaped pattern. The presence of adjustment cost in the model implies that out of the steady state Tobin's q differs from 1. The initial drop in real marginal costs and the real rental rate are more than compensated by a substantial decline in the nominal interest rate, which drives Tobin's q, and hence investment, up.

4.3.3   Alternative set-up

The first exercise considers an exogenous growth pattern, finding that a mark-up contraction has an unambiguous positive effect on GDP and employment. To check this result, it might be useful to consider an alternative scenario where growth is obtained endogenously. For this purpose, we use QUEST III (see Roeger *et al.*, 2008), the DSGE model employed in the Directorate General for Economic and Financial Affairs of the European Commission for quantitative policy analysis. QUEST III is populated by households, final and intermediate goods producing firms, a research industry, a monetary and a fiscal authority. In the final goods sector, firms produce differentiated goods that are imperfect substitutes for goods produced abroad. Households buy the patents of designs produced by the R&D sector and license them to the intermediate goods producing firms. The intermediate sector is composed of monopolistically competitive firms which produce intermediate products from rented capital input using the designs licensed from the household sector.

To check for the differences and similarities between the two growth-rate environments, we run a similar simulation using QUEST and introduce a permanent mark-up shock to the final goods sector. The intermediate sector is not the best candidate to simulate the shock implied by the SD as the endogenous growth peculiarities of the model impose a new role for the intermediate firm's margins. Essentially, a mark-up becomes necessary to cover the sunk costs implied by the patent licences, therefore a lower mark-up would impede the entry of new firms and thus the rate of technological progress. This trade-off implies a smaller impact of the Services Directive. A smaller mark-up deters the entry of newcomers and therefore slows technological progress, partially cancelling the positive effect coming from capital accumulation and capital stock building. The results shown in Figure 4.11 highlight the positive and lasting effect on GDP, productivity and the external balance triggered by higher competition in the final goods sector. The endogenous growth mechanism stimulates the entry of new firms and increases R&D via an increased demand for capital. As Roeger *et al.* (2008) remark, the increased demand for labour will affect employment and real wages differently because of differences in the labour supply response of the different skilled workers (low, medium and high skills). The direct effect of the shock on the capital stock exceeds the increase in GDP despite the opposition of a loss in the terms of trade, which is also tempering the impact on consumption.

The dynamics in Figure 4.12 reflect similarities with the first simulation in terms of qualitative results. Despite the different set-up, REMS results turn out to be robust to growth assumptions, yielding similar quantitative results and profiles. However, we can pinpoint another basic difference. QUEST dynamics take longer to reach the new steady state of the economy, as the endogenous growth mechanism dilutes the effects of the shock. Once the new stable path is reached (after 25 years), we observe an increase in GDP of 0.89 per cent, and no long-term effects on total hours worked. The slight deviation with respect to REMS results might lie in the different calibration of the mark-up variable.[6]

4.4 Conclusions

In the decade previous to the recession of 2008–9, Spain showed a persistent inflation differential, a growing external deficit and low relative productivity. As discussed in this chapter, these three problems are closely related and are an indication of the lack of overall competitiveness of the Spanish economy. During the 2008–9 crisis, some of the imbalances were reduced, but the cost in terms of unemployment was dramatic. For this reason, the Spanish economy faces the challenge of reducing unemployment over the next few years and improving competitiveness, while at the same time, implementing the necessary structural reforms.

Among these structural reforms, the implementation of the Services Directive is particularly relevant. For this reason, we evaluated its long- and short-run effects using REMS. As shown in section 3, the unexpected and permanent reduction in the margin with which firms operate would effectively shift the steady state of the Spanish economy. According to our results, Spanish GDP would increase by 1.21 per cent because of both demand and supply factors, while the economy would become more productive. While employment also increases slightly, the total number of hours per adult scarcely increase, allowing labour productivity to go up by more than 1 per cent. As long as productivity is the key determinant of competitiveness in the long run, the implementation of the Services Directive would effectively put Spain on the road to closing the labour productivity gap *vis-à-vis* the rest of the EMU and the United States, and becoming a more competitive player.

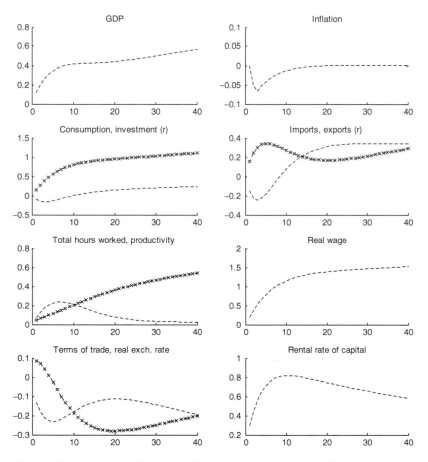

Figure 4.12   Transitional dynamics after permanent reduction in final goods sector mark-up, using QUEST III; periods = years

Notes

1. The World Bank's Doing Business variables used in this index refer to how easy it is to start a business (number of procedures, time and cost), to handle permits and to conduct foreign trade.
2. Among others, see Kox *et al.* (2004, 2005), Breuss and Badinger (2005), Copenhagen Economics (2005) and Bajo and Gómez-Plana (2005).
3. In the cost minimisation problem of firms discussed in Chapter 2, we show the adjusting effect of the fixed-cost parameter κ_f, so that no extraordinary profits exist in the long run and the number of firms in the industry stabilises.
4. After 40 quarters, the economy will have reached its new steady state.

5. The change in labour supply can be decomposed into two labour-supply components, varying in response to a wage change: the extensive margin referring to changes in the number of workers in the labour market, and the intensive margin pointing to variations in hours of work.

6. The catch-up effect is larger in REMS as its starting point is above the initial value of QUEST III: 1.32 in REMS versus 1.20 in QUEST III.

5
The Effects of Public Investment

A. de la Fuente and R. Doménech

5.1 Introduction

The public sector accounts for a significant fraction of fixed capital formation in most countries. Public administrations, together with public organisations and enterprises, are often the main suppliers of transport and other key infrastructures and devote large amounts of resources to investment in educational, health care and administrative facilities. Spain is no exception to this. Over the twenty years between 1985 and 2005, the Spanish public administrations accounted on average for over 16 per cent of total investment.

In this chapter we explore the impact of public investment on aggregate output. The chapter is divided into five sections. Section 5.2 compares Spain's pattern of public investment with that of other industrial countries. Section 5.3 briefly surveys the existing literature on the contribution of public investment to output growth, with an emphasis on the effects of the infrastructure component of this aggregate. Section 5.4 describes how public investment and the public capital stock enter the REMS model. This model is then used to simulate the aggregate effects of a permanent positive shock to public investment. Section 5.5 concludes.

5.2 Public investment and public capital stocks in the OECD

This section reviews the evolution of public investment and the public capital stock in Spain since 1950. To put Spain's situation in context, we shall adopt a comparative perspective, taking as our reference the sample comprising the main member states of the Organisation for

Economic Co-operation and Development (OECD), excluding the most recent entrants into this organisation and some small economies for which it is difficult to find the required data. We shall refer to this aggregate as OECD-21.[1]

One important complication that should be kept in mind when interpreting an exercise of this nature is that public investment means different things in different countries, for at least two reasons. The first is that, in some countries, the available data refer only to capital expenditure by central governments while others also include investment by regional and municipal administrations, and in some cases, but not in others, capital spending by public enterprises. The second is that the relative weights of the public and private sectors vary considerably across countries, particularly in the education and health care sectors, but also in other areas, such as transport and energy supply networks.

Our data on public investment ratios are taken from the OECD's Economic Outlook database and from the National Accounts published by the same organisation. Using a perpetual inventory procedure with geometric depreciation, we have constructed stocks of public capital for the countries in our sample. As described in Appendix 1, our depreciation rates are taken from Kamps (2006), and starting stocks at the beginning of the sample period are approximated using the same procedure as de la Fuente and Doménech (2006a).

Figure 5.1 plots the evolution of Spanish public investment measured as a fraction of GDP, along with the maximum, minimum and average values of the same ratio in the OECD-21. Figure 5.2 provides a snapshot of the situation of each individual country during the last years of the period being studied (2000–5). The average public investment rate in our sample of reference has varied between 3 per cent and 4 per cent of GDP during the entire sample period, with a slight upward trend between 1950 and the early 1970s, and a slight downward trend thereafter. Spain was above the sample average only after the mid-1980s. Spain's public investment rate increased sharply during the 1980s, rising from 1.75 per cent of GDP in 1980 to a peak of 4.86 per cent in 1991 and decreasing thereafter to a level only slightly above the sample mean. During the period 2000–5, Spain ranked seventh in the sample in terms of its public investment ratio, behind Japan, New Zealand, Ireland, Italy, the United States and Finland.

Figure 5.3 is identical to Figure 5.1 except that it focuses on the share of the public sector in total investment. In the average OECD-21 country, public investment accounted for around one sixth of total fixed capital formation, with a slight downward trend during the second half of the

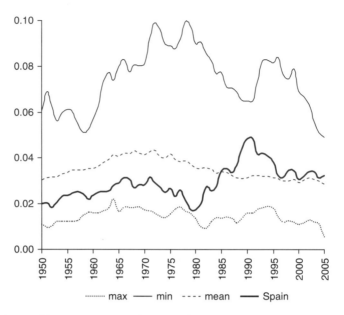

Figure 5.1   Public investment as a fraction of GDP, evolution over time, 1950–2005

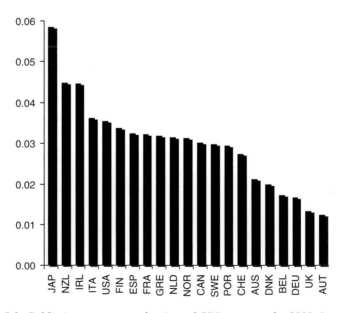

Figure 5.2   Public investment as a fraction of GDP, averages for 2000–5

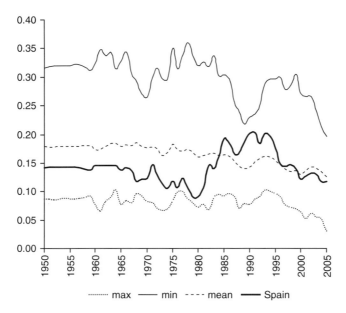

Figure 5.3 Public investment as a fraction of total investment, evolution over time, 1950–2005

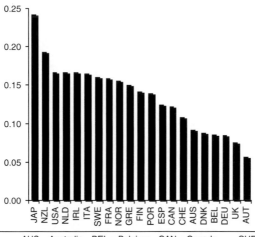

AUT = Austria	AUS = Australia	BEL = Belgium	CAN = Canada	CHE = Switzerland
DNK = Denmark	FIN = Finland	FRA = France	DEU = Germany	GRE = Greece
IRL = Ireland	ITA = Italy	JAP = Japan	NLD = Netherlands	NOR = Norway
NZL = New Zealand	POR = Portugal	ESP = Spain	SWE = Sweden	UK = United Kingdom
USA = United States				

Figure 5.4 Public investment as a fraction of total investment, averages for 2000–5

sample period. The profile of this indicator in the case of Spain is similar to the one shown in the previous figure: starting from a relatively low level of public investment intensity, the country climbed above the sample mean during the 1980s and reverted to this level in the final part of the period.

Figures 5.5 to 5.10 show the evolution of the stock of public capital, measured in per capita terms, and as a fraction of the total capital stock and of GDP. In terms of the first indicator, Spain remained significantly below the OECD-21 average throughout the sample period. Except for a brief period between 1975 and 1985, during which the unemployment rate increased steadily from 4.5 per cent to 20.6 per cent, however, the country's relative position improved consistently over time, as its per capita stock increased from 28 per cent of the OECD average in 1950 to 80 per cent in 2005.

When public capital is measured as a fraction of the total capital stock or of GDP, the situation is somewhat different. While Spain started out well below the OECD average, by the end of the sample period it had practically converged to the mean in terms of both indicators. This suggests that public capital was not particularly scarce relative to private

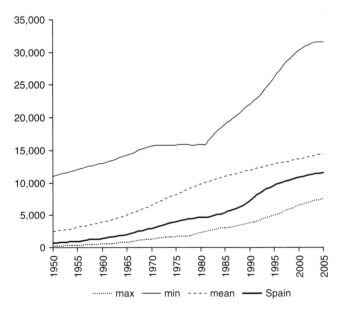

Figure 5.5   Stock of public capital per capita, evolution over time

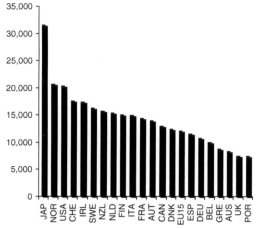

Figure 5.6   Stock of public capital per capita in 2005

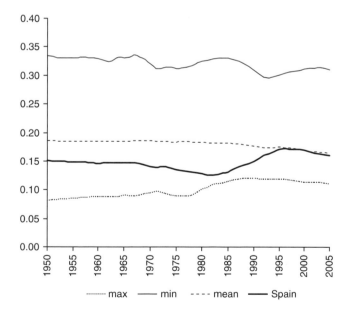

Figure 5.7   Public capital as a fraction of the total stock of capital, evolution over time, 1950–2005

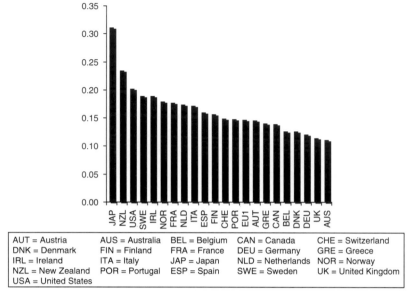

Figure 5.8   Public capital as a fraction of the total stock of capital in 2005

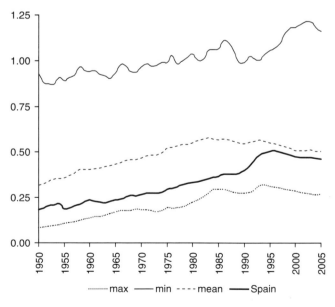

Figure 5.9   Stock of public capital as a fraction of GDP, evolution over time, 1950–2005

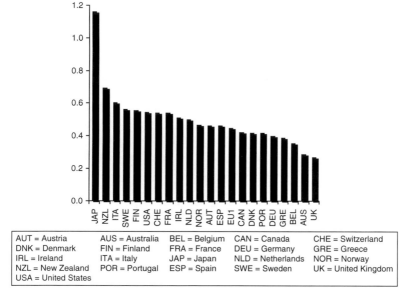

AUT = Austria   AUS = Australia   BEL = Belgium   CAN = Canada   CHE = Switzerland
DNK = Denmark   FIN = Finland   FRA = France   DEU = Germany   GRE = Greece
IRL = Ireland   ITA = Italy   JAP = Japan   NLD = Netherlands NOR = Norway
NZL = New Zealand POR = Portugal   ESP = Spain   SWE = Sweden   UK = United Kingdom
USA = United States

Figure 5.10   Stock of public capital as a fraction of GDP in 2005

capital in recent years, and that the country's stock of public capital was roughly in line with its income level.

5.3   Infrastructures and productivity: a brief survey

An important part of public investment expenditure finances the construction and maintenance of infrastructures (such as transport, energy and water supply networks) that provide productive services to the private sector of the economy as well as direct consumption benefits. This section briefly surveys the literature that has tried to measure the impact of such expenditure on productivity, mainly through the estimation of aggregate (national or regional) production functions in which public capital enters as an input, or through cross-country growth regressions.[2]

While research in this area has been quite active for two decades, analysts are still far from reaching a consensus on infrastructure's contribution to economic growth. A good many studies have addressed the issue using different statistical techniques and various regional and national samples, with mixed results. Some conclude that the rate of return on infrastructure capital is very high and that public investment is an important determinant of the rate of growth of national or regional income. Other studies, however, have much more pessimistic results and conclude that the contribution of public capital to aggregate output is very small or non-existent – or at least cannot be detected using the traditional framework of an aggregate production function.

5.3.1   Early optimism: Aschauer and Munnell

One of the earliest and most influential attempts to quantify the impact of public capital on productivity is by Aschauer (1989). This author estimated a Cobb–Douglas production function that included public capital as one of its inputs, using United States aggregate data, and concluded that the elasticity of output with respect to this factor is extremely large (0.39).

Aschauer's work received a considerable amount of attention and can be considered the point of departure of the large literature on the subject. Perhaps the main reason for its great impact is that it appeared at a time when both academics and policy-makers were searching without success for the causes of the alarming productivity slowdown that started in the mid-1970s in most industrial countries. In this context, Aschauer's results were appealing as they offered a plausible diagnosis of the problem and provided a simple policy prescription: increase public investment in infrastructure (see Munnell, 1990a).

Aschauer's results and prescriptions were reinforced by the findings of Munnell (1990b) using state-level data. This author constructed estimates of the private and public capital stocks for the states of the US and estimated a production function using a specification in levels without specific state effects. Her results coincided with those of Aschauer in that the effect of the stock of infrastructures on productivity was positive and significant. On the other hand, Munnell's estimate of the coefficient of public capital was much lower than Aschauer's but still quite high (around 0.17 rather than 0.39). One possible explanation for this difference relates to the existence of interregional spillovers which would be captured by the estimates based on national aggregates but would not show up in the state data. In a second exercise Munnell disaggregated the public capital stock into various types of infrastructures. Confirming Aschauer's results once again, she found that the infrastructures having the greatest impact on productivity are roads and the water supply network.

5.3.2   Second thoughts and econometric problems

The optimistic findings of Aschauer and Munnell were soon questioned on various grounds. Several authors have argued that Aschauer's estimate of the elasticity of output with respect to public capital was too high to be credible and suggested that his results might have resulted from various econometric problems.[3] The first difficulty is the possibility of reverse causation. In this interpretation, public investment would be a superior good, and the observed correlation between this variable and productivity growth would simply reflect the fact that governments tend to invest more in periods of rapid growth. Aschauer, however, was aware of this possibility and supplied some evidence that this was not the problem. First, he observed that his results did not change substantially when public capital was lagged. Moreover, if there was a reverse causation problem, we would expect to see a strong correlation between productivity growth and many components of public consumption and investment. A significant positive correlation, however, is found for only the component of public investment devoted to productive infrastructure. As we shall see below, Fernald (1999) used sectoral data to provide additional evidence that causation runs from infrastructure investment to productivity growth, and not the other way around. His key finding was that increases in the stock of roads seems to induce faster productivity growth in those industries that are more intensive users of such infrastructures – a pattern we would not expect to find if causation ran from output growth to public investment.

A second and probably more serious objection is that Aschauer's analysis does not control for other possible determinants of productivity growth. As Holtz-Eakin (1994) observed, the American postwar data contain essentially a single observation: the simultaneous fall in public investment and productivity growth which started in the mid-1970s. It is possible, however, that this pattern is only a coincidence. The fall in the US rate of public investment at the beginning of the 1970s seems to relate mainly to two factors: the completion of the interstate highway network, and the stabilisation and subsequent decrease in the school-age population (Gramlich, 1994). On the other hand, the productivity slowdown could be a result of the rapid increase in energy prices following the oil shocks of the 1970s and 1980s, which may have rendered obsolete a significant fraction of the private capital stock,[4] or of some other factor. In any event, the coincidence of the two processes may simply be by chance, and the apparent significance of public investment may reflect the fact that this variable serves as a proxy for some other omitted factor/s that were the true cause of the problem. The results of Ford and Poret's (1991) work would seem to be consistent with this interpretation. These authors replicated Aschauer's analysis for eleven OECD countries and found a significant positive correlation between public investment and productivity growth in only half the cases.

The third criticism of Aschauer's work takes us to relatively complex econometric issues. Some studies argue that Aschauer's results may be an example of the 'spurious regressions' problem discussed by Granger and Newbold (1974).[5] These authors argue that in many cases the apparently good results of regressions in levels between non-stationary variables (that is, between variables which display a trend) are not reliable and suggest the use of a specification in first differences in order to obtain consistent estimates.

When this is done, the results are often, but not always, less favourable to the hypothesis that infrastructure investment has a substantial effect on productivity growth. It must also be noted that the estimation in first differences presents some shortcomings of its own. Munnell (1992) observed that this specification frequently yields implausible estimates of the parameters of private factors in the aggregate production function and argued that it would not be reasonable to expect a stable relationship between public investment and output growth over a one-year period. Second, some recent developments in econometrics suggest that the level estimates may be more reliable than it was first thought. In particular, the estimation in levels of a relationship between non-stationary variables works well (is consistent) when the variables are cointegrated; that is, when a linear combination of them exists that is stationary. In fact, the ordinary least squares (OLS) estimates obtained in this manner would be better than usual in large samples, though it is also true that, since their distributions will not be the standard ones, the usual significance tests lose their validity.

The econometrics literature provides various cointegration tests and different procedures for estimation and inference with cointegrated variables. Some of these techniques have been applied in the public capital literature, with generally favourable results. In the Spanish case, Bajo and Sosvilla (1993), Argimón *et al.* (1993) and Mas *et al.* (1993), among others, found evidence of cointegration among the relevant series, which would in principle rule out the possibility of spurious regressions and ensure the consistency of the estimates, and they concluded that infrastructure investment has a significant and large positive effect on productivity.[6]

5.3.3   Some sectoral evidence

Fernald (1999) analysed the impact of road construction on productivity growth using industry-level United States data. As we have already noted, his results support the view that the correlation between infrastructure and productivity does not reflect a reverse causation problem. If this were the case, we would expect to see no systematic variation across industries in the strength of the correlation. If road construction does increase productivity, on the other hand, the effect should be stronger in those sectors that are intensive users of road transport. Fernald found that this is indeed the case and concluded that investment in highways is productive.

Fernald's findings are also broadly consistent with Aschauer's conclusions on the high rate of return on infrastructure investment, but with one important qualification: while the construction of the interstate highway system seems to have contributed substantially to productivity growth in the 1950s and 1960s, there are no reasons to expect that additional investment in roads will yield similar results. According to Fernald's estimates, highway construction contributed about 1.4 percentage points to aggregate annual productivity growth before 1973 and only about 0.4 points after that year. Hence, infrastructure investment may indeed account for a substantial share of the observed slowdown in United States productivity. It does not follow, however, that an increase in public investment will trigger substantial productivity gains in the future, as the rate of return on road construction seems to have fallen dramatically after the completion of the basic interstate network.

5.3.4 Mixed results in cross-country and cross-regional studies

Many studies have explored the relationship between infrastructure and productivity using pooled data sets that combine observations for several years and different countries or regions. Using pooled data allows the researcher to exploit the cross-section variation of the data in addition to their time-series dimension and should mitigate some, but not all, of the econometric problems that arise in time-series studies for a single country. In particular, panel results are less open to the spurious regressions problem arising from common trends in the data. On the other hand, relying on the cross-section variation in the data does not eliminate and may even aggravate the reverse causation problem that may affect studies of the productivity effects of public capital. The direction of the bias, however, is not clear *ex ante* and will depend on the way public investment is financed. At the country level, it seems likely that rich nations will demand more public capital than poor ones, a fact that is likely to generate an upward bias in the estimated coefficient of public capital. A similar situation will tend to arise within a given country if regional governments are financed by 'domestic' tax revenues, but

Table 5.1 Summary of results on infrastructures and growth

	No. of eqs.	(+)	(0)	(−)	Avge ζ	Avge. t
1. *Data in levels without specific effects*						
US states	10	100%	0%	0%	0.204	9.43
Spanish regions	3	0%	100%	0%	0.03	1.16
Cross country	29	45%	45%	10%	n.a.	1.11
2. *Data in levels with specific effects*						
US states	16	31%	56%	13%	0.004	0.51
Spanish regions	21	95%	5%	0%	0.129	3.99
Cross country	4	50%	25%	25%	n.a.	0.25
Regions of other countries	11	91%	9%	0%	0.176	9.19
3. *Data in differences*						
US states	15	7%	87%	7%	−0.030	−0.58
Spanish regions	8	63%	38%	0%	0.190	2.17
Cross country	8	75%	25%	0%	0.121	0.79
Regions of other countries	2	100%	0%	0%	0.318	2.58

Source: de la Fuente (2009).

the bias may be reversed if infrastructure investment is financed centrally and used as a mechanism for regional redistribution. It is generally agreed that, in order to avoid the potential endogeneity bias, it is important to control for fixed country or regional effects, as their omission will generate a correlation between the error term and infrastructure variables that will render OLS estimates of production function coefficients inconsistent.

Table 5.1 summarises the results of a large number of cross-country and cross-regional studies that are surveyed in de la Fuente (2009). For each of four samples (comprising, respectively, the states of the US, the regions of Spain, various groups of countries, and the regions of different nations) and three broad groups of specifications (convergence equations and production functions estimated with the data in levels, with and without specific (fixed or random) effects, and production functions estimated with the data in differences), the table shows the total number of equations reported in the cited paper and the fraction of this total in which the estimated coefficient of the relevant public capital or infrastructures variable is positive and significant (+), negative and significant (−) and insignificantly different from zero (0), using a t−value of 1.8 as the cut-off point for significance. Whenever possible, the table also contains estimates of the average coefficient of infrastructures or public capital in the production function (ζ) and of the relevant t ratio for each group of estimates. Average coefficient values should be interpreted with care because different studies use different infrastructure or public capital aggregates. It should also be kept in mind that the two averages reported in the table are generally computed over different sets of regressions as some studies report t ratios or coefficient estimates that cannot be compared with the rest for various reasons.[7]

As can be seen in Table 5.1, the cross-country evidence is inconclusive, with approximately half the studies reporting significant positive effects while the other half find no clear evidence of growth effects from infrastructure. This evidence is also very hard to assess because of differences across studies in sample composition and econometric specification, and the poor quality and possible lack of homogeneity of cross-country data on public investment or capital stocks. A recent study by Kamps (2006) that attempts to tackle the latter problem by constructing a homogeneous series of public capital stocks using OECD data obtains rather positive results using pooled data and a specification in first differences that implicitly allows for fixed country effects.

Regional studies should be free of most of these problems, but they also display a mixed pattern of results that only allows for the drawing of rather tentative conclusions. Early positive results with regional samples by Munnell and other authors are probably unreliable because they failed to control for specific effects that are quite likely to be there and can generate substantial biases. The elimination of specific effects through differencing often leads to the loss of significance of public capital variables. As we have already noted, however, such specifications can be questioned on the grounds that first-differenced data may contain too much short-term noise to allow for the estimation of a production function. The fact that estimates of the coefficients of private inputs obtained with these data are typically quite unreasonable seems to point in this direction, notwithstanding the results of formal tests that are invoked in some studies to select differenced specifications.

This leaves us with estimations in levels with specific regional effects as the most likely source of reliable results. Focusing on those studies that have followed this approach, the one thing that stands out in Table 5.1 is the difference in results across the two main regional samples considered in de la Fuente (2009). Public capital variables are almost always significant in panel data specifications for the Spanish regions and often insignificant in similar exercises conducted with United States data. Working with US state data, García-Milà *et al.* (1996), Evans and Karras (1994), Baltagi and Pinnoi (1995) and Holtz-Eakin (1994), among other authors, all report similar results: the public capital variable displays a positive and significant coefficient when the production function is estimated in levels without specific effects, but generally loses its significance when specific effects are introduced or the equation is estimated in first differences. In the Spanish case, by contrast, infrastructure generally maintains or even increases its significance when these specifications are adopted to control for specific regional effects (see, among others, Mas *et al.* (1996), González-Páramo and Argimón (1997), Dabán and Lamo (1999), de la Fuente (2002), Álvarez *et al.* (2003), and de la Fuente and Doménech (2006b)).

Fernald (1999) provides a plausible explanation for the surprising discrepancy between US state-level studies and those focusing on the regions of other countries. He observes that the existing data for the US states starts in 1970 – that is, at approximately the time when the interstate highway system was completed – and conjectures that this may explain the negative results of most US studies. The evidence from Spain and other Mediterranean countries is consistent with this hypothesis, as the per capita stock of infrastructure is much smaller in these territories than in the United States, and so are the findings by Mas *et al.* (1996) and Fernald (1999) that the coefficient of infrastructure tends to fall as the sample period is extended.

5.3.5   A tentative conclusion

On the whole, our reading of the evidence is that there are sufficient indications that public infrastructure investment contributes significantly to productivity growth, at least for countries where a saturation point has not been reached. The returns to such investment are probably quite high in the early stages, when infrastructures are scarce and basic networks have not been completed, but fall sharply thereafter. Hence, appropriate infrastructure provision is probably a key input for development policy, even if it does not hold the key to rapid productivity growth in advanced countries where transportation and communications needs are already adequately served.

On the other hand, the great disparity of results we found in the literature is worrying, to say the least, and points to the need for further work in this area. It seems reasonable to interpret some of the results we have reported as an indication of the persistence of various data and econometric problems, as well as of the possible need for a more flexible framework than the one generally used in the literature. First, there is in all likelihood an important data problem that may bias estimates of infrastructure coefficients towards zero. Many of the public capital series used in the literature (particularly at the cross-country level) are rather tentative estimates constructed from incomplete primary sources and covering relatively short periods. Second, it is likely that we have not yet fully solved other relevant econometric problems, starting with the possible endogeneity of the regressors. A third factor to consider is that the monetary cost of a given infrastructure may not be a good measure of the productive services it supplies. The usual specifications of the production function assume implicitly that a dollar spent on roads has a similar impact in all regions (holding the stocks of other inputs constant). It seems clear that this is not the case, as both construction costs and the productive impact of different types of infrastructure may differ across regions, reflecting factors for which most studies do not control, such as *geography* and climate. There are some indications in the literature that controlling for these factors and using physical infrastructure indicators helps to improve the results to some extent.

5.4 Effects of a permanent increase in public investment

5.4.1 The long-run effects of public investment

To assess the effects of changes in public investment on the main macroeconomic variables of the Spanish economy we shall rely, as in previous chapters, on the model described in Chapter 2.

Recall that the aggregate production function of the REMS model is of the form:

$$y_t = z_t \left(\left[a k_t^{-\rho} + (1-a) e_t^{-\rho} \right]^{-\frac{1}{\rho}} \right)^{1-\alpha} (n_t l_{1t})^{\alpha} \left(k_t^p \right)^{\zeta} \qquad (5.1)$$

where y is total output, z a technology shock, k private capital, e energy, n employment, l average hours per worker and k^p the stock of public capital. It is assumed that $\alpha = 0.594$ and $\zeta = 0.06$. Government investment (g_t^i which is exogenous in the model) increases the stock of public capital, which, given the depreciation rate δ^p, obeys the following law of motion:

$$\gamma_A \gamma_N k_{t+1}^p = g_t^i + (1 - \delta^p) k_t^p \qquad (5.2)$$

where γ_A is the exogenous rate of technological progress and γ_N the exogenous rate of population growth.

The policy experiments we shall conduct later in this chapter are extremely sensitive to the value assigned to the elasticity of output with respect to public capital (ζ). Unfortunately, the existing literature on the subject is only of limited help in setting the value of this parameter because, as we saw in the previous section, different studies provide very different and often contradictory results in this regard. As discussed previously, the great disparity of empirical results we find in the literature is of little guidance. For this reason, we have used an alternative procedure to set the value of ζ. In an economy in which total output (y) and value added (y^n) are the same, it can be shown (see, for example, Cassou and Lansing, 1998) that the optimal steady-state government investment rate is given by:

$$\frac{g^i}{y^n} = \frac{\beta \delta^p \zeta}{1 - \beta(1 - \delta^p)} \tag{5.3}$$

In Figure 5.11 we have represented the optimal value of the public investment rate (solid line) against different values of ζ, for the calibrated values of β and δ^p used in REMS. The two dashed horizontal lines represent the maximum (5.1 per cent) and minimum

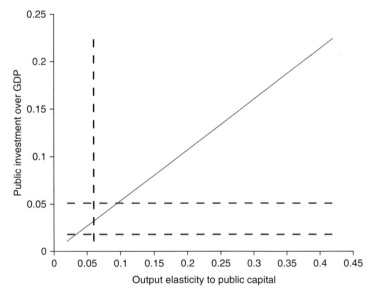

Figure 5.11 Optimal public investment rate as a function of the output elasticity of public capital (solid line)

Notes: The horizontal lines represent the maximum and minimum values of the investment rate from 1980 to 2009; the vertical line is the calibrated value of $\zeta = 0.06$, used in REMS

(1.8 per cent) levels of the public investment rates observed in the Spanish economy from 1980 to 2009. As we can see, this range is compatible with values of ζ between 0.03 and 0.10, supporting the choice of $\zeta = 0.06$ (vertical dotted line), which is only slightly greater than the value of $\zeta = 0.05$, proposed by Baxter and King (1993).[8] An interesting result from Figure 5.11 is that values of ζ as high the one estimated by Aschauer, or by some authors for the Spanish economy, would imply unrealistically high levels for the optimal rate of public investment – or, equivalently, that the Spanish government is further away from this optimal rate than would seem reasonable.[9]

Given that public capital affects the marginal productivity of private capital and labour, an increase in government investment not only has a direct effect on output, but also an indirect effect that works through changes in private investment and labour supply decisions. In Table 5.2 we show the long-run multipliers of a permanent increase of 1 per cent of GDP in government investment, for different values of the output elasticity of public capital. These multipliers are in line with the results found by Baxter and King (1993), despite the fact that REMS incorporates many extensions not included in the basic RBC model of these authors, showing that the bulk of the impact of public investment comes from its direct supply-side effects. In our baseline scenario, where $\zeta = 0.06$, the long-run effect on value added (y^n) of an increase in government investment of 1pp of GDP is equal to 3.34pp of GDP, of which approximately half is explained by an increase in private consumption (c), with a multiplier equal to 1.43. Private investment (i) also increases in the long run with a multiplier equal to 0.34. This positive effect on private investment is accumulated over time, inducing a higher stock of private capital (k). The higher marginal productivity of labour translates into employment, with a long-run elasticity equal to 1.63.

Table 5.2 Long-run effects of public investment

Values of ζ	$\Delta y^n / \Delta g^i$	$\Delta c / \Delta g^i$	$\Delta i / \Delta g^i$	$\Delta k / \Delta g^i$	$\Delta k^p / \Delta g^i$	$\frac{\Delta n}{n} / \frac{\Delta g^i}{g^i}$
0.02	1.69	0.28	0.24	10.81	64.37	1.44
0.04	2.46	0.85	0.31	14.14	64.37	1.53
0.06 (Baseline)	3.34	1.43	0.39	17.51	64.37	1.63
0.08	4.04	2.01	0.46	20.92	64.37	1.73
0.10	4.84	2.60	0.54	24.37	64.37	1.83
0.12	5.66	3.19	0.61	27.88	64.37	1.94

Table 5.2 also shows the sensitivity of fiscal multipliers to changes in the output elasticity of public capital. As may be expected, a higher value of this parameter translates into a larger estimate of the impact of public investment on the variables of interest, with private consumption rising faster than GDP. With Aschauer's estimate $\zeta = 0.4$, the long-run GDP multiplier would be 18.32, almost six times larger than in our baseline, suggesting again that very large values of ζ are not realistic.

5.4.2   The short-run effects of public investment

After discussing the long-run effects of an increase in government investment we turn to its short-run effects and to their sensitivity to changes in some of the relevant parameters.

In Figure 5.12 we show the impulse-response functions of the main variables to a permanent increase in government investment by

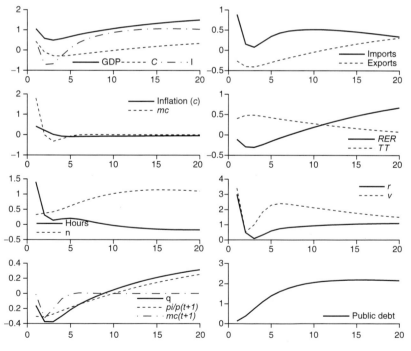

Figure 5.12   Impulse–response functions to a permanent increase in government investment equivalent to 1 per cent of GDP

1 per cent of GDP. In the first panel we can see that the impact effects on GDP, consumption and private capital are all positive despite public capital being fixed in the short run and increasing only slowly over time as investment accumulates. As described in Chapter 2, the positive response of private consumption to public investment is driven by the presence of RoT consumers. With only Ricardian households in the economy, the response of private consumption to a permanent increase of g^i would be close to zero or even negative, particularly when habits are not present.[10]

Private investment rises on impact but then declines for several quarters before gradually rising again to its long-run level. The positive impact response of private investment is consistent with the observed increase in aggregate demand and hours worked (third row, left), which increases the marginal productivity of capital (third panel right). To understand the dynamics of private investment it is convenient to recall the following two expressions involving Tobin's q:

$$q_t = \frac{1 + \pi_{t+1}^c}{1 + r_t^n} \left[r_{t+1}(1 - \tau_{t+1}^k) + \tau_{t+1}^k \delta + \frac{p_{t+1}^i}{P_{t+1}} \frac{\phi}{2} \frac{j_{t+1}^2}{k_{t+1}^2} + q_{t+1}(1 - \delta) \right]$$

(5.4)

and

$$q_t = \frac{P_t^i}{P_t} \left[1 + \phi \left(\frac{j_t^o}{k_t^o} \right) \right]$$

(5.5)

where r is the rental cost of private capital, τ^k the tax rate on capital incomes, j gross private investment and P^i/P the relative price of investment goods. As shown in Figure 5.12 (fourth row, left), the dynamics of Tobin's q are well explained by expected marginal costs and relative investment prices. The higher aggregate demand induces a sharp increase in marginal costs (second row, left) on impact. As we have seen, the REMS model displays many Keynesian features in the short run, departing from the typical dynamics of neoclassical models, such as the one proposed by Baxter and King (1993). However, the economy rapidly accommodates the shock, and the higher production capacity in $t+1$ translates into a fall in marginal costs, which in turn induces a reduction in q_t according to Equation (5.4). In addition, higher marginal costs also imply higher price levels. As part of the private demand for investment goods is filled by imports (which have a greater share in investment than in GDP), relative investment prices (P_{t+1}^i/P_{t+1}) fall, also contributing to the dynamics of q_t. However, these effects are short-lived, so Tobin's q eventually converges to a higher steady state consistent with a higher level of private investment.

The higher price level, initially caused by the permanent increase in government investment, produces an increase in the terms of trade (P^x/P^m), as shown in Figure 5.12 (second row, right), a fall in exports and a rise in imports (first row, right). Again, these effects are short-lived, since the procedure described in Chapter 2 to close the small open economy model ensures the external equilibrium in the long run.

Regarding the main labour market variables, given the law of motion of employment in our search model and the costs associated with posting and filling a vacancy, hours adjust quickly on impact to the increase in aggregate demand, as Figure 5.12 (third row, left) shows. Given the incentives of firms to hire more workers, they post more vacancies (third row, right) and eventually employment grows, converging to its higher steady-state level (Table 5.2).

The last panel of Figure 5.12 shows the dynamics of public debt. Despite the higher tax revenues induced by the increase in economic activity, the permanent increase in public investment generates a budget deficit that accumulates over time, raising the stock of public debt, until the fiscal rule described in Chapter 2 guarantees the budgetary neutrality of this expansionary fiscal policy.

We have also performed a sensitivity analysis of short-run effects of the permanent increase in public investment to changes in some parameters of the model, which are particularly relevant in shaping its dynamics. Table 5.3 shows the results of this exercise for the main variables. For each of them we have computed the percentage deviation on impact from the initial steady state. Thus the first row in Table 5.3 corresponds to the impact response of GDP (y^n), consumption (c), private investment (i), employment (n) and hours (l_1) represented in Figure 5.12, the

Table 5.3   Impact effects of a permanent increase in public investment

	y^n	c	i	n	l_1
(1) Baseline	1.05	0.43	0.42	0.33	1.40
(2) No RoT consumers ($\lambda^r = 0$)	0.87	−0.15	0.73	0.31	1.20
(3) No price rigidities+(2)	0.46	−0.21	−1.01	0.18	0.54
(4) No wage rigidities+(3)	0.45	−0.21	−1.08	0.23	0.66
(5) No habits ($h = 0$)+(4)	0.38	−0.58	−0.58	0.21	0.57
(6) Independent central bank+(1)	0.76	0.20	−1.39	0.26	1.02

first period after the shock. In the second row, we explore the situation in which there are no RoT households in the economy ($\lambda^r = 0$). As expected, the response of consumption then becomes negative. However, as in this case in which the economy is populated only by Ricardian consumers with access to capital markets, the response of private investment is now larger than in the baseline. Nevertheless, the GDP effect is smaller than in the economy with RoT consumers, and the hours response is similar, response of hours, whereas the response of employment is unaffected. In the third row, in addition to $\lambda^r = 0$ we assume that there are no price rigidities. In this case, all firms change their prices in response to higher marginal costs. As expected, the response of output is now smaller, given the rapid adjustment of prices, and private investment falls on impact. As commented earlier, the dynamics of Tobin's q are partially driven by the relative price of investment goods and the fact that the share of imports is greater for investment than for GDP. Consistent with the smaller response of output, the impact effects on hours and employment are also now less important. In row (4) we eliminate the real wage rigidities from the previous case. Now the responses of employment and hours are slightly greater, since the effects of higher public investment on wages are now also greater in the short run. In row (5) we remove habits from the previous economy. Now the response of private consumption is larger: a higher public investment increases households' incentives to save and invest in private capital. Finally, in row (6) we come back to the baseline situation but now assuming that the exchange rate is flexible (and, as a result, that the uncovered interest parity holds) and that the short-term interest rates are governed by a standard Taylor rule:

$$\ln \frac{1+r_t}{1+\bar{r}} = 0.75 \ln \frac{1+r_{t-1}}{1+\bar{r}} + 1.75(1 - \rho^r)\ln(\pi_t - \overline{\pi}) \qquad (5.6)$$

Since the response of the nominal interest rate is now larger than in the case of a currency area with an asymmetric shock in public investment, private investment falls on impact instead of increasing as in the baseline, thus reducing the short-run effects on GDP.

5.5   Conclusions

In this chapter we have explored the effects of public investment on aggregate output. First we compared the situation of the Spanish economy with other OECD countries regarding different aspects of public investment and capital. Empirical evidence shows that public investment as a share of GDP was below the OECD average until the 1980s, but has remained slightly above since then. A similar pattern is found for the share of public capital in the total capital stock. Despite this improvement, the stock of public capital per capita is still slightly below the average for the OECD, though very close to the average of the EU15, suggesting that public capital has not been particularly scarce relative to private capital in recent years, and that the country's stock of public capital is roughly in line with its income level.

Second, we have summarised the empirical evidence of the effects of public investment on productivity growth. Our reading of this evidence is that there are sufficient indications that these effects are positive and significant. Therefore, appropriate infrastructure provision is probably a key input for development policy. However, the great disparity of results found in the literature is worrying. Some of the disparities result from various data and econometric problems, as well as from differences in the methodology used to assess the effects of public investment.

Finally, we have evaluated the effects of a permanent increase in public investment on the main macroeconomic variables of the Spanish economy, using REMS. Given the wide range of estimates of the output elasticity of public capital available in the literature, we have shown that a value of this parameter close to 0.06 is reasonable and fits quite well with the public investment rate in the Spanish economy from 1980 onwards. Given this elasticity, the long-run multiplier of a permanent increase of 1 percentage point of GDP in government investment is equal to 3.34, showing the relative importance of the supply-side effects of this economic policy. After discussing the long-run effects of public investment, we analysed its short-run effects and their sensitivity to changes in some relevant parameters, which affect the transitional dynamics to the steady state. In our baseline, the impact multiplier on GDP is slightly above unity, suggesting that this supply-side policy has not only significant long-run effects, but also relevant stabilisation effects.

Notes

1. In particular, our reference sample includes the EU-15, with the exception of Luxembourg, plus the United States, Canada, Australia, New Zealand, Japan, Switzerland and Norway.
2. This section is based on de la Fuente (2009).
3. Munnell (1992), for example, finds it difficult to believe that the coefficient of public capital may be larger than that of private capital – particularly because a large part of public investment finances 'non-productive' activities that are not captured by existing national income statistics.

4. Tatom (1991b) finds that controlling for the price of oil reduces the coefficient of public capital in Aschauer's specification to one third.
5. See Aaron (1990), Hulten and Schwab (1991), Jorgenson (1991) and Tatom (1991a, 1991b). These authors find that public capital loses its significance when a specification in first differences is used.
6. A number of other studies analyse the relationship between public capital and productivity in different countries using cointegration techniques. Among others, see Ligthart (2000) for Portugal; Mamatzakis (1999) for Greece; Otto and Voss (1996) for Australia; Flores de Frutos et al. (1998) for Spain; Ramírez (2000) and Albala-Bertrand and Mamatzakis (2001) for Chile; Ramírez (2002) for Mexico; Everaert and Heylen (2001) for Belgium; and Kavanagh (1997) for Ireland. With the exception of the last one, all these papers estimate significant and relatively large positive coefficients for public capital. Some of these authors also report the results of Granger causality tests, which suggest that causality runs from public capital to output but not in the reverse direction.
7. For example, many cross-country studies estimate ad hoc growth specifications from which it is not possible to recover production function coefficients. See de la Fuente (2009) for additional details on the construction of Table 5.1 and for a complete listing of the underlying studies.
8. In REMS, an elasticity equal to 0.06 for gross output is equivalent to an elasticity of 0.08 for value-added, exactly the same value as the weighted average output elasticity of public capital proposed by Bom and Ligthart (2008), after correcting for publication bias in their meta-analysis of 76 studies. These values are, for example, in the middle of the range of estimates obtained by Boscá *et al.* (2002) for the Spanish regions.
9. In fact, this value of $\zeta = 0.06$ is in line with the results of de la Fuente and Doménech (2008).
10. The interactions between habits and RoT households are very relevant in shaping the dynamics of many macroeconomic aggregates. In particular, the labour market search model gains extra power to reproduce some of the stylised facts characterising labour markets, as well as other business cycle facts concerning aggregate consumption and investment behaviour, as Boscá, *et al.* (2009b) have shown.

6
On Ricardian Equivalence and Twin Divergence

M. Cardoso and R. Doménech

6.1 Introduction

In 2007 the Spanish economy showed a large current account deficit (10 per cent of GDP), a public budget surplus (2.2 per cent of GDP), and a relatively low household saving rate (6.5 per cent of GDP), at least when compared with its investment rate (almost 10 per cent of GDP). However, with the economic crisis of 2008–9, the situation changed dramatically, as Figures 6.1, 6.2 and 6.3 show. The public budget surplus turned into a huge deficit, estimated at 11.2 per cent of GDP in 2009, the household saving rate increased enormously, to above 11 per cent of GDP, and the current account deficit, at 5.0 per cent of GDP in 2009, was correcting very quickly.[1]

This empirical evidence is very interesting, since it seems to contradict well-known economic theory, as, for example, the existence of twin deficits. At the same time, the rise in private savings and the accumulation of fiscal deficits during the crisis of the late 2000s is observationally equivalent to the Ricardian equivalence hypothesis, for which it is difficult to find robust empirical support (see Seater, 1993). In fact, the recent experience of the Spanish economy seems to corroborate the empirical findings by Kim and Roubini (2008) about what they call 'twin divergence'; that is, the accepted empirical fact in the United States that when the public budget worsens the current account improves and vice versa (see also Corsetti and Müller, 2007, and Cavallo, 2005, 2007 on this issue). Thus the negative correlation between the public budget surplus and the current account was not a specific characteristic of the 2008–9 crisis, since it was also the rule in previous expansions and recessions, as Figure 6.4 shows. The correlation between both variables is −0.74 and falls slightly to −0.67 after controlling for the output gap. In

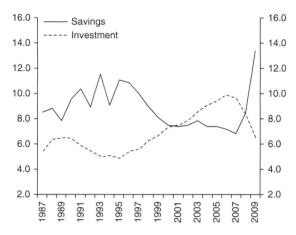

Figure 6.1   Household saving and investment rates (% of GDP), Spain, 1987–2009
Source: BBVA Research based on INE.

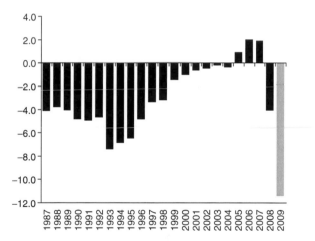

Figure 6.2   General government balance (% of GDP), Spain, 1995–2009
Source: BBVA Research based on MEH.

a related paper, Erceg *et al.* (2005), using an open economy DGE model
(SIGMA) for the USA, found that fiscal deficits have relatively small effects
on the trade balance, irrespective of whether its source is a spending
increase or a tax cut, even introducing non-Ricardian consumers, which

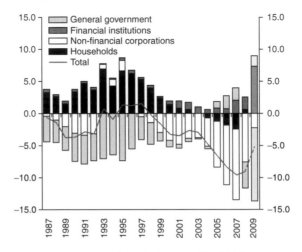

Figure 6.3   Current account (% of GDP), Spain, 1987–2009
Source: BBVA Research based on INE and MEH.

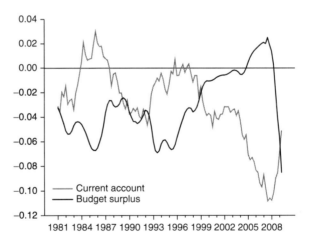

Figure 6.4   Current account and the budget surplus (% of GDP), quarterly frequency, 1981–2009
Source: BBVA Research based on INE and MEH.

help to increase the effects of fiscal policy on private consumption (see Galí *et al.*, 2007; Andrés *et al.*, 2008).

The aim of this chapter is to understand the effects of government shocks on household behaviour and the current account in a small open economy in a currency area, as is the case of Spain. For this purpose we use the model presented in the Chapter 2 (REMS) to analyse the effects of expansionary fiscal policies. As discussed previously, REMS builds on recent advances in DGE models, sharing many features of the SIGMA model, such as nominal and real rigidities or the presence of constrained households, but departs from SIGMA in two important aspects.[2] First, REMS models a small open economy (Spain) in a monetary union (EMU). Second, it includes a richer and deeper characterisation of the labour market, distinguishing between the intensive and extensive margin in a search and matching model.

Despite the presence of a large share of non-Ricardian consumers (liquidity constrained households), the expansionary fiscal policy has only small negative effects on the current account, as Erceg *et al.* (2005) also found for the United States. Additionally, the current evidence about the large increase in the household saving rate, at the same time as the government has incurred a large deficit, seems to be motivated mainly by precautionary saving in response to the greater uncertainty and high unemployment rate (18 per cent in 2009), as well as the desire to reduce levels of debt after the dramatic fall in their wealth and the expectation of future higher real interest rates, as a consequence of the international finance turmoil. Given these explanations, while this evidence is observationally equivalent to Ricardian equivalence, it seems that only a fraction of the increase in the household saving rate is explained by the large current deficit in the government's budget. In fact, our results show that private agents compensate only partially for the effects of fiscal policies on the saving rate. Therefore, the emphasis on fiscal consolidation should be based more on the sustainability of government debt than on its effects on external imbalances. According to these results, the current facts of the Spanish economy could be explained by the presence of a large negative output shock, as suggested by Kim and Roubini (2008) for the United States, that the Spanish government has tried to counteract with a large positive fiscal stimulus.

The structure of this chapter is as follows. In section 6.2 we analyse the effects of an increase in public consumption. Section 6.3 presents the results of an increase in public investment. The effects of a reduction of the labour income tax rate are shown in section 6.4. In section 6.5 we discuss the sensitivity of our results to changes in some crucial parameters. Finally, section 6.6 presents the main conclusions.

6.2   Fiscal policy and the current account: a shock in public consumption

We first analyse the effects of a temporary but persistent increase in public consumption on the main macroeconomic variables in our model. The initial shock in public consumption is equivalent to 1 per cent of GDP (an increase of more than 5 per cent in terms of public consumption), similar to the size of the expansionary policies implemented through public expenditure in 2008 and 2009 by the Spanish government.[3] Figure 6.5 presents the impulse-response functions of the main endogenous variables. The response of output is clearly positive on impact and the short-term multiplier is equal to 1.0, in line with the results of Hall (2009), Corsetti *et al.* (2010) and Woodford (2010), and slightly higher than in Cwik and Wieland (2009) and Cogan *et al.* (2009). As expected, the response of private consumption is also positive, because

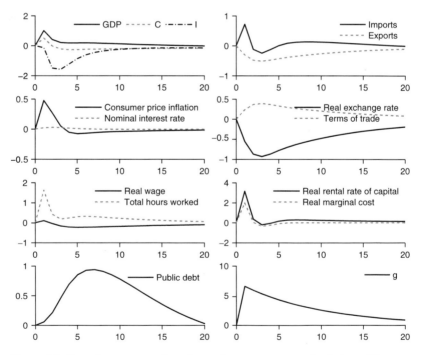

Figure 6.5   Impulse–response functions after a temporary shock in public consumption

of the presence of rule-of-thumb (RoT) consumers, since the consumption of optimising households falls, given the negative wealth effects of higher government spending. The higher level of output is obtained with a higher level of total hours worked (labour supply also rises with the negative wealth effect of optimising households), which is accompanied by slightly higher real wages, in spite of their rigidities. In contrast, private investment decreases, reaching its lowest levels after three quarters. The fall of investment is driven by the fall in Tobin's q.

The increase in marginal costs also pushes the inflation rate up. Higher domestic prices as well as higher levels of output and private consumption cause an increase in imports on impact. However, this increase in imports has a short life since imports are more sensitive to private investment, which falls from $t + 1$ to $t + 3$. The increase in domestic prices also has a negative effect on foreign competitiveness, thus inducing a reduction in exports. As shown in Figure 6.5, the real exchange rate appreciates and the terms of trade (P^x/P^m) increase. In spite of the higher inflation rate, the nominal interest rate increases very slightly, given the small value of the Spanish economy in EMU inflation (around 10 per cent). Finally, as expected, public debt increases, reaching its highest level seven quarters after the shock, and then falls steadily as a result of the fiscal rule.

A very interesting way of analysing the effects of the positive shock in public consumption on the external imbalances is given by Figure 6.6. In this figure we have represented the absolute deviations of savings, investment and public consumption, all in relative terms with respect to GDP, from their steady-state levels (that is, $x_t - \bar{x}$). As we can see, the public consumption rate rises above 0.8 percentage point (pp), and the saving rate falls by almost 0.6pp. In fact, private savings compensate for only 46.6 per cent of the increase of public consumption on average over the first 20 quarters. Therefore, there is only partial Ricardian equivalence in the Spanish economy.

However, the fall in the investment rate partially compensates for the fall in the saving rate and therefore the increase in the current account deficit is very small: its impact is equal to 0.2pp of GDP, smaller than a quarter of the increase in the public consumption rate. In other words, though there is some evidence of twin deficits, only a small fraction of the government budget deficit translates into a current account deficit. Surprisingly, despite the large differences between SIGMA and REMS, our results are very similar to those obtained by Erceg *et al.* (2005), who found that a fiscal deficit has a relatively small effect on the United States

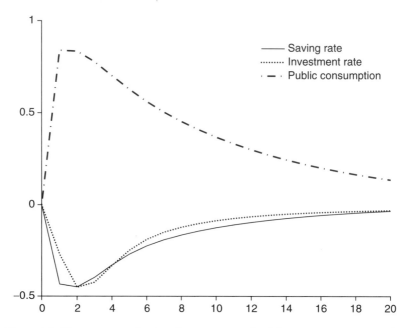

Figure 6.6   The response of saving, investment and public consumption rates after a temporary shock in public consumption, absolute deviations from their steady-state values

trade balance, irrespective of whether the source is a spending increase or tax cut. In their benchmark calibration, whereas in REMS non-Ricardian consumers represent 50 per cent of total households, they find that a rise in the fiscal deficit of 1pp of GDP induces the current account to deteriorate by less than 0.2pp of GDP. Our results are also in line with Abbas *et al.* (2010), who find that an improvement in the fiscal balance by 1pp of GDP is associated with an improvement in the current account of 0.2–0.3pp of GDP.

6.3   A temporary increase in public investment

As a second exercise of expansionary fiscal policy we analyse the effects of a temporary increase in public investment. As in the case of public consumption, the initial shock in public investment is equivalent to 1 per cent of GDP (slightly more than 20 per cent in terms of public investment) and similar in its magnitude to the Fund for Local Investment implemented by the Spanish government in 2009.[4]

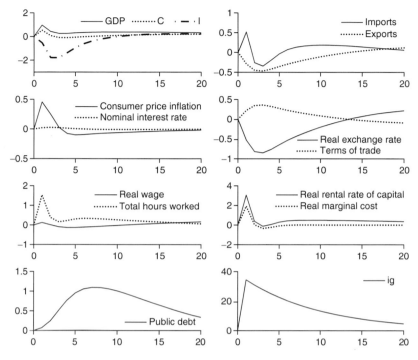

Figure 6.7 Impulse–response functions after a temporary shock in public investment

As can be seen from Figure 6.7, the response of output is again clearly positive on impact, though the short-term multiplier is slightly smaller (0.97), and the response of private consumption is also positive (the consumption of optimising households falls). Notice that the transitory nature of the shock and the accumulation of public capital may explain the slightly higher fiscal multiplier than in the case of the public consumption shock. As in the previous case, the positive shock in public investment induces a higher level of total hours worked and slightly higher real wages, and a fall in private investment. The rest of the variables show similar responses to those observed previously after a public consumption shock. The main difference is in the persistence of the shock, since public investment accumulates into public capital, which depreciates slightly.

The effects of the positive shock in public investment on the external imbalances are analysed in Figure 6.8. In this case, the public investment

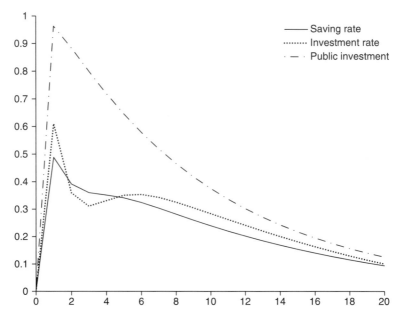

Figure 6.8   The response of saving, investment and public investment rates (% of GDP) after a temporary shock in public investment, absolute deviations from their steady-state values

rate increases above 0.9 percentage points, whereas the total investment rate increases by only 0.6pp on impact, since private investment falls. The saving rate also increases in this case, because public savings are higher as a consequence of greater public revenues, and the economy exhibits a very small current account deficit (0.12 per cent of GDP), again confirming the previous results. While the current account deficit is very persistent, its size in terms of GDP is small, implying a weak relationship between the deficits in the government budget and the current account.

6.4   A temporary reduction of labour income taxes

The next exercise we consider is a temporary reduction of 10 per cent in the labour income tax rate. The *ex ante* effects of this reduction in the tax rate are equivalent to 0.5 per cent of GDP, very close in its magnitude to the tax rebate implemented by the Spanish government in 2008 and 2009.[5] Figure 6.9 shows the impulse–response functions after the shock.

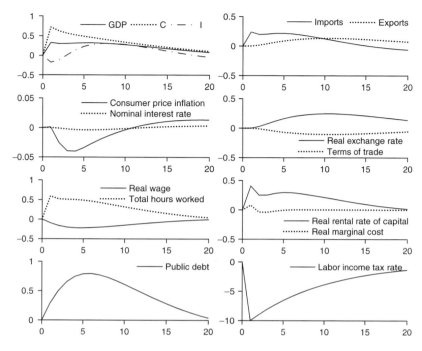

Figure 6.9 Impulse–response functions after a temporary reduction in the labour income tax rate

Output increases on impact (the tax multiplier is equal to −0.61, smaller than for public consumption and investment), and remains above its steady-state level over many quarters.

The increase in private consumption is even higher than for GDP, and is explained by the increase in the consumption of non-Ricardian households, since optimising households do not change their consumption levels. The crowding-out effects on private investment are now smaller, as well as the increase in the marginal cost and the rental rate of capital. The fall in the labour income tax rate induces a reduction in the real wage (before taxes) and, as expected, an increase in total hours worked, as households take advantage of lower taxes. The fall in the labour income tax rate translates into a small depreciation of the real exchange rate and into a small fall in the terms of trade, which gives place to higher exports. However, imports increase more than exports, particularly on impact, first through higher private consumption and later through higher private investment from $t + 3$ onwards.

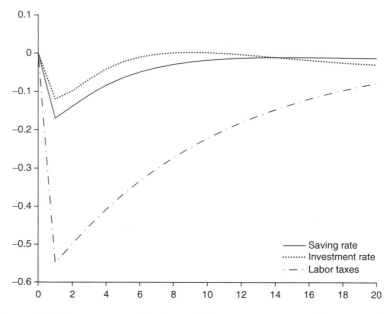

Figure 6.10 The response of saving and investment rates, and revenues from labour income taxes over GDP after a temporary reduction of the labour income tax rate, absolute deviations from their steady-state values

The effects of the temporary reduction in the labour income tax rate on external imbalances are analysed in Figure 6.10. In this case, revenues from labour income taxes fall by more than 0.5pp of GDP, the investment rate only decreases by 0.12pp on impact and the saving rate also falls by 0.17pp. Given the small responses of the investment and saving rates, the economy exhibits a very small current account deficit (0.05 per cent of GDP), only slightly smaller than the decline in the case of the public consumption and investment shocks.

6.5   Sensitivity analysis

To check the robustness of our results, we again analysed the effects of a shock in public consumption (equivalent to 1 per cent of GDP) under different specifications in our model. The results of these exercises are shown in Table 6.1. For each exercise we show the fiscal multiplier, the investment rate, the saving rate and the current account balance in terms of GDP. All these variables refer to the same quarter in which the fiscal

Table 6.1 Sensitivity analysis

	Multiplier	I/GDP	S/GDP	CA/GDP
(1) Baseline	1.01	23.55	23.38	0.17
(2) $\lambda^r = 0.8$	1.19	23.44	23.20	0.23
(3) $\lambda^r = 0.0$	0.82	23.64	23.54	0.09
(4) $\lambda^w = 0.9$	1.08	26.92	26.67	0.25
(5) $ptm = 0.0$	0.96	23.33	23.16	0.16
(6) $\sigma_x.\sigma_c, \sigma_i \times 2$	0.81	22.66	22.46	0.20
(7) $s^x, \omega_c, \omega_i \times 0.5$	1.01	21.68	21.61	0.08
(8) $h = 0.0$	0.94	23.64	23.49	0.15
(9) $\rho^w = 0.9$	1.05	23.45	23.29	0.16
(10) $\phi_b = 0.06$	0.96	23.48	23.35	0.13
(11) $\lambda^r = \lambda^w = 0.9, \phi_b = 6 \times 10^{-6}$	1.53	26.67	26.21	0.46
(12) Spending reversal fiscal rule	1.06	23.77	23.56	0.22
(13) Independent central bank	0.60	23.73	23.73	0.01

Notes: The variables in the columns refer to the impact fiscal multiplier, the investment and saving ratios, and the current account surplus in terms of GDP, in the same period in which public consumption increases by 1% of GDP.

stimulus is implemented. To facilitate comparisons, the first row shows only the results of our baseline.

In the second row we show the results for $\lambda^r = 0.8$; that is, when we increase the share of RoT consumers in the economy. As expected, the fiscal multiplier increases, by almost 20 per cent with respect to the baseline. Additionally, as the share of Ricardian consumers is smaller, the effect of the fiscal deficit on the current account deficit is also greater, increasing to −0.23 per cent of GDP, almost a quarter of the initial fiscal stimulus. Conversely, when we reduce the share of RoT consumers, as in row (3), both the fiscal multiplier and the current account deficit are smaller, since the Ricardian equivalence is greater. These results are similar to the ones obtained by Erceg *et al.* (2005).

In the fourth row we increase the bargaining power of workers ($\lambda^w = 0.9$). A higher value of λ^w increases the sensitivity of wages to marginal labour productivity, since workers have the power to set wages up to the highest feasible level. In this case, both the fiscal multiplier and the effects on the current account balance are higher than in the baseline.

In row (5) we set the pricing-to-market parameter to zero; that is, export prices are exactly equal to domestic prices. Therefore, as the fiscal stimulus increases domestic prices, export prices also increase by the same amount, and relative prices remain constant. As expected, the loss in competitiveness induces a smaller fiscal multiplier and a slightly smaller current account deficit with respect to the baseline.

In the sixth row we multiply by 2 the elasticity of imports and exports to relative prices. In this case the fiscal multiplier is 20 per cent smaller than in the baseline, but the current account balance increases only slightly to −0.20. In row (7), instead of increasing the sensitivity of exports and imports to relative prices, we reduce the openness of the economy, dividing the scale factors in export and import equations (s^x, ω_c and ω_i) by 2. While the fiscal multiplier is not affected by this change in the specification of the model, as expected the effects on the current account balance are now smaller than in the baseline, approximately half of its current account deficit, in line with the results of the analysis by Corsetti and Muller (2009).

In rows (8) and (9), we show that the baseline results are also robust to changes in the habit parameter ($h = 0$) and in the coefficient of real wage inertia ($\rho^w = 0.9$). In both cases the fiscal multiplier and the effects on the current account balance do not change very much. In row (10) we increase the sensitivity of the risk premium to the external debt. As expected, this change reduces both the fiscal multiplier and the current account balance.

Combining those changes with greater effects in the external position, in row (11) we have increased the share of the RoT consumer up to the (improbable) value of 90 per cent, the bargaining power of workers ($\lambda^w = 0.9$) and have reduced significantly the coefficient ϕ_b, which measures the sensitivity of the risk premium to external debt, and this now converges to the steady state very slowly. Even in this unrealistic situation in which the fiscal multiplier increases by 50 per cent with respect to the baseline, the current account deficit becomes 0.46 of GDP, less than half of the initial fiscal stimulus.

In row (12) we have changed the specification of the fiscal rule. In contrast to the baseline, in which fiscal consolidation is achieved with lump-sum transfers, in this case public spending also reacts to the deviations of the debt-to-GDP ratio from its steady-state level:

$$g_t^c = 0.9 g_{t-1}^c + 0.1 \overline{g^c} - 0.002 \left[\frac{b_{t-1}}{gdp_t} - \overline{\left(\frac{b}{gdp} \right)} \right] - \varepsilon_t^g \tag{6.1}$$

The effects of this type of rule over the fiscal multiplier have also been analysed by Corsetti *et al.* (2009) and Wieland (2010). According to these authors, the effects of fiscal stimulus depend not only on short-term tax and spending policies, but also on the expectations of agents regarding offsetting measures in the future. They find that accounting for such fiscal rules that make explicit spending reversals brings new Keynesian models in line with the crowding-in of private consumption. As can be seen in row (12), these results are confirmed, though the effects are relatively small: both the fiscal multiplier and the current account deficit increase with a fiscal rule for public expenditure which is sensitive to the deviations of the public debt-to-GDP ratio from its steady-state level.

Finally, in row (13) we have evaluated the implications of being in a currency area with no independent monetary policy. In principle, for a relatively small country such as Spain, both the fiscal multiplier and the effects of the fiscal stimulus on the current account balance should be greater, since monetary policy reacts only slightly increasing interest rates. Davig and Leeper (2009) have found that government spending generates positive consumption multipliers and a higher fiscal multiplier for GDP when monetary policy is passive; that is, in a regime in which the monetary authority does not increase real interest rates in response to expansive fiscal policies. In the limiting case in which the zero bound on nominal interest rates is binding, Christiano *et al.* (2009) and Woodford (2010) have found similar results. In row (13) we have changed the specification of the model, assuming that the exchange rate is flexible (therefore the uncovered interest parity holds) and that the short-term interest rates are governed by a standard Taylor rule:

$$\ln \frac{1+r_t}{1+\bar{r}} = 0.75 \ln \frac{1+r_{t-1}}{1+\bar{r}} + 1.75(1-\rho^r)\ln(\pi_t - \bar{\pi}) \tag{6.2}$$

As expected, the fiscal multiplier is now much smaller and the effects on the current account balance almost negligible.

In summary, this sensitivity analysis confirms the main results obtained in our baseline. The effects of fiscal policy on the current account balance are relatively small. To obtain greater effects on the current account in line with the twin deficit hypothesis we have to impose values of some parameters as, for example, a seemingly improbable share of RoT consumers.

6.6 Conclusions

In this chapter we explored the effects of different expansionary fiscal policies on the trade deficit in Spain, a small open economy in a currency union and therefore with no independent central bank. Using

REMS, we found that expansionary fiscal policies have only small negative effects on the current account, even assuming a large proportion of non-Ricardian consumers. Though Ricardian equivalence holds only partially, the crowding-out effects on private investment implied by fiscal policies compensate for the behaviour of national savings, thus avoiding large effects on the trade deficit.

An additional interpretation of these results is that the current negative correlation between the large deficit in the government balance budget and the quick correction of the current account during 2009 cannot be explained by the twin divergence hypothesis in the Spanish economy, and it may be explained by a large output shock that more than compensates for the effects of fiscal policy.[6] Additionally, the large increase in the household saving rate in 2009 seems to be motivated by precautionary saving and the desire to reduce levels of debt, as a response to the international financial turmoil and the huge increase in unemployment, rather than by the large fiscal stimulus, as proposed by the Ricardian equivalence hypothesis.

From a policy perspective, our results suggest that the emphasis on future fiscal consolidation should be based more on the sustainability of government debt than on the negative effects on external imbalances.

Notes

1. BBVA (2009d) offers a deep analysis of the structural changes in Spanish public accounts, as a consequence of the recent economic crisis.
2. Nominal and real rigidities not only affect the response of output to fiscal policy, but also the volatility of output to supply shocks in economies where taxes are distortionary, as in all advanced economies. For example, Andrés and Doménech (2006) show that, contrary to what has been found in RBC models, distortionary taxes tend to reduce output volatility relative to lump-sum taxes when significant rigidities are present.
3. In particular, the law of movement of public consumption is given by:

$$g_t^c = 0.9 g_{t-1}^c + 0.1 \overline{g^c} + \varepsilon_t^g$$

   where $\overline{g^c}$ is the steady-state level of public consumption and ε^g is the shock.
4. As for public consumption, the law of movement of public investment is given by:

$$i_t^g = 0.9 i_{t-1}^g + 0.1 \overline{i^g} + \varepsilon_t^i$$

   where $\overline{i^g}$ is the steady-state level of public consumption and ε^i is the shock.
5. The law of movement of the labour income tax rate is given by:

$$\tau_t^l = 0.9 \tau_{t-1}^l + 0.1 \overline{\tau^l} + \varepsilon_t^\tau$$

where $\overline{\tau^l}$ is the steady-state level of the labour income tax rate and ε^τ is the shock.

6. Notice that given a parameterisation of our model, it may be possible to perform stochastic simulations to generate artificial data and compute the implied distributions of the correlation between the government budget deficit and the current account for different types of shocks.

7
Tax Reforms and Economic Performance

J. E. Boscá, R. Doménech and J. Ferri

7.1 Introduction

Despite the integration of Spain into the European Union and the high rates of growth recorded between 1995 and 2007, relative per capita income in Spain with respect to the United States was only 69 per cent in 2007, slightly lower even than in the mid-1970s. As in many other European countries, it seems that Spain faces a 'glass ceiling' which constrains complete convergence with the United States. Though the lower level of GDP per hours worked accounts for three-quarters of the gap between Spain and the United States, a lower use of labour at both the intensive (hours per employed) and extensive (employment) margins also explains a significant part of it. For these reasons, to understand the macroeconomic performance of the Spanish economy relative to the United States, it is very important to take into account the differences in labour utilisation between the two countries.

In recent years, fiscal policy, and in particular taxes, have attracted much attention in explaining the differences in labour utilisation and macroeconomic performance between European countries and the United States. While the argument that taxes were one of the reasons why European labour markets performed worse than those in the United States has been around since the mid-1990s (see, for example, European Commission, 2004, and Nickell, 2006, for a survey of the empirical literature), the evidence offered by Prescott (2004) that taxes explain the bulk of the difference between the United States and Europe in the evolution of hours per adult has generated a renewed interest in the effects of tax structure on the labour performance of advanced economies. A recent exemplary contribution to this literature has been made by Coenen *et al.* (2008). Using a New Area-Wide Model (NAWM) for the EMU, these authors find that lowering tax distortions in the EMU to the levels prevailing in the United States would increase hours worked per adult and output by more than 10 per cent.

In this chapter we follow a similar approach to Coenen *et al.* (2008) and use REMS to analyse the effects of lowering the overall tax wedge to the same level as in the United States. REMS shares many features with NAWM, such as nominal and real rigidities or the presence of constrained households, but also has two significant differences. First, REMS models a small open economy (Spain) in a monetary union (EMU), whereas NAWM is a two-country model calibrated for the EMU and the United States. Second, it includes a richer and deeper characterisation of the labour market, distinguishing between the intensive and extensive margins in a search and match model.

In the analysis of the effects of taxation on the labour market, as in many previous contributions, we break down the overall tax wedge into consumption and labour income taxes and social security contributions. As shown in the second section of this chapter, while the overall tax wedge is between the levels prevailing in the EU and the United States, there are also some significant differences in its composition, since social contributions in Spain are higher than in the EU, whereas labour income taxes are below the level in the United States.

Our results partially confirm previous findings in the literature as a reduction in the overall tax wedge of 19.5 points, in order to reach United States levels, has a positive effect in the long run, increasing total hours by about 8.9 per cent and GDP by about 8.3 percentage points (pp). In terms of GDP per adult, these results account for a quarter of the gap with respect to the United States, but imply a slight increase of about 0,5pp in the labour productivity gap. The rise in total hours per adult is explained by a similar increase in both hours per employee and the employment rate of about 4.5 percentage points, allowing hours per adult to converge to levels only slightly lower than those in the United States. When, in addition to the change in the overall tax wedge, we allow for a variation in capital tax rates to the levels of the United States we find that overall GDP increases by only 6.25 points, because of the negative effects generated by increasing capital tax rates by 4.9 points. In contrast, total hours rise by 8.5 percentage points, given that higher capital taxes have no significant effect on hours worked per employee, but produce a mild decrease in employment rates.

The rest of the chapter is organised as follows. In the section 7.2 we document the differences between the United States, the EU and Spain in terms of GDP per adult, employment and participation rates, hours and taxes, evaluating this evidence in terms of previous contributions to the literature. In section 7.3 we present the main results of our analysis, both in terms of the long-run effects and the transitional dynamics of the main variables. In section 7.4, we carry out a sensitivity analysis of the results. Section 7.5 summarises our conclusions.

7.2   Macroeconomic performance, taxes and the labour market

A useful and convenient way of analysing the empirical evidence on macroeconomic and labour market performance and the tax wedge in the Spanish economy is to use the following equation as a starting point:

$$\frac{GDP}{L^{16-64}} \equiv \frac{GDP}{H} \frac{H}{L^d} \frac{L^d}{L^s} \frac{L^s}{L^{16-64}} \tag{7.1}$$

where GDP over the working-age population (L^{16-64}) is broken down as the product of labour productivity (GDP per hour, H), the average number of annual hours worked per employee (H/L^d), the employment rate (the ratio of the employed over total workers, L^d/L^s) and the participation rate (the ratio of total workers over the working-age population). As the employment rate is equal to one minus the unemployment rate (u), we can then rewrite Equation (7.1) as

$$\frac{GDP}{L^{16-64}} \equiv \frac{GDP}{H} \frac{H}{L^d} (1-u) \frac{L^s}{L^{16-64}} \tag{7.2}$$

In other words, per capita income (measured in terms of the working-age population) depends on labour productivity, unemployment and participation rates, and the average number of hours per employee.

In Figure 7.1 we have represented the evolution of GDP over the working-age population in Spain and the EU-15 in relative terms to the United States.[1] As can be seen, relative per capita income peaked in 1975 (at 72.0 per cent), decreased significantly until the mid-1980s (60 per cent) and then, with some cyclical fluctuations, started to increase until the end of the sample, when relative income was 69 per cent in 2007. In the EU-15, after the increase in the 1960s and 1970s, relative per capita income has fluctuated between 75 per cent and 80 per cent, with no perceptible trend since the 1980s. Despite the international integration of many markets and the process of technology diffusion, it seems that European countries face a 'glass ceiling' that constrains complete convergence with the United States.

The breakdown provided by Equation (7.1) clearly illustrates the factors behind this 'glass ceiling'. In Figure 7.2 we have represented the

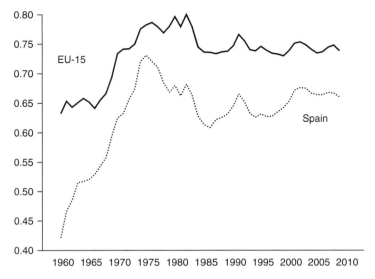

Figure 7.1   GDP over working-age population, relative to the United States, 1960–2010
Source: OECD National Accounts, various issues.

evolution of the four variables that determine per capita income. Spanish labour productivity reached 90 per cent of the level of the United States in the mid-1990s, but decreased during the 2000s as a result of the increase in productivity growth in the United States and the significant reduction in the unemployment rate in the Spanish economy, which implied the entry of many workers to low-productivity jobs. As a result, relative Spanish labour productivity in 2007 was 76 per cent (85 per cent in the EU-15). Hours per employee were higher in the EU-15 and in Spain than in the United States until the mid-1980s. In the case of the EU-15, the downward trend has been highly persistent since then (reaching 92 per cent in 2007), whereas in the case of Spain, relative hours per employee remained fairly constant from 1985 to 2000, then experiencing a slight decline over the next few years, to reach 96.4 per cent in 2007. The employment rate $(1 - u_t)$ was higher in Spain and the EU-15 than in the United States until the beginning of the 1980s. However, with the increase in structural unemployment in European countries, particularly in Spain, the relative (to the US) employment rate fell below 100 per cent. In the Spanish economy, the relative employment rate dropped to 84 per cent in 1994, to recover later to 96 per cent in 2007. Dew-Becker and Gordon (2008) have documented the trade-off between labour productivity and

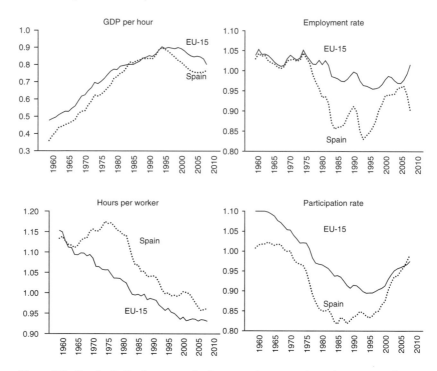

Figure 7.2   Productivity, hours worked per employee, and employment and participation rates in relative terms to the United States, 1960–2010
Source: OECD National Accounts, various issues, and Groningen Growth and Development Centre (GGDC) Productivity Level Database, various years.

the employment rate in both raw data and regressions that control for the two-way causality between productivity and employment growth, showing that there was a robust negative correlation between productivity and employment growth in European countries from 1980 onwards. This evidence is the opposite in the case of the United States. Ball and Mankiw (2002) found that the correlation between productivity growth and the structural unemployment rate has been positive in the United States. The last panel in Figure 7.2 shows that the correlation between the participation rate and employment rate has been positive, in both Spain and the EU-15.

One key result of Figure 7.2 is that, in order to understand the macroeconomic performance of Spain and the EU-15 relative to the United States, it is very important to take into account the changes in both the intensive (hours per employed worker) and extensive (employment) margins of the labour market. In fact, Alesina and Giavazzi (2006) use these pieces of empirical evidence, together with other facts, to document their expectations about the economic and political eclipse of Europe. According to these authors, Europe has much to learn from market liberalism in the United States in relation to worker productivity, labour market regulations, support for higher education, technology research efforts and fiscal policy.

In the late 2000s, fiscal policy and in particular taxes have attracted much attention as a possible explanation for the differences in labour utilisation on each side of the Atlantic. The argument that taxes are one of the main reasons for lower labour utilisation in Europe than in the United States is based on the observation that the tax wedge (the difference between the effective consumption wage received by workers and the total effective cost paid by firms) is lower in the latter than in the former. In Figure 7.3 we present the evolution of consumption taxes (τ^c), labour income taxes paid by workers (τ^l), social security contributions

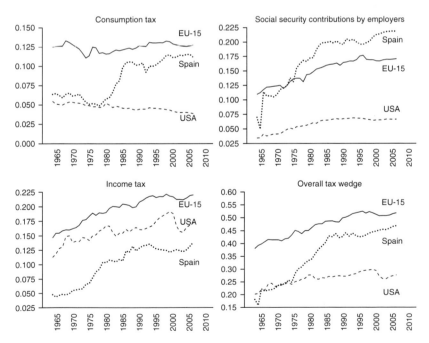

Figure 7.3 Taxes on consumption and labour income, social security contributions and the overall tax wedge in Spain, EU-15 and the United States, 1965–2007

paid by employers (τ^{ss}) and the total tax wedge (τ) approximated as:

$$\tau = 1 - \frac{(1-\tau^l)}{(1+\tau^c)(1+\tau^{ss})} \simeq \tau^l + \tau^c + \tau^{ss} \tag{7.3}$$

We have updated the information from Boscá *et al.* (2005) to 2007, the last year for which information is available, using their methodology, and have computed EU-15 averages using GDP in PPP as weights. As can be seen, both in Spain, and in particular in the EU-15, taxes forming the tax wedge are higher than in the United States, with the only exception being income taxes, which are lower in Spain. Additionally, these figures show that European countries exhibit a trend in the overall tax rate, which is more pronounced in the case of Spain.

However, to offer a complete view of the distortions created by the different tax systems, we represent in Figure 7.4 the time profile of capital tax rates (τ^k) in the three economic areas of interest. As can be seen, capital taxation has been persistently higher in the United States than in Europe, in contrast to the overall tax wedge. Nevertheless, Europe as a whole, and particularly Spain, present a marked trend in capital taxation that has seen capital taxes converge almost to United States levels by the end of the sample period.

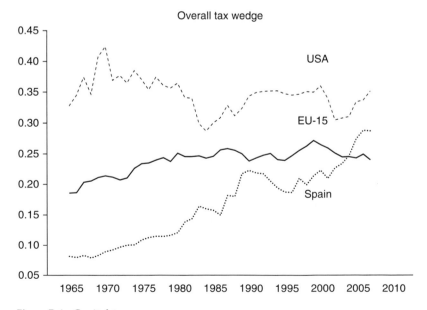

Figure 7.4 Capital tax

Several papers have investigated the effects of taxes on hours worked, but with no distinction between the intensive and extensive margins; that is, focusing on the ratio of total hours over the working-age population (see Causa, 2008, for a review of this literature). Prescott (2004) has argued that the differences in the tax wedge can explain the differences between the United States and several European countries in the evolution of hours worked per adult. Rogerson (2006, 2008) has shown that both technology and taxes can account for the evolution of hours per adult in the United States and several continental European countries. Pissarides (2007) has pointed out that the effects of taxes on hours worked per adult are sensitive to the specification of the model, which may be appropriate for some countries (the United States and continental Europe), but not for others (Scandinavian countries, for example), a result also stressed by Rogerson (2007). Ohanian *et al.* (2008) present economic evidence in which changes in labour taxes account for a large share of the trend differences in hours worked per adult in a sample of 21 OECD countries from 1956 to 2004, even accounting for other explanatory variables, such as the duration of unemployment benefits or measures of employment protection regulation. In the case of the Spanish economy, Conesa and Kehoe (2005) found that taxes can account for the level of hours worked per adult in 1970 and 2000, but not simultaneously for the fall in the first part of the sample and the increase in the later 2000s.[2] Of the two margins, the effect of taxes on the employment rate has received much more attention than the case of hours worked per employee. While summarising this empirical literature is beyond the scope of this chapter (interested readers may turn to Nickell, 2006, and Causa, 2008) and the empirical research offers a wide range of results, as alleged by Doménech and Garcia (2008), whereas cross-section evidence (for example, Jackman *et al.*, 1996; Nickell, 1997; Nickell and Layard, 1999) shows a null or low correlation between labour taxes and unemployment rates, the time series or panel data correlation (for example, Bean *et al.*, 1986, Elmeskov *et al.*, 1998; Blanchard and Wolfers, 2000; Nickell *et al.*, 2005; Planas *et al.*, 2007) is usually positive and, in many cases, statistically significant.[3]

The effect of taxes on average hours worked by the employed (the intensive margin) has been analysed by a shorter list of authors. Using a sectorial database of wealthy countries in the mid-1990s, Davis and Henrekson (2004) found that higher taxes lower the number of hours worked. Similar results were found by Faggio and Nickell (2007) in a sample of OECD countries, from 1981 to 1999, although their results are sensitive to the inclusion of variables that control for the distribution of earnings. More recently, Causa (2008) found that high marginal tax rates levied on second home owners are a significant disincentive on the intensive margin of labour supply, whereas the labour supply of men is insensitive to taxation.

The empirical evidence on the relative performance of labour markets supports the relevance of analysing the effects of taxes on both margins. As shown in Figure 7.2, and pointed out by Fang and Rogerson (2008), there are important differences between countries in the contribution of the intensive and extensive margins in explaining the number of hours worked per adult. In Figure 7.5 we have represented[4] the evolution of the three components of hours worked per adult in relative terms to the United States, using the following breakdown in logs:

$$\ln \frac{H_{it}}{L_{it}^{15-64}} - \ln \frac{H_{USt}}{L_{USt}^{15-64}} = \left(\ln \frac{H_{it}}{L_{it}^d} - \ln \frac{H_{USt}}{L_{USt}^d} \right) + \left(\ln \frac{L_{it}^d}{L_{it}^s} - \ln \frac{L_{USt}^d}{L_{USt}^s} \right)$$

$$+ \left(\ln \frac{L_{it}^s}{L_{it}^{15-64}} - \ln \frac{L_{USt}^s}{L_{USt}^{15-64}} \right) \qquad (7.4)$$

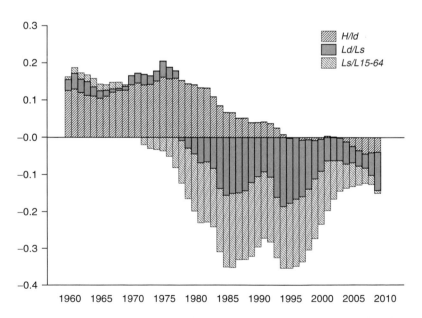

Figure 7.5 Intensive (hours per employee) and extensive margins (employed per adult population) in Spain, relative to the United States, 1960–2007.

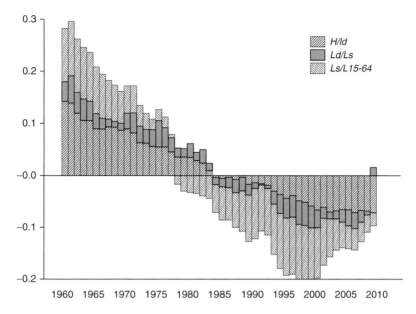

Figure 7.6 Intensive (hours per employee) and extensive (employed per adult population) margins in EU-15, relative to the United States, 1960–2007

As can be seen from Figure 7.5, most of the volatility of hours per adult comes from the changes in employment and participation rates, particularly in the 1980s and 1990s. In the 1960s, the hours per adult were approximately 15 per cent higher in Spain than in the United States, and 10 per cent lower in 2007, the greatest difference being −35 per cent in 1986. This figure also shows that the fall in the relative number of hours per adult between 1975 and 1985 was only partially explained by hours per employee (25 per cent of the total fall), and its contribution was even negative in explaining the recovery between 1995 and 2007. However, the relevance of the intensive margin in explaining the relative performance of the EU-15 with respect to the United States has been much greater, and similar to the relevance of the participation rate, as can be seen from Figure 7.6, whereas the contribution of the employment rate has been smaller.

7.3 Tax reform and economic performance in Spain

In this section we run some simulations to illustrate how changing the tax distortions in Spain to the levels prevailing in the United States affects the performance of the labour market and output. In all cases, fiscal shocks are considered to be unexpected and permanent. To highlight comparability with respect to Coenen *et al.* (2008), we chose the same selected variables but, given the presence of search and match in the labour market in our model, we separate the extensive and intensive margins of labour utilisation, also adding information on the reaction to vacancies. In all the experiments we assume that the loss of government revenues is offset by an increase in a lump-sum tax charged to households such that public investment and consumption, and the government debt-to-output ratio, remain constant in the long run.

7.3.1   Long-run effects

Table 7.1 reports the long-run effects for each individual component of the overall tax wedge, the first column representing a reduction in the consumption tax wedge, the second an increase in the labour tax wedge and the third a reduction in firms' social security contributions. The overall tax wedge is displayed in the last column. Figures in the table represent percentage changes with respect to the initial steady state.

According to our results, the reduction in the overall tax wedge would have an unequivocally positive effect on the Spanish economy in the long run that would be summarised by an increase in total hours per adult of about 8.9 per cent, and in GDP of about 8.3pp. Consequently,

Table 7.1   Long-run benefits of lowering tax wedges in Spain

	Components of overall tax wedge			Overall wedge
	$\Delta\tau^c = -7.5$	$\Delta\tau^l = 3.0$	$\Delta\tau^{sc} = -15.0$	$\Delta\tau = -19.5$
GDP	3.41	−1.63	6.46	8.29
Consumption	4.06	−1.95	7.67	9.82
Investment	1.40	−0.67	2.64	3.38
Exports	1.78	−0.86	3.34	4.26
Imports	0.41	−0.20	0.76	0.97
Total hours per adult	3.69	−1.78	6.95	8.88
Hours per employed	1.77	−0.84	3.36	4.32
Employment rate	1.92	−0.94	3.59	4.56
Real wage	−0.98	0.49	11.92	11.36
After tax real wage*	5.72	−2.68	10.96	14.17
Effective labour cost	−0.98	0.49	−1.82	−2.31
Terms of trade	−1.39	0.66	−2.65	−3.41
Vacancies	4.61	−2.20	8.74	11.22

Note: (∗) Deflated with the price of consumption good

there is no reduction, but a very small increase in the labour productivity gap with respect to the United States (which actually amounts to 24 percentile points). While these results represent a significant effect in terms of hours per capita and output, in terms of per capita GDP they account for only one-third of the gap with respect to the United States, and for an insignificant fraction in the case of labour productivity.

The rise in total hours per capita is explained by an equal increase in both hours per worker and the employment rate of about 4.5pp. These figures are in line with the empirical evidence. According to Nickell's (2004) discussion regarding panel data estimations for the main OECD countries, a reduction equivalent to our 19.5 pp in the tax wedge would raise the employment rate by between 3 and 5.3pp. This effect is significant but modest, implying for the Spanish economy around one-third of the average difference in the employment rate since 1985 between Spain and the United States. However, the increase in hours per employee would imply the convergence of this variable to United States levels.

The results shown in Table 7.1 are very similar to those obtained by Coenen *et al.* (2008). In general, the effects in our simulation represent approximately two-thirds of the effects estimated by these authors, a difference that is consistent with the fact that the relative tax wedge in the Spanish economy with the United States is smaller than in the case of the EU-15. GDP per hour also decreases in our simulation, albeit with a very limited quantitative effect (0.6pp), compared with the results provided by Coenen *et al.* (2008), where output increased by 11.89 per cent and hours worked by 13.72 per cent, with productivity subsequently falling by 1.83pp.

Higher labour input pushes up the marginal productivity of capital and therefore its rate of return, thus affecting Tobin's q positively, and hence also investment. Given the long-run level of labour and capital, the supply side of domestic goods is determined. On the demand side, the increase in the rental rate of capital, together with higher wages and more working hours, induces a boost in household income and therefore in consumption (especially where RoT households are concerned).[5] In order to balance the demand and the supply side of domestic goods, the terms of trade (p^x/p^m) fall, to improve the external position. Because Spanish export prices deviate from international prices as a result of the pricing-to-market assumption, the increase in relative export prices (P^x/P) is lower than in relative import prices (P^m/P), thus provoking a fall in the terms of trade. Finally, the increase in output per worker and the decrease in firms' effective labour costs push up the marginal value of a new worker, driving firms to advertise more vacancies.

Moving on to the steady-state effects of changes in the different components of the tax wedge, the first thing to note is that, as expected, the signs and individual contributions of tax variations are in line with the reduction of the total tax wedge in the last column of Table 7.1. Notice that, in the case of Spain, the labour tax rate has to be increased to reach United States levels ($\Delta \tau^l > 0$). This means that, in general, the effects are contrary to those of the other tax components. Hours per worker are determined by the condition derived in the model through the Nash bargaining framework. Under that condition, firms' social security contributions, labour income tax and consumption tax (through the shadow price of income) have a negative effect on hours per employee. Given this mechanism, the increase in consumption tax and in firms' social security contributions increases the number of hours per worker, but the augmentation in the labour tax rate decreases them.

The only qualitative difference across the different components of the tax wedge is related to the effects on real wages, after-tax real wages and effective labour costs. In REMS, the real wage is a bargained variable that depends on the three components of the overall tax wedge: the consumption tax rate (which affects consumption prices and hence the shadow price of income), the labour income tax rate (which directly influences bargained wages and indirectly through the marginal utility of newly created jobs) and firms' social security contributions (that directly influence negotiated wages). In the case of a reduction in consumption taxes, the after-tax real wage increases because the direct effect on consumption prices prevails. However, real wages and effective labour costs are reduced, mainly because the decrease in consumption prices increases the marginal shadow value of household income. This in turn makes households more sensitive to accepting lower real wages (measured in terms of the overall price deflator). In the case of changes in labour income tax, similar reasoning applies: an increase in labour taxes reduces after-tax labour wages, pushing up real wages in the bargaining. With respect to the decrease in social security contributions, as expected, this is the only case where the effect on real wages is the opposite of reductions in consumption and labour taxes. This can be explained easily because a reduction in social security contributions lowers effective labour costs, making firms more able to accept higher real wages in the bargaining process.

In order to offer the whole picture of the effects of bringing the Spanish tax system in line with that prevailing in the United States, in Table 7.2

Table 7.2 Long-run effects of increasing capital taxes in Spain

	Overall wedge	Capital tax	Capital tax and overall wedge
	$\Delta\tau = -19.5$	$\Delta\tau^k = 4.9$	$\Delta\tau^k = 4.9$ and $\Delta\tau = -19.5$
GDP	8.29	−1.81	6.25
Consumption	9.82	−0.83	8.89
Investment	3.38	−3.34	−0.22
Exports	4.26	−1.50	2.64
Imports	0.97	−0.35	0.60
Total hours per adult	8.88	−0.49	8.48
Hours per employed	4.32	0.07	4.37
Employment rate	4.56	−0.42	4.11
Real wage	11.36	−1.20	9.98
After tax real wage*	14.17	−0.80	13.22
Effective labour cost	−2.31	−1.20	−3.53
Terms of trade	−3.41	1.14	−2.08
Vacancies	11.22	−0.98	10.05

Note: (∗) Deflated with the price of consumption good

we present the results of pushing up the Spanish capital tax rate to the level of the United States. In the first column we summarise the results related to the overall tax wedge. In the second, we isolate the effect of increasing the capital tax rate, and in the last column we interact the capital tax and the overall tax rates. While they are close, the results of this last column are not equal to those obtained by adding up the first and second columns directly, because of the existence of interaction effects. The main conclusions of this exercise are as follows. First, changing the Spanish capital tax rate to United States levels would not have a significant affect on labour market variables (hours per employed person and employment rate). Second, GDP would decrease by 1.81pp because of the large decrease in productive investment driven by the increase in capital taxation. Finally, as a consequence of this, there would be a further fall in Spanish labour productivity of 2.2pp.

7.3.2 Transitional dynamics

Looking at the transitional dynamics produced by the unexpected permanent reduction in the overall tax wedge shown in Figure 7.7, we can appreciate similar behaviour on behalf of both real wages (deflated by the price of the production good) and total hours per capita. Both magnitudes increase on impact and follow each other very closely over the medium term, though the impulse in hours disappears before that

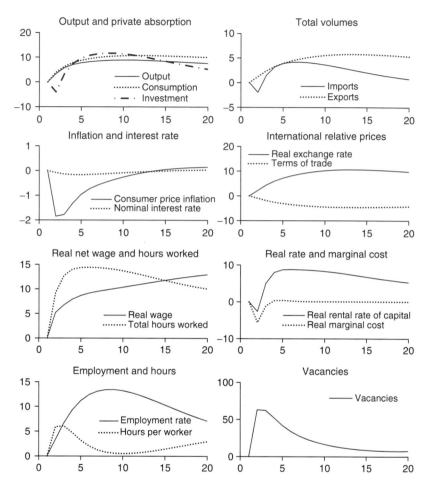

Figure 7.7 Transitional dynamics after a permanent reduction in the overall tax wedge

in wages. Interestingly, the breakdown of hours between hours per employee and the unemployment[6] rate shows that, over the medium term, the increase in labour income stems mainly from more employment rather than from these employees spending more hours at the workplace.

Our model also features a rapid decline in vacancies after a very pronounced initial jump, resulting from the steady reduction in the search effort and an increase in market tightness.

Another interesting fact is related to the short-run dynamics of investment. As can be seen, investment falls in the first few quarters and then recovers. The initial fall in investment is related to the original fall in marginal costs, resulting from the reduction in effective labour costs. As marginal costs go down, consumption inflation dampens, provoking a fall in Tobin's q and, consequently, a reduction in investment. After a number of quarters, given that the rental rate of capital recovers through an increase in the productivity of capital, investment experiences a steady increase towards its new higher long-run level.

With respect to the foreign sector variables, the change in the overall tax wedge generates a continuous increase in exports, driven by both real depreciation and a fall in the terms of trade. Given that our model is a small open economy, the rest of the world is exogenous and there are no spillovers across countries that induce additional effects. However, imports fall on impact because the negative effect of the initial increase in the relative price of imports more than compensates for the positive income effect produced by the increase in aggregate demand.

The transitional dynamics for each individual component are given in Appendix 6. The temporal path of the variables is, in all cases, very similar to that discussed above for the overall tax wedge. However, in the case of the capital tax rate, and contrary to the result obtained for steady-state values, hours per employee begin to fall sharply during the first year and recover later.

The dynamics of aggregate consumption depicted in Figure 7.7 hide the distinctive behaviour of optimising and RoT consumption. The distribution of lump-sum endogenous transfers among both types of agents affects their consumption possibilities. In Figure 7.8 we show the deviation (in percentage points) with respect to the steady state of total aggregate consumption (left panel), consumption of Ricardian households (central panel) and restricted households (right panel). The solid line corresponds to the case in which the whole burden is borne by optimising households, while the dotted line depicts the opposite situation, where RoT consumers are the only ones burdened. Finally, the dashed line corresponds to an intermediate situation where both agents share the burden of lump-sum taxation. Given that, in our model, the reduction in the overall tax wedge requires a negative lump-sum transfer (that is, a lump-sum tax), the distribution of this burden has quite marked effects on the dynamics of individual consumption. On impact, the consumption of Ricardian agents decreases when they support the whole burden of taxation, while this does not happen when restricted households face the entire payment of the lump-sum tax. As

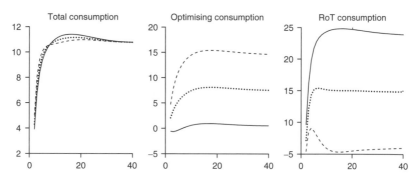

Figure 7.8   Dynamics of consumption after a permanent reduction in the overall tax wedge

was to be expected, the short-run impact on RoT consumption is highly significant, compared to agents that smooth consumption over their lifetime. However, the dynamics of aggregate consumption are not greatly affected by the distribution of the burden of lump-sum transfers.[7]

7.4   Sensitivity analysis

In Tables 7.3 and 7.4 we report a sensitivity analysis regarding the long-run effects of bringing tax wedges and capital taxes in Spain to the levels prevailing in the United States. First, we show in these tables how the long-run effects on key macroeconomic variables depend on the labour supply elasticity of households. As in Coenen *et al.* (2008), we change our baseline labour-supply elasticity of 0.5 to a value of 3, which is the same as that calibrated in Prescott (2004).

With respect to the results of lowering the tax wedge, they are, as to be expected, similar to those reported by Coenen *et al.* (2008). However, the magnitude of these effects on output and hours worked is less important than in their results. In our search and match labour market context, total hours per adult increase in the new steady state by 10.39 per cent compared to the 8.88 per cent increase for the baseline calibration of the reduction in the overall tax wedge. These effects are smaller because workers in our model have more room to manoeuvre when faced with shocks, as is readily apparent, bearing in mind that extensive and intensive margins respond very differently when labour-supply elasticity is increased. We observe that hours per employee increase significantly by 10.92 per cent in the new steady state, compared to 4.32 per cent

Table 7.3 Sensitivity of long-run benefits of lowering tax wedges in Spain

	Components of overall tax wedge			Overall wedge
	$\Delta\tau^c = -7.5$	$\Delta\tau^l = 3.0$	$\Delta\tau^{sc} = -15.0$	$\Delta\tau = -19.5$
Labour supply elasticity value of 3				
GDP	4.23	−1.99	8.07	10.41
Consumption	5.08	−2.41	9.67	12.44
Investment	1.43	−0.67	2.72	3.50
Exports	2.09	−1.00	3.95	5.07
Imports	0.48	−0.23	0.90	1.15
Total hours per adult	4.18	−1.95	8.02	10.39
Hours per employed	4.40	−2.06	8.44	10.92
Employment rate	−0.22	0.11	−0.42	−0.53
Real wage	−0.06	0.02	13.83	13.76
After-tax real wage*	6.63	−3.11	12.71	16.43
Effective labour cost	−0.06	0.02	−0.15	−0.21
Terms of trade	−1.64	0.76	−3.15	−4.08
Vacancies	−0.82	0.40	−1.53	−1.95

Note: (∗) Deflated with the price of consumption good.

Table 7.4 Sensitivity of long-run effects of increasing capital taxes in Spain

	Overall wedge	Capital tax	Capital tax and overall wedge
	$\Delta\tau = -19.5$	$\Delta\tau^k = 4.9$	$\Delta\tau^k = 4.9$ and $\Delta\tau = -19.5$
Labour-supply elasticity value of 3			
GDP	10.41	−1.94	8.18
Consumption	12.44	−0.79	11.53
Investment	3.50	−3.50	−0.28
Exports	5.07	−1.61	3.31
Imports	1.15	−0.37	0.75
Total hours per adult	10.39	−0.37	9.94
Hours per employed	10.92	−0.15	10.70
Employment rate	−0.53	−0.22	−0.76
Real wage	13.76	−1.42	12.10
After-tax real wage*	16.43	−1.01	15.23
Effective labour cost	−0.21	−1.42	−1.66
Terms of trade	−4.08	1.23	−2.63
Vacancies	−1.95	−0.81	−2.78

Note: (∗) Deflated with the price of consumption good.

in the baseline scenario. In contrast, the employment rate decreases slightly (−0.53 per cent), while in our baseline calculations it rose by 4.56 per cent. Thus, in line with Fang and Rogerson (2008) there seems to be a trade-off between hours per employee and the employment rate that makes total hours vary less. The smaller reduction in effective labour costs and greater willingness on behalf of workers to spend more time working result in an important increase in hours worked by employees, so firms hire fewer workers and post fewer vacancies. In line with these labour market effects, GDP also experiences a stronger effect than in the baseline simulation, rising by 10.41 per cent compared with the 8.29 per cent increase in the baseline scenario. If we now look at the robustness of our simulations in the case of capital tax, comparing the second columns in Tables 7.2 and 7.4, we can appreciate that changing labour-supply elasticity had no noticeable effect on any of the macroeconomic variables in the tables. In fact, none of the steady-state variations are larger than 0.25pp.

In addition to the previous findings regarding labour supply elasticity, we have performed other exercises (not reported in the tables) to check the robustness of our results against different parameter values. These exercises are mainly related to relevant parameters in equations affecting the labour market. Concentrating only on the effects of lowering the tax wedge, given that the results for capital taxes are quite robust, if we assume, for example, a more efficient matching technology (increasing χ_1 by 20 per cent) our steady-state impacts on relevant macroeconomic variables are not altered in a significant manner either. Only the number of vacancies increases by almost 2pp more in the new steady state compared with our baseline calculations. Also, increasing the elasticity of matches to vacancies (augmenting the value of χ_2 by 20 per cent) has only mild (albeit noticeable) effects on the long-run response of vacancies (the steady-state increase for this variable dropping from 11.22 per cent to 10.13 per cent) and on the extensive and intensive margins. Hours per employed person increase by only 4.01 per cent in the new steady state, compared to 4.32 per cent in the baseline scenario. In contrast, the employment rate rises by 5.25 per cent, more than half a point more than in our baseline calculations, where it increased by 4.56 per cent. No noteworthy effects on other relevant macroeconomic aggregates are observed in these exercises. This is also the case when we check our simulation results against changes in worker bargaining power (λ^w). To get an idea of the robustness of our results, a 25 per cent reduction in λ^w implies that GDP (or investment) increases in the new steady state by 8.47 per cent (3.52 per cent) compared to an 8.29 per cent (3.38 per cent) increase in the baseline calibration of the reduction in the overall tax wedge.

7.5 Conclusions

This chapter employed a rational expectations model for simulation and policy evaluation of the Spanish economy (the REMS model) to perform a simulation exercise consisting of reducing the overall tax wedge prevailing in Spain to United States levels. This exercise is very similar in its objectives to other studies applied to European countries, such as Coenen *et al.* (2008), but using a model that characterises a small open economy in a currency area. As our model also specifies a labour market in which there are searching and matching between workers and firms, where a richer and deeper analysis of the effects of taxes on both the intensive and extensive margins of labour can be performed.

According to our results, a reduction in the overall tax wedge of 19.5 points, in order to reach United States levels, has an unequivocally positive effect in the long run on output and labour in the Spanish economy: total hours increase by about 8.9 per cent, and GDP rises by about 8.3 percentage points. In terms of GDP per adult, these results account for one third of the gap with respect to the United States, but imply a slight increase of about 0.5pp in the labour productivity gap. The rise in total hours per adult is explained by a similar increase in both hours per employee and the employment rate of about 3.5 percentage points. This effect accounts for around one-third of the average difference in the employment rate between Spain and the United States since 1985. The increase in hours per employee, however, would allow this variable to converge to United States levels. When, in addition to the change in the overall tax wedge, we allow for a variation in capital tax rates to the levels of the United States, we find that overall GDP increases by only 6.25 points because of the negative effects generated by increasing capital tax rates by 4.9 points. In contrast, total hours rise by 8.5pp, given that higher capital taxes have no significant effect on hours worked per employee, but produce a mild decrease in employment rates.

With respect to other macroeconomic aggregates, our simulation exercise predicts higher steady-state levels of consumption, private investment, exports, imports, real wages and vacancies. In contrast, terms of trade and real effective labour costs would fall. In the short run there are no important transition costs, except for the case of investment, which falls in the first few quarters. Vacancies, however, experience a boom over the first few years.

In summary, this chapter has presented estimates of the costs of distortionary taxation in the Spanish economy. Nevertheless, as long as the intertemporal budget constraint of the government is satisfied, a lower level of taxation also implies a lower level of public expenditure. Taking into account this trade-off, the challenge is how to increase the efficiency of taxes without having a negative effect on the provision of essential public services, which promote equal opportunities for all and a fair distribution of income, as well as the sustainability of the pension system.

Notes

1. Data for the EU-15 refer to the 15 initial members of the European Union, excluding Luxembourg (because of a the lack of data) and Spain (for a better comparison as it represents 10.6 per cent of the EU-15 GDP in 2006).
2. Fernández de Córdoba and Torregrosa (2005) and Doménech and Pérez (2006) have also analysed the effects of changes in fiscal structure on labour and output in the Spanish economy.
3. As surveyed by González-Páramo and Melguizo (2008), an alternative research area in the empirical literature has analysed the effects of taxes on wages instead of on unemployment. According to their results, in the long run workers bear between three-quarters of the tax burden in continental and Anglo-Saxon economies and the whole tax burden in Scandinavian countries.
4. Notice that we performed a similar exercise in Chapter 1.
5. These results are due to the assumption in our model that lump-sum taxes are borne only by optimising consumers. Obviously, a different assumption would imply other redistributive effects. We shall come back to this issue in the next section.
6. It is worth recalling that unemployment in our model is an equilibrium unemployment. Thus it can consider involuntary unemployment to be a result only of frictions in search, and not disequilibrium unemployment caused, for example, by hysteresis in the labour market or other types of long-term unemployment.
7. The dynamics of other macroeconomic variables are also affected by the assumption made about the distribution of transfers. However, as is the case with total consumption, the effects are quite moderate. In any case, steady-state values are always the same, so the results in Table 7.3 remain unaffected.

8
Conclusions

J. E. Boscá, R. Doménech, J. Ferri and J. Varela

From 1995 to 2007 the Spanish economy enjoyed one of the longest periods of economic growth in recent decades, with an average growth rate of 3.7 per cent higher than in the majority of the economies in the European Union (EU). Total population also grew more in Spain during this period than in other countries, because of massive immigration flows. But despite population growth, as discussed in Chapter 1, economic growth was compatible with per capita income convergence, since Spain reduced the gap with the European average by 8 points.

However, this period of sizeable economic growth was also characterised by some elements that raised doubts and concerns about the quality of growth in the Spanish economy. The first was the persistent inflation differential with respect to the Economic and Monetary Union (EMU) which, with a monetary policy determined by the ECB which regulated the behaviour of the euro-zone as a whole, gave rise to *ex-post* real interest rates that were exceptionally low and even negative for some years. Negative real interest rates and intense population growth induced a significant residential investment boom with great consequences. The second concern was the increasing current account deficit, which went from zero to ten per cent of GDP in 2008. The third problem was the weak growth in productivity in the 1995–2007 period. Productivity per worker had converged to the EU level in the second half of the twentieth century, reaching 99.5 per cent of the EU-12 in 1995. But from then until 2006 it diminished again to as low as 89 per cent. This performance was even more conspicuous if we take into account that in this period productivity in the United States was outstandingly dynamic, growing at higher rates than in Europe. Therefore, from 1995 onwards Europe lagged behind the United States in terms of productivity, and Spain underperformed to an even greater extent. To many economists, these three problems:

inflation differential, external imbalance and a weak increase in productivity, are linked: it is frequently said that the inflation differential and a high current account deficit are the consequence of weak productivity growth.

By 2007 some of the drivers of economic growth in the previous few years were heading towards exhaustion. The benefits derived from economic integration and the stability of monetary and fiscal policies had already materialised. Spain gradually stopped being a net beneficiary of European cohesion policies that had contributed greatly to public capital accumulation and therefore to the improvement in infrastructures. Finally, there was little margin for improvement in participation rates (except in the case of women) as they converged towards the levels prevailing in advanced economies such as the United States or the European Union. Under these circumstances, the imbalances accumulated were not sustainable for a longer period. Additionally, the adjustment of these imbalances has coincided with the deepest international crisis since the Great Depression, inducing a very intense fall in activity, and particularly in employment. The consequence has been a rapid increase in the unemployment rate to 20 per cent of the labour force, in just two years reaching the levels of the previous recession in 1993–4. Given the experience of the crisis of 2008–9, it is clear that future growth cannot be based on the same determinants as in the economic expansion from 1995 to 2007. Future improvements in Spanish per capita income will require a larger increase in labour productivity and, in particular, in total factor productivity and human capital, an issue that has caught the attention of many authors.

In this book we have presented a series of essays on the Spanish economy, based on the results of simulations and evaluation with REMS (the rational expectation model of the Spanish economy) of different macroeconomic policies. As described in Chapter 2, REMS is a dynamic general equilibrium model constructed primarily to serve as a tool for simulation and for the understanding of the transmission channels through which policy action affects the domestic economy. As far as economic theory is concerned, REMS can be characterised as a New Keynesian model with the optimising behaviour of households and firms being rooted deeply in the rational expectations hypothesis. The supply side of the economy is modelled through a neoclassical production function, implying that the long-term behaviour of the model closely reproduces the Solow growth model; that is, the economy reaches a steady-state path with a growth rate determined by the rate of exogenous technical progress plus the growth rate of the population. However, some prominent features differentiate this model from the neoclassical paradigm in the long term. First, trading, both in the goods and the labour market, is not achieved under Walrasian conditions. Firms in goods markets operate under monopolistic competition, setting prices sluggishly. In the labour market, firms and workers negotiate wages to distribute the rents generated in the matching process. Consequently, in our model, equilibrium unemployment will persist in the long term. Second, some households behave as myopic consumers that do not optimise intertemporally. Additionally, consumers take into account past consumption (habits) in their decisions. As a result, aggregate consumption increases in response to a positive fiscal shock, departing from the typical reduction that characterises neoclassical models. Thus, in the short term, REMS is influenced by the New Keynesian literature, allowing for a stabilising role of demand-based policies.

While the book is not about the Spanish economic crisis initiated after the subprime financial crisis that began in 2007, it offers a different analysis on the simulation effects of stabilisation policies and structural reforms that were discussed or implemented during this crisis. In this vein, the book focuses more on the effects of alternative demand and supply-side policies, some of them implemented in 2008–10, rather than in explaining the determinants and characteristics of the Spanish economic crisis. The book also offers evidence that economic growth in Spain could be greatly improved by raising significantly the growth rate of productivity per hour worked. More particularly, the level of education seems to be a key factor in the next few decades if Spain is to catch up with most advanced countries in terms of productivity and welfare.

From a business cycle perspective, important for any stabilisation policy, the most recent data used in this book show characteristics of the cycle that are similar to those obtained by other related studies using older data. Thus a low volatility of Spanish GDP compared with other industrialised economies is detected, together with a relatively high volatility of private consumption, a strong counter-cyclical behaviour of net exports, a very high relative volatility of vacancies and a counter-cyclical pattern of government debt, which lags behind the output cycle.

The evidence also shows that the Spanish economy has experienced a trade-off between job creation and stable employment since the 1980s. From 1997 onwards, Spain strongly championed employment growth in Europe; however, since 2008 it has led in job destruction. Specialisation in low-productivity activities and the abundance of unskilled workers explain this pattern to a great extent in an economy in which growth has been fuelled by unprecedentedly low real interest rates. But the inadequate legal framework of labour relations should also be blamed for the extraordinary increase in unemployment. Low investment in active labour market policies, the unfriendly design of passive policies and collective bargaining and, above all, the extraordinarily high number of temporary workers are some examples of this ill-designed legislation.

The chances of easy and cheap access to external financing for the foreseeable future are very slight, so Spain must seek to promote alternative incentives to growth, mainly by investing in activities with higher value-added and a more intensive use of skilled workers. Politicians and many commentators advocate a change in the growth model, and rightly so. This book shows (in Chapter 3) is that changes in the economic structure do not make labour reforms any less necessary, but rather the reverse if Spain wants to shorten employment recovery significantly.

An accurate reform that deals with the main inadequacies of Spanish labour regulations (at least in the legislation up to the summer of 2010) is called for in order to ease the employment growth–stability trade-off. Simulations in the book show that such reforms might significantly speed up the process of unemployment reduction, while also fostering productivity and real wage growth in line with what has been seen in Europe. These reforms act as a powerful tool to increase the extensive margin (job creation) while reducing the intensive margin (hours per worker).

In addition, a deep reform of product markets, in particular in services, will complement and reinforce the effects of a labour market reform. An incomplete Single Market for services, as well as many regulatory obstacles at the national level, obstructs free competition. Measures aimed at fostering market competition, such as the Services Directive, would therefore have a bearing on economic efficiency and relative prices in the European services sector. The transposition of the Services Directive into Spanish legislation tries to take advantage of the potential that the Directive offers and to maximise its economic effects. This ambitious character is not reflected in a wider scope, but rather by the depth of some chapters proposed by the Directive: a deeper administrative simplification, the reinforcement of economic freedom (for example, with the limitation of the use of negative silence), and a strict and credible sanctioning regime for the different levels of public administration. Softening the regulatory framework and making it more homogeneous across the member states would yield economic gains both for producers – such as greater economies of scale, downward pressure on costs or greater labour productivity growth; and for consumers, via the preservation of their purchasing power to cushion the impact of the 2008–9 crisis and greater transparency, which would reduce uncertainty.

In Chapter 4 the effects of the Services Directive on Spain are simulated through potential gains via higher competition – that is, a reduction in mark-ups in the services sector. As a consequence of this, a gradual and sustained GDP growth would be observed, while inflation would drop initially, only to return to its initial level after a few quarters. On the demand side, the main components of Spanish GDP, consumption and investment, would present a positive evolution as a result of greater opportunities and increased efficiency that would boost the real wage and rental rate of capital. In this case, supply-side effects would transcend the traditional trade-off between employment and productivity observed in the Spanish economy since the mid-1990s. Both increase as a result of the Directive, though in the short run we observed an overshooting effect in employment, with 0.75 per cent growth with respect to its steady-state value after 12 quarters (around 150,000 new jobs). In the medium to long run, the economic effects are found to be more capital-intensive, as the permanent effect on productivity is about 1 per cent.

These effects are particularly relevant in a country such as Spain, traditionally presenting losses in competitiveness because of low productivity rates and persistent inflation differentials with respect to the rest of the euro area, as already noted. Supply-side policies enhancing market competition in the product market, such as the implementation of the Services Directive, therefore seem necessary to support more efficient and flexible markets, to avoid artificially low potential output growth and to guarantee a rapid recovery from the current recession.

But, in addition to a change in the rules regarding the behaviour of the labour and product markets, the amount of public investment is an important policy variable for increasing output growth and productivity in a new growth model. The public sector accounts for a significant fraction of fixed capital formation in Spain. Public administrations, together with public organisms and enterprises, are often the main suppliers of transport and other key infrastructures, and invest resources heavily in educational, health care and administrative facilities.

Chapter 5 shows how, over the years between 1985 and 2005, Spanish public administrations accounted, on average, for over 16 per cent of total investment. The public investment rate increased sharply during the 1980s, rising from 1.75 per cent of GDP in 1980 to a peak of 4.86 per cent in 1991, and decreasing thereafter to a level only slightly above the sample mean. During the period 2000–5, Spain ranked seventh in the sample in terms of its public investment ratio, behind Japan, New Zealand, Ireland, Italy, the United States and Finland. In terms of per capita public capital stock, Spain remains slightly below the OECD average, but when public capital is measured as a fraction of the total capital stock or of GDP, the situation is somewhat different. While Spain starts out well below the OECD average, by the end of the sample period it has practically converged to the mean in terms of both indicators. This suggests that public capital has not been particularly scarce relative to private capital in recent years, and that the country's stock of public capital is roughly in proportion with its income level.

To answer the question of how public investment affects productivity and output growth, this book first reviewed the existing literature and then offered some simulations for Spain in a general equilibrium setting. From the review of the literature it appears that there are sufficient indications that investment in public infrastructure contributes significantly to productivity growth. The returns to such investment are probably quite high in the early stages, when infrastructures are scarce and basic networks have not been completed, but fall sharply thereafter. Hence, appropriate infrastructure provision is probably a crucial input for development policy, even if it does not hold the key to rapid productivity growth in advanced countries where transportation and communications needs are already adequately served.

However, the great disparity of results found in the literature is worrying. Some of the disparities are caused by a range of data and econometric problems, as well as differences in the methodology used to assess the effects of public investment. Given the wide range of estimates of the output elasticity of public capital available in the literature, we have shown that a value of this elasticity close to 0.06 is reasonable and fits quite well with the public investment rate in the Spanish economy from 1980 onwards.

Chapter 5 also evaluated the effects of a permanent increase in public investment on the main macroeconomic variables of the Spanish economy. The long-run multiplier of a permanent increase of 1 percentage point of GDP in government investment is equal to 3.34, showing the relative importance of the supply-side effects of this economic policy. After discussing the long-run effects of public investment we also analysed its short-run effects as well as their sensitivity to changes in some relevant parameters, which affect the transitional dynamics to the steady state. In our baseline, the impact multiplier of GDP is slightly above unity, suggesting that this supply-side policy not only has significant long-run effects but also relevant stabilisation results.

In 2007, the Spanish economy exhibited a large current account deficit of 10 per cent of GDP, a public budget surplus of 1.9 per cent of GDP and a relatively low household saving rate of around 6.5 per cent of GDP, when compared with their investment rate of almost 10 per cent of GDP. However, with the economic crisis of 2008–9, the situation changed dramatically. The public budget surplus turned into a huge deficit in 2009 that the government estimated at 11.2 per cent of GDP, the household saving rate increased enormously to a value above 11 per cent of GDP, and the current account deficit, 5.1 per cent of GDP in 2009, is correcting very quickly.

However, despite the presence of a large share of non-Ricardian consumers, the expansionary fiscal policy has had only a small negative effect on the current account. Additionally, the evidence the time of writing regarding the large increase in the household saving rate, at the same time as the government has incurred a large deficit, seems to be motivated mainly by precautionary saving in response to greater uncertainty and the high unemployment rate, and the desire to reduce indebtedness, after the dramatic fall in household wealth and expectations of future higher real interest rates, as a consequence of the international finance turmoil.

In fact, Chapter 6 shows that private agents compensate only partially for the effects of fiscal policies on the saving rate, and the fall in the investment rate only partially compensates for the fall in the saving rate, therefore the increase in the current account deficit is very small. In other words, though there is some evidence of twin deficits, only a small fraction of the government budget deficit translates into a current account deficit.

Given these explanations, while the evidence of increasing public deficits together with rising saving rates is observationally equivalent to Ricardian equivalence, it seems that only a fraction of the increase in the household saving rate is explained by the large current deficit in the government's budget. Therefore, at the time of writing, the emphasis on future fiscal consolidation should be based more on the sustainability of government debt than on the effects on external imbalances. According to these results, recent factors of the Spanish economy could be explained appropriately by the presence of a large negative output shock, which the Spanish government has tried to counteract with a large positive fiscal stimulus.

Related to fiscal policy issues, taxes have recently attracted much attention as an explanation of the differences in labour utilisation and macroeconomic performance between European countries and the United States. In Chapter 7 we presented simulations of the costs of distortionary taxation in the Spanish economy. Thus a reduction in the overall tax wedge of 19.5 points, to reach United States levels, is shown to have an unequivocally positive effect in the long run on output and labour in the Spanish economy: total hours would increase by about 8.9 per cent and GDP would rise by about 8.3 percentage points. In terms of GDP per adult, these results would account for one-third of the gap with respect to the United States, but imply a slight increase of about 0.5pp in the labour productivity gap. The rise in total hours per adult is explained by a similar increase in both hours per employee and the employment rate of about 3.5pp. This effect accounts for around one-third of the average difference in the employment rate between Spain and the United States since 1985. The increase in hours per employee, however, would allow this variable to converge to United States levels.

When, in addition to the change in the overall tax wedge, a variation in capital tax rates to the levels of the United States is allowed, the finding is that overall GDP increases by only 6.25 points, because of the negative effects generated by increasing capital tax rates by 4.9 points. In contrast, total hours rise by 8.5pp, given that higher capital taxes have no significant effect on hours worked per employee, but produce a mild decrease in employment rates. Simulations also predict higher steady-state levels of consumption, private investment, exports, imports, real wages and vacancies. In contrast, terms of trade and real effective labour costs would fall. In the short run there are no important transition costs of changing the tax wedge, except for the case of investment, which falls in the first few quarters, whereas vacancies experience a boom over the first few years.

Given the magnitude of the challenges that the Spanish economy is currently facing and that it will have to overcome in the future, new modelling tools, complementary to the one presented in this book, will be needed. Some of them may be accommodated in REMS – as, for example, different groups of labour force according to their skills, the endogenous nature of technical progress or additional linkages between the financial and the real sectors. Over and above this, Bayesian estimation techniques may improve the fit of the model and our understanding of the driving forces behind the economic growth of the Spanish economy. With all these improvements in mind, REMS is expected to continue to help in the design and evaluation of economic policies in Spain in the near future.

Appendix 1
Dataset for International Comparisons

A.1.1 Definitions and sources of international data

- *GDP at purchasing power parity.* In some countries it has been necessary to rescale GDP slightly to enable relative per capita income comparisons with data available in Eurostat in August 2008.
  Sources: Economic Outlook, OECD, and National Accounts, OECD, various years. Summers and Heston (1991) 'Penn World Tables' (PWT 6.2) for the period 1950–9, growth rates used for backward extrapolation.
- *Population, working-age population, labour force and unemployment rate.*
  Sources: Economic Outlook, OECD, and National Accounts and Employment Outlook, OECD, various years. PWT 6.2 for the period 1950–9, growth rates used for backward extrapolation. The working-age population refers to the population aged between 15 and 64 years, and 16 to 64 for Norway, Spain, Sweden, the United Kingdom and the United States. The employed population is consistent with national accounts, so may not be the same as that stated in the OECD Labour Force Survey.
- *Hours worked*: number of hours worked per employee per year across the economy as a whole.
  Sources: Economic Outlook, OECD, 2008(1), Austria 2004–7, Employment Outlook, OECD, 2008. The data for Greece in 2007 refer to 2006. For years previous to those available from the OECD, the hours estimated by Groningen Growth and Development Centre, are extrapolated backwards using their growth rates.
- *Private productive capital stock.* The same methodology as for the permanent inventory method in de la Fuente and Doménech (2006a) has been used to calculate the initial capital stock in 1950, but distinguishing between the private productive capital series, and residential investment and public capital. The depreciation rates are those published by Kamps (2006). See Appendix A.1.2 for further details.
  Sources: Economic Outlook, OECD, and National Accounts, various years. PWT 6.2 for the period 1950–9, growth rates used for backward extrapolation.

- *Years of schooling* among the population aged over 25 years. Source: de la Fuente and Doménech (2006a). Data for the most recent years have been extrapolated up to 2009 using the forecasts provided by Arnold *et al.* (2007). These estimates are very similar to those provided in Cohen and Soto (2007).
- *Cost of regulations* affecting economic activity. Corresponds to the average of the standardised values, for the 21 OECD countries in 2006, of the cost of setting up and closing down a company, red tape, regulations on hiring employees, the cost of registering ownership and accessing credit, investor protection and contract protection (both variables with a negative sign), the tax burden and ease of foreign trade (also with a negative sign). Source: Doing Business 2007, World Bank.
- *Inflation.* Rate of growth of the private consumption deflator. Source: Economic Outlook, OECD.
- *Structural unemployment rate.* NAIRU estimated by the OECD, unless otherwise stated. Source: Economic Outlook, OECD.
- *Public Deficit.* Source: Economic Outlook, OECD.

A.1.2   Estimation of the capital stocks

We construct series of physical capital stocks in the OECD for the period 1950–2009 using a perpetual inventory procedure with annual depreciation rates taken from Kamps (2006). From 1960 onwards, data for investment rates are from OECD Economic Outlook Database and National Accounts, where three different types of investment are distinguished: business capital, public investment and housing. We correct investment data for differences in PPP across countries. Prior to that date, we use IMF data and price deflators and, for some countries where no information is available, we extrapolate investment backwards using the growth rates provided in Summers and Heston (1991) PWT 5.6 for total investment, which is divided into the three types of capital using the averages of shares during the 1960s.

To estimate the initial capital stock we modify the procedure proposed by Griliches (1980) to take into account that the economies in our sample may be away from their steady states. The growth rate of the stock of capital, γ_K, can be written in the form

$$\gamma_{K_i} = \frac{I_i}{K_i} - \delta_{it}$$

for each type of capital, where I_i is investment, δ_i the depreciation rate and K_i the stock of physical capital. Solving this expression for K and assuming that the growth rate of investment is a good approximation to the growth rate of the capital stock (that is, $\gamma_K \simeq \gamma_I$), we obtain an expression that can be used to estimate the initial capital stock using data on investment flows:

$$K_i = \frac{I_i}{\gamma_{K_i} + \delta_i} \simeq \frac{I_i}{\gamma_{I_i} + \delta_i}$$

When implementing this approach, it is common to use the level of investment in the first year in the sample period and the growth rate of the same variable over the entire period. In our case, however, this does not seem to be the best way to proceed because (i) investment may be subject to transitory disturbances that make it dangerous to rely on a single observation; and (ii) rates of investment and factor accumulation will tend to vary over time in a systematic way as countries approach their steady states.

In an attempt to control for these factors, we use the growth rate of investment over the period 1950–60 and the HP-filtered level of investment in 1955. Hence our version of the preceding equation is of the form:

$$K_{i,1950} = \frac{I_{55}^{HP}}{\gamma_{I_{50,60}^{HP}} + \delta_i}$$

where I_{55}^{HP} is the Hodrick–Prescott trend of investment (with a smoothing parameter equal to 10). We use 1955 as the base year instead of 1950 because it is known that this filter may display anomalies at sample endpoints.[1]

Once we have an initial capital stock for each of the three types of capital we use the standard perpetual inventory procedure:

$$K_{it} = I_{it} + (1 - \delta_{it})K_{it-1}$$

Note

1. Because of data limitations and other anomalies we have used a different base year for some countries. In particular, we used 1953 for Canada and Norway, and 1960 for the UK, Greece and Ireland.

Appendix 2
The REMS Database (REMSDB)

The database comprises national aggregates. All series cover the period 1980–2010, which in turn can be divided into two sub periods depending on the nature of the data. The first spans from 1980 to the last available data released by the various statistical sources – that is, 2010 in the current version of the database. The second, which covers a four-year period, relies mainly on the official forecasts included in the Stability and Growth Program (SGP). Additionally, to generate a baseline scenario for the REMS model, the whole set of variables are extended towards a 2050 horizon. Though not part of REMSDB, this forward extrapolation obviously builds on the database and further complies with the requirements imposed by the balanced-growth hypothesis.

For simulation purposes, all series have been collected on a quarterly basis. When quarterly data were not readily available from the existing statistical sources, high-frequency series were obtained by applying the Kalman filter and smoother to an appropriate state–space model where the observations correspond to the low-frequency data.[1] The frequency of monthly series has also been treated and converted into quarterly data with techniques that are specific to each series. Needless to say, all series take the form of seasonally adjusted data. Where the series provided by official statistical sources does not take seasonal effects into account, these were adjusted using TRAMO/SEATS. The dataset has not been subject to any transformation other than the extraction of the seasonal component or the mere application of linking-back techniques. This is not the case with the variables used to construct a baseline scenario of the REMS model, most of which have been expressed in efficiency units so as to display a stationary pattern. Put differently, every series included in the baseline scenario exhibits a number of statistical properties that comply with the balanced-growth hypothesis. Section 4.2 details the treatment given to the baseline-type series.

The database considers five types of variables. While each of these groups is somewhat stylised, they gather sets of variables of a different nature. The taxonomy is as follows. The first category includes various production and demand aggregates, along with their corresponding deflators. A second group brings together population and labour market series. The third block is made up of monetary and financial variables, and the fourth includes relevant government aggregates. A final set gathers a number of heterogeneous variables that play a role in the baseline scenario and for which no direct statistical counterpart is available in official sources.

A.2.1   Data sources

Whenever possible, the information collected for the database is taken from official sources. The key series are taken from the Spanish Quarterly National Accounts (SQNA) provided by the Instituto Nacional de Estadística (INE, National Statistical Institute). The remaining series come from various statistical sources, all of which have been chosen to ensure the most coherent dataset possible.

Lack of official back-linking between the two currently published SQNA series – that is, 1980–2004 and 1995–2009, with base years respectively in 1995 and 2000 – complete series for the period 1980–2009 have been built up on the basis of back-cast figures using the level registered in 1995Q1 and the growth rates of the SQNA 1980–2004 series. Apart from that, any treatment given to the series by the INE has been adopted accordingly and the base year 2000 respected.

Following the System of National Accounts methodology (SNA93), the new European System of National Accounts (ESA95) recommends the use of chain indices for quantifying growth rates in volume and price measures. The INE duly implemented this methodology as of spring 2005. On the plus side, according to the theory of index numbers, the chaining method displays relative superiority over the more traditional method of fixed-base indices, as it better captures the rapid evolution of the economic reality. On the minus side, an important consequence of using chain indexes is that the associated volume measures are not additive. Empirically, it can easily be shown that the adoption of the chaining technique has a modest effect on the results obtained in terms of growth rates in the indices. That said, in REMSDB we produce series at constant market prices following traditional methodology, and adopt 2000 as the base year.

Details about the series, namely their statistical sources and units of measurement, are presented in this Appendix. A thorough explanation of the five categories of series is provided below.

A.2.2   Description of the series

A.2.2.1   Historical data (1980–2009) and forecast period

Production and demand variables

Production and demand variables are central to the database. They have been taken from the SQNA provided by the INE with other official sources complementing these data.

The forecast period spans five additional years beyond the last available data released by official sources. In particular, the demand and production series are extended in line with the forecasts included in the SGP. To enable forecasting on a quarterly basis from the macroeconomic scenario reflected in the SGP, three month growth rates are benchmarked to their corresponding year-on-year growth rates under the assumption of similar growth rates across all quarters. Excluding the demand and production block, the remaining series have been extended following specific rules as explained below.

The forecast of GDP at constant market prices is made consistent with official forecasts for *GDP at current market prices?* and the corresponding deflator. A similar strategy is applied to the various demand aggregates, to maintain consistency with total GDP.

It is also assumed that *Non-Market Services' Gross Value Added* keep pace with *Government Current Expenditures*. This makes it much easier to obtain a forecast period for both *Private GDP at market prices* and *Private GDP at basic prices*, the latter being calculated by deducting the *Net Taxes on Products* from the former.[2] In turn, *Net Taxes on Products* includes three tax categories – namely, the *Value Added Tax (VAT)*, *Taxes and Duties on Imports*, and *Taxes on Products, excluding VAT and Import and Export Taxes*. The latter includes, among others, taxes levied on alcoholic beverages, tobacco consumption, hydrocarbon products and the like. This means that, to forecast *Net Taxes on Products*, several hypotheses are made regarding its three components. First, it is assumed that both the *VAT* and *Taxes on Products, excluding VAT and Import and Export Taxes* change in line with *Private Consumption*. Second, *Taxes and Duties on Imports* grow as fast as *Goods and Services Imports*.

The *Capital Stock* series has been constructed according to the perpetual inventory method. This applies both to the historical data and the forecast period. The relevant data come originally from the BDMORES database (see Dabán *et al.*, 2002). More precisely, the initial capital stock refers to 1979 in BDMORES whereas the depreciation rate stands at 5 per cent. To estimate the depreciation rate, BDMORES assumes that the capital stock is made up of private and public equipment and structures, including residential capital.

As an indicator for *Energy Demand* we use the total amount of energy commanded by any productive sector in the economy. The total amount of inter industry energy consumption has been constructed as a weighted average of both gas/oil and electricity consumption, as reported by the *Indice de Produccion Industrial* (Industrial Production Index: IPI) provided by the INE. A scale correction is then performed to enable the total amount of inter-industry energy consumption to match its ratio to GDP that prevailed in the economy in 1995 according to the system of Input–Output Tables.

Prices and costs

Price deflators for *GDP at market prices*, aggregate *Private and Public Consumption, Exports and Imports* are obtained from the SQNA series at current prices and our own estimates of their counterparts at constant market prices. Similarly, the deflator of the private component of total GDP is calculated using as inputs our own estimates of private GDP at both current and constant market prices. This general procedure does not apply to *Energy Demand*, for which we select the *Indice de Precios Industriales* (Industrial Price Index: IPRI).

In general, assumptions on the forecast period rely on the SGP. This is particularly the case for *GDP* and *Private Consumption* deflators. *Public Consumption* and *Exports* and *Imports* deflators resemble the pattern observed in *Private*

Consumption. Forward estimates of the *Energy Demand* deflator are in keeping with long-run trends in energy prices as dictated by future markets.

The data on *Compensation per Employee* are also taken from the SQNA. We subsequently use the *Labour Cost per Employee* series as provided by the SGP to complete the forecast period.

Demographic and labour market series

As a general rule, demographic and labour market variables are taken from the INE, which in turn draws on a number of sources to collect the relevant series. Forecasting procedures are nevertheless specific to each series. We provide further details on the variables belonging to this block.

First, *Total Population* matches INE annual estimates from 1996 to 2009. Published census data available for 1980 and 1991 have subsequently been linked through the use of historical adjusted inter-census population estimates provided by the INE at sometime in the past. This procedure has enabled us to compile complete series for *Total Population* covering the period 1980–2009. Forecasts rely on population flows as captured by the so-called 'Scenario 2' released by the INE.

Estimates of *Adult Population* (that is, population aged over 16) are then made consistent with the *Total Population* series computed in the manner described above, under the assumption that the demographic age structure remains pretty much the same as captured by official sources. The figures covering the forecast period 2007–10, *Adult Population*, is obtained by assuming a constant ratio of this group to *Total Population*, in accordance with experts' views on demographic trends.

Regarding the unemployment rate, the data included in REMSDB are coherent with *Labour Force Survey* (LFS) figures for *Total Employment, Unemployment* and *Labour Force*. These series, which are released for two distinctive periods (1976–95 and 1996–2009) imply the same unemployment rate for the last quarter of 1995 and the first quarter of 1996, meaning that no specific treatment was needed to ensure homogeneity across the two quarters spanning the transition. The time span of the series is extended to 2010 on the basis of the forecasts reflected in the SGP.

Total Employment and *Employment Full-time Equivalents* both replicate SQNA data, while forecasts are taken from the SGP. SQNA is also the statistical source for the retrieval of historical data for *Employment in Non-Market Services* and *Employment Full time Equivalents in Non-Market Services*. These two series are extended under the assumption that the *Gross Value Added of Non-Market Services* at constant market prices grows in line with public consumption as captured by the SGP, and that the services' labour productivity movements in the years to come will reflect past patterns in its growth rate.

Labour Force figures over the period 1980–2009 are determined endogenously by dividing total employment, as provided by the SQNA, over one minus the unemployment rate.[3] Then the magnitude of *Total Unemployment* is computed by multiplying the unemployment rate by the labour force calculated in the manner described above.

Hours worked are computed as the product of the number of employed workers, as provided by the SQNA, and the number of hours per employed worker, as given by the *Encuesta de Población Activa* (EPA, LFS). The series obtained in this manner for the period 1980–2009 have been made as coherent as possible, with the figures on hours provided by the annual National Accounts for the period 2000–9.[4] Regarding the quantification of the latter series, the various statistical sources differ significantly in their magnitude.[5] Beyond national data, which have been duly consulted, OECD statistics have been studied in depth as a countercheck. However, a strategy has been devised by which EPA data covering the period 1987–2004 have been adjusted to allow for different employment statuses, most remarkably self-employed workers versus employees, and part-time versus full-time employment. Retropolation between 1980 and 1987 has been completed by applying the percentage change in hours worked per employee taken from the Labour Costs Index (LCI) to the available 1987 level. Forward extrapolation (realistically) assumes that the number of hours per employed worker will remain broadly consistent.

On the other hand, REMSDB includes two labour market variables with no statistical counterpart in official sources, namely the number of vacancies and matches per quarter.[6] To construct the former we follow Antolín (1995). This methodology amounts to adjusting the series *Puestos de trabajo ofrecidos para gestión pendientes de cubrir* (job vacancies posted by firms) as reflected in the *Movimiento labboural Registrado* (Recorded Labour Flows (MRL)) managed by the former Instituto Nacional de Empleo (National Employment Institute (INEM)), by introducing a scale factor which accounts for the incomplete coverage of the series and also deals with the two-level shifts that show up in December 1995 and August 1999. These anomalies may be attributable to methodological changes. To estimate the quarterly number of matches we rely on the *Total de contratos registrados* (Total number of recorded contracts), also included in the MRL. Nevertheless, to provide an accurate picture of the number of matches we adjust for the chaining of successive fixed-term contracts by which workers are hired and fired simultaneously, one period after another. This adjustment removes from the series any hire-and-fire practices not reflecting genuine matches between former unemployed workers and unfilled vacancies. More specifically, we assimilate these 'virtual' contracts with those signed before 2001 and captured either by the *Contratos por obra y servicio* (works and services contracts), *Contratos eventuales por circunstancias de la producción* (temporary contracts contingent on production) or *Contratos a tiempo parcial* (part-time contracts).

Monetary and financial variables

The main provider of historical data on monetary and financial variables is the Bank of Spain. Two monetary aggregates have been collected, namely the *Contribution of Domestic Monetary and Financial Institutions to M1/M3*. Both are monthly data ranging from September 1997 to November 2003. Both a retropolation to 1980 and an extrapolation to 2010 have therefore been produced for them to be included in REMSDB. Also, the quarterly frequency is taken as the simple arithmetical average calculated over each set of three quarters.

Two short-term interest rate series have been retained, namely *Spanish Non-transferable three-month deposits* and *US three-month interest rates*. Originally provided as monthly data, both series of interest rates have been converted into quarterly data by calculating the simple arithmetical average over each set of three quarters.

The quarterly nominal dollar/ecu-euro exchange rate builds on the corresponding monthly series released by the Bank of Spain. The high-frequency series has been obtained by calculating the simple arithmetical average for each three-month period. The forecast period relies on the SGP estimates.

Public sector variables

A further data requirement for the implementation of REMS concerns the series on government expenditures and tax receipts. To meet our needs, the *Account of Expenditures and Receipts of the Public Administration* has been elaborated following the classification used by the Intervención General de la Administración del Estado (State's Accounts Department (IGAE)). Though this accounting exercise is performed on an annual basis, a quarterly version has been produced by using a quadratic interpolation, which ensures additive consistency with annual data.[7] The series obtained in this manner are compatible with *Government Final Consumption,* one of the components of final demand. A final remark on this set of series concerns *Government Debt,* for which quarterly data are obtained by applying the *Kalman filter* directly to annual data covering the period 1980–9. Once the quarterly counterpart is available we use it to produce a complete series together with *Public Debt according to the Excessive Deficit Procedure* as released by the Bank of Spain.

All tax categories in the model, namely consumption tax, labour income tax, social security contributions tax and capital income tax, are taken from the corresponding average effective tax rates estimated by Boscá *et al.* (2005).

Notes

1. The tools for temporal disaggregation closely resemble the methodology described in Harvey (1989, ch. 6). In doing so, we proceed along the lines of Chow and Lin (1971) and Fernández (1981).
2. Net taxes are calculated by subtracting all subsidies to taxes of the same nature.
3. In practice, this implies that the derived labour force figures differ significantly from the information on the same series provided by the Labour Force Survey.
4. The release of quarterly data on hours worked by the SQN was subsequent to the completion of REMSDB.
5. The number of hours captured by surveys addressed to firms, such as the Labour Cost Index and the Wage Survey, is well below the number of hours that show up in surveys that collect data revealed by workers, for example, the LFS.
6. For further details on the construction of these two series see Díaz (2007).
7. The use of quarterly data provided by either IGAE or SQNA has been avoided because of non-meaningful time distribution from an economic perspective resulting from accountancy procedures. In general, criteria based on National Accounts rules are more relevant from a macroeconomic point of view. The related annual series have been adjusted accordingly to reflect these accounting criteria on a quarterly basis.

Appendix 3
Nash Bargaining with RoT Consumers

A.3.1 Maximisation problem

The Nash bargain process maximises the weighted product of the parties' surpluses from employment.

$$\max_{w_t, l_{1t}} \left(\frac{\partial V_t}{\partial n_t} \right)^{1-\lambda^w} \left(\frac{1-\lambda^r}{\lambda_{1t}^o} \frac{\partial W_t^o}{\partial n_t} + \frac{\lambda^r}{\lambda_{1t}^r} \frac{\partial W_t^r}{\partial n_t} \right)^{\lambda^w} = \max_{w_t, l_{1t}} \left(\lambda_{ft} \right)^{1-\lambda^w} \left(\lambda_{ht} \right)^{\lambda^w}$$

(A3.1)

where $\lambda_{ft} \equiv \frac{\partial V_t}{\partial n_t}$ and $\lambda_{ht} \equiv \frac{1-\lambda^r}{\lambda_{1t}^o} \frac{\partial W_t^o}{\partial n_t} + \frac{\lambda^r}{\lambda_{1t}^r} \frac{\partial W_t^r}{\partial n_t}$.

Deriving w.r.t. w_t

$$(1-\lambda^w) \left(\frac{\lambda_{ht}}{\lambda_{ft}} \right)^{\lambda^w} (-l_{1t})(1+\tau^{sc}) + \lambda^w \left(\frac{\lambda_{ht}}{\lambda_{ft}} \right)^{\lambda^w - 1}$$
$$\times \left(\lambda_{1t}^o \frac{1-\lambda^r}{\lambda_{1t}^o} \left(1 - \tau^l \right) l_{1t} + \lambda_{1t}^r \frac{\lambda^r}{\lambda_{1t}^r} \left(1 - \tau^l \right) l_{1t} \right) = 0$$

(A3.2)

or

$$(1-\lambda^w)\lambda_{ht} = \lambda^w \frac{\left(1 - \tau^l \right)}{(1+\tau^{sc})} \lambda_{ft}$$

(A3.3)

Therefore, optimisation of this joint surplus w.r.t. wages implies that

$$\lambda^w \frac{\partial V_t}{\partial n_t} = (1-\lambda^w) \left(\frac{1-\lambda^r}{\lambda_{1t}^o} \frac{\partial W_t^o}{\partial n_t} + \frac{\lambda^r}{\lambda_{1t}^r} \frac{\partial W_t^r}{\partial n_t} \right)$$

(A3.4)

A.3.2 Solution for hours

Deriving Equation (A3.1) w.r.t. l_{1t}

$$(1 - \lambda^w) \left(\frac{\lambda_{ht}}{\lambda_{ft}} \right)^{\lambda^w} \left(\alpha mc_t \frac{y_t}{n_t l_{it}} - w_t \left(1 + \tau^{sc} \right) \right)$$
$$+ \lambda^w \left(\frac{\lambda_{ht}}{\lambda_{ft}} \right)^{\lambda^w - 1} \left(w_t \left(1 - \tau^l \right) + \left[\frac{1 - \lambda^r}{\lambda_{1t}^o} + \frac{\lambda^r}{\lambda_{1t}^r} \right] U_{lt} \right) = 0 \qquad (A3.5)$$

where U_{lt} is the marginal (dis)utility of hours.

$$U_{lt} = -\phi_1 (1 - l_{1t})^{-\eta} \qquad (A3.6)$$

From Equation (A3.3)

$$(1 - \lambda^w) \frac{\lambda_{ht}}{\lambda_{ft}} = \lambda^w \frac{\left(1 - \tau^l \right)}{\left(1 + \tau^{sc} \right)} \qquad (A3.7)$$

Therefore, Equation (A3.5) can be written as

$$\frac{\left(1 - \tau^l \right)}{\left(1 + \tau^{sc} \right)} \alpha mc_t \frac{y_t}{n_t l_{1t}} = \phi_1 (T - l_{1t})^{-\eta} \left[\frac{1 - \lambda^r}{\lambda_{1t}^o} + \frac{\lambda^r}{\lambda_{1t}^r} \right] \qquad (A3.8)$$

A.3.3 Solution for wages

From the firm's side, we have the following FOC

$$\beta E_t \frac{\lambda_{1t+1}^o}{\lambda_{1t}^o} \frac{\partial V_{t+1}}{\partial n_{t+1}} = \frac{\kappa_v v_t}{\chi_1 v_t^{\chi_2} \left[(1 - n_t) l_{2t} \right]^{1 - \chi_2}} = \frac{\kappa_v}{\rho_t^f} \qquad (A3.9)$$

Therefore

$$(1 - \lambda^w) \left(1 + \tau^{sc} \right) E_t \frac{\beta}{\lambda_{1t}^o} \left((1 - \lambda^r) \frac{\partial W_{t+1}^o}{\partial n_{t+1}} + \lambda^r \frac{\lambda_{1t+1}^o}{\lambda_{1t+1}^r} \frac{\partial W_{t+1}^r}{\partial n_{t+1}} \right)$$
$$= \lambda^w \left(1 - \tau^l \right) E_t \beta \frac{\lambda_{1t+1}^o}{\lambda_{1t}^o} \frac{\partial V_{t+1}}{\partial n_{t+1}} = \lambda^w \left(1 - \tau^l \right) \frac{\kappa_v}{\rho_t^f} \qquad (A3.10)$$

From Equation (A3.3) and combining Equations (2.19), (2.25), (2.44) and (A3.4):

$$\frac{\lambda^w}{(1-\lambda^w)}\frac{\left(1-\tau^l\right)}{(1+\tau^{sc})}\left(\alpha mc_t\frac{y_t}{n_t} - w_t\left(1+\tau^{sc}\right)l_{1t} + (1-\sigma)\frac{\kappa_v}{\rho_t^f}\right)$$

$$= (1-\lambda^r)w_t\left(1-\tau^l\right)l_{1t}$$

$$- (1-\lambda^r)\left(1-\tau^l\right)ub_t + \frac{(1-\lambda^r)}{\lambda_{1t}^o}\left(\phi_1\frac{(1-l_{1t})^{1-\eta}}{1-\eta} - \phi_2\frac{(1-l_2)^{1-\eta}}{1-\eta}\right)$$

$$+ \lambda^r w_t\left(1-\tau^l\right)l_{1t} + \frac{\lambda^r}{\lambda_{1t}^r}\left(\phi_1\frac{(1-l_{1t})^{1-\eta}}{1-\eta} - \phi_2\frac{(1-l_2)^{1-\eta}}{1-\eta}\right)$$

$$+ (1-\sigma-\rho_t^w)\left(\frac{1-\lambda^r}{\lambda_{1t}^o}\beta E_t\frac{\partial W_{t+1}^o}{\partial n_{t+1}} + \frac{\lambda^r}{\lambda_{1t}^r}\beta E_t\frac{\partial W_{t+1}^r}{\partial n_{t+1}}\right) \quad \text{(A3.11)}$$

Collecting terms:

$$\frac{\lambda^w}{(1-\lambda^w)}\frac{\left(1-\tau^l\right)}{(1+\tau^{sc})}\left(\alpha mc_t\frac{y_t}{n_t} - w_t\left(1+\tau^{sc}\right)l_{1t} + (1-\sigma)\frac{\kappa_v}{\rho_t^f}\right)$$

$$= w_t\left(1-\tau^l\right)l_{1t} - \left(1-\tau^l\right)ub_t + \left(\frac{(1-\lambda^r)}{\lambda_{1t}^o} + \frac{\lambda^r}{\lambda_{1t}^r}\right)$$

$$\times \left(\phi_1\frac{(1-l_{1t})^{1-\eta}}{1-\eta} - \phi_2\frac{(1-l_2)^{1-\eta}}{1-\eta}\right)$$

$$+ (1-\sigma-\rho_t^w)\frac{\beta E_t}{\lambda_{1t}^o}\left((1-\lambda^r)\frac{\partial W_{t+1}^o}{\partial n_{t+1}} + \lambda^r\frac{\lambda_{1t+1}^o}{\lambda_{1t+1}^r}\frac{\partial W_{t+1}^r}{\partial n_{t+1}}\right.$$

$$\left. + \lambda^r\frac{\lambda_{1t}^o}{\lambda_{1t}^r}\frac{\partial W_{t+1}^r}{\partial n_{t+1}} - \lambda^r\frac{\lambda_{1t+1}^o}{\lambda_{1t+1}^r}\frac{\partial W_{t+1}^r}{\partial n_{t+1}}\right) \quad \text{(A3.12)}$$

or

$$w_t\left(1-\tau^l\right)l_{1t} = \lambda^w\left[\frac{\left(1-\tau^l\right)}{(1+\tau^{sc})}\alpha mc_t\frac{y_t}{n_t} + \frac{\left(1-\tau^l\right)}{(1+\tau^{sc})}\frac{\kappa_v v_t}{(1-n_t)}\right]$$

$$+ (1-\lambda^w)\left[\left(\frac{(1-\lambda^r)}{\lambda_{1t}^o} + \frac{\lambda^r}{\lambda_{1t}^r}\right)\left(\phi_2\frac{(1-l_{2t})^{1-\eta}}{1-\eta}\right.\right.$$

$$\left.\left. - \phi_1\frac{(1-l_{1t})^{1-\eta}}{1-\eta}\right) + \left(1-\tau^l\right)g_{ut}\right] + (1-\lambda^w)$$

$$\times (1-\sigma-\rho_t^w)\lambda^r\beta E_t\frac{\lambda_{3t+1}^r}{\lambda_{1t+1}^r}\left(\frac{\lambda_{1t+1}^o}{\lambda_{1t}^o} - \frac{\lambda_{1t+1}^r}{\lambda_{1t}^r}\right) \quad \text{(A3.13)}$$

Appendix 4
Net Foreign Asset Accumulation

From the government budget constraint:

$$\gamma_A \gamma_N b_{t+1} = g_t^c + g_t^i + g_{ut}(1 - n_t) + g_{st} - t_t + \frac{(1+r_t^n)}{1+\pi_t} b_t$$

and assuming $\gamma_A \gamma_N b_{t+1} - \frac{(1+r_t^n)}{1+\pi_t} b_t = 0$ we obtain

$$t_t = g_t^c + g_t^i + g_{ut}(1 - n_t) + g_{st} \tag{A4.1}$$

Recall the aggregate resource constraint:

$$c_{ht} + i_{ht} + g_t^c + g_t^i + \frac{p_t^x}{P_t} ex_t = y_t - \frac{p_t^e}{P_t}(1 - \alpha_e)e_t - \kappa_v v_t - \kappa_f \tag{A4.2}$$

Multiplying the optimising household budget constraint by $(1 - \lambda^r)$ and the RoT budget constraint by λ^r, we obtain after aggregation

$$\left(r_t(1 - \tau_t^k) + \tau_t^k \delta\right) k_t + w_t \left(1 - \tau_t^l\right) \left(n_t l_{1t} + \bar{\pi}(1 - n_t) l_{2t}\right)$$

$$+ \left(1 - \tau_t^l\right) g_{st} - trh_t + \frac{m_{t-1}}{1 + \pi_t^c} + (1 + r_t^n) \frac{b_t}{1 + \pi_t^c}$$

$$+ er_t^n(1 + r_t^{nw}) \frac{b_t^w}{1 + \pi_t^c} - (1 + \tau_t^c) c_t \frac{P_t^c}{P_t} - \frac{P_t^i}{P_t} j_t \left(1 + \frac{\phi}{2}\left(\frac{j_t}{k_t^o}\right)\right)$$

$$- \gamma_A \gamma_N \left(m_t + b_t + \frac{er_t^n b_{t+1}^w}{\phi_{bt}}\right) = 0$$

and rearrange terms to leave taxes on the left-hand side

$$r_t \tau_t^k k_t - \tau_t^k \delta k_t + w_t \tau_t^l n_t l_{1t} + \overline{\pi} w_t \tau_t^l (1 - n_t) l_{2t} - \left(1 - \tau_t^l\right) g_{st} + trh_t + \tau_t^c c_t \frac{P_t^c}{P_t}$$

$$= r_t k_t + w_t n_t l_{1t} + \overline{\pi} w_t (1 - n_t) l_{2t} - \frac{P_t^c}{P_t} c_t$$

$$- \frac{P_t^i}{P_t} j_t \left(1 + \frac{\phi}{2}\left(\frac{j_t}{k_t}\right)\right) + er_t^n (1 + r_t^{nw}) \frac{b_t^w}{1 + \pi_t^c} - \gamma_A \gamma_N \frac{er_t^n b_{t+1}^w}{\phi_{bt}} \qquad (A4.3)$$

where we have assumed that $\gamma_A \gamma_N b_{t+1} - \frac{(1+r_t^n)}{1+\pi_t} b_t = 0$ and $\frac{m_{t-1}}{1+\pi_t^c} - \gamma_A \gamma_N m_t = 0$
From the definition of government tax revenues,

$$t_t = (\tau_t^l + \tau_t^{sc}) w_t (n_t l_{1t}) + \tau_t^k (r_t - \delta) k_t$$

$$+ \tau_t^c \frac{P_t^c}{P_t} c_t + \tau_t^e \frac{P_t^e}{P_t} e_t + trh_t + \tau_t^l \overline{\pi} w_t (1 - n_t) l_{2t} + \tau_t^l g_{st}$$

and using Equation (A4.1) it follows that

$$g_t^c + g_t^i + \overline{\pi} w_t (1 - n_t) l_{2t} + g_{st}$$

$$= (\tau_t^l + \tau_t^{sc}) w_t (n_t l_{1t}) + \tau_t^k (r_t - \delta) k_t$$

$$+ \tau_t^c \frac{P_t^c}{P_t} c_t + \tau_t^e \frac{P_t^e}{P_t} e_t + trh_t + \tau_t^l \overline{\pi} w_t (1 - n_t) l_{2t} + \tau_t^l g_{st}$$

Rearranging terms, the left-hand side of Equation (A4.3) turns out to be:

$$r_t \tau_t^k k_t - \tau_t^k \delta k_t + w_t \tau_t^l n_t l_{1t} + \overline{\pi} w_t \tau_t^l (1 - n_t) l_{2t} - \left(1 - \tau_t^l\right) g_{st} + trh_t + \tau_t^c c_t \frac{P_t^c}{P_t}$$

$$= g_t^c + g_t^i + \overline{\pi} w_t (1 - n_t) - \tau_t^e \frac{P_t^e}{P_t} e_t - \tau_t^{sc} w_t n_t l_{1t}$$

Introducing this result into Equation (A4.3) we obtain

$$g_t^c + g_t^i + \overline{\pi} w_t (1 - n_t) l_{2t} - \tau_t^e \frac{P_t^e}{P_t} e_t - \tau_t^{sc} w_t n_t l_{1t}$$

$$= r_t k_t + w_t n_t l_{1t} + \overline{\pi} w_t (1 - n_t) l_{2t} - \frac{P_t^c}{P_t} c_t$$

$$- \frac{P_t^i}{P_t} i_t + er_t^n (1 + r_t^{nw}) \frac{b_t^{ow}}{1 + \pi_t^c} - \gamma_A \gamma_N \frac{er_t^n b_{t+1}^{ow}}{\phi_{bt}}$$

Rearranging terms:

$$\frac{P_t^c}{P_t} c_t + \frac{P_t^i}{P_t} i_t + g_t^c + g_t^i - \tau_t^e \frac{P_t^e}{P_t} e_t - \tau_t^{sc} w_t n_t l_{1t} - r_t k_t - w_t n_t l_{1t}$$

$$= er_t^n (1 + r_t^{nw}) \frac{b_t^{ow}}{1 + \pi_t^c} - \gamma_A \gamma_N \frac{er_t^n b_{t+1}^{ow}}{\phi_{bt}}$$

Now, using Equation (A4.2) and taking into account that $P_t^c c_t = P_t c_{ht} + P_t^m c_{ft}$, $P_t^i i_t = P_t i_{ht} + P_t^m i_{ft}$ and $P_t^m im_t = P_t^m c_{ft} + P_t^m i_{ft} + P_t^e \alpha_e e_t$:

$$y_t - (1 + \tau_t^e)\frac{P_t^e}{P_t}e_t - \kappa_v v_t - \kappa_f - \tau_t^{sc} w_t n_t l_{1t} - r_t k_t - w_t n_t l_{1t} + \frac{P_t^m}{P_t}im_t - \frac{P_t^x}{P_t}ex_t$$

$$= er_t^n(1 + r_t^{nw})\frac{b_t^{ow}}{1 + \pi_t^c} - \gamma_A \gamma_N \frac{er_t^n b_{t+1}^{ow}}{\phi_{bt}}$$

Notice that GDP measured at factor costs is given by:

$$gdp_t = y_t - (1 + \tau_t^e)\frac{P_t^e}{P_t}e_t - \kappa_v v_t - \kappa_f - \tau_t^{sc} w_t n_t l_{1t}$$

or, alternatively:

$$gdp_t = r_t k_{t-1} + w_t n_t l_{1t}$$

Therefore:

$$\gamma_A \gamma_N \frac{er_t^n b_{t+1}^{ow}}{\phi_{bt}} - er_t^n(1 + r_t^{nw})\frac{b_t^{ow}}{1 + \pi_t^c} = \frac{P_t^x}{P_t}ex_t - \frac{P_t^m}{P_t}im_t$$

Appendix 5
Using Behavioural Equations to Produce Non-observable Data

Several variables included in the model have no direct statistical counterparts from official sources. Such variables include consumption by and employment of both RoT and optimising consumers, Lagrange multipliers, Tobin's q, the composite capital stock, the marginal cost and a measure of total factor productivity. To sidestep the lack of data availability affecting these variables, one may use the model's related behavioural equations. For Example, consumption by RoT consumers is obtained from the first-order condition represented by the budget restriction:

$$c_t^r = \frac{1}{(1+\tau_t^c)} \frac{P_t}{P_t^c} \left[w_t \left(1 - \tau_t^l \right) \left(n_t^r l_{1t} + rr_t \left(1 - n_t^r \right) l_{2t} \right) + g_{st} \right]$$

while consumption of optimising households is obtained from consumption of RoT consumers and aggregate consumption according to:

$$c_t^o = \frac{c_t - \lambda^r c_t^r}{(1 - \lambda^r)}$$

With regard to the employment rates of the different household types, under the assumption of identical ρ_t^W and σ, it follows that $n_t = n_t^o = n_t^r$. To see this more clearly, one may write the law of motion for employment in terms of the number of employees E_t^o and E_t^r:

$$E_1^o = (1 - \sigma)E_0^o + \rho_t^W(N_0^o - E_0^o)$$

$$E_1^r = (1 - \sigma)E_0^r + \rho_t^W(N_0^r - E_0^r)$$

Let the initial condition satisfy $\frac{N_0^o}{N_0} = 1 - \lambda^r$ and $\frac{E_0^o}{E_0} = 1 - \lambda^r$. Then it is convenient to write E_1^o in terms of E_1^r as:

$$E_1^o = \frac{1 - \lambda^r}{\lambda^r} \left[(1 - \sigma)E_0^r + \rho_t^W(N_0^r - E_0^r) \right] = \frac{1 - \lambda^r}{\lambda^r} E_1^r$$

that in per capita terms turns out to be:

$$\frac{N_0^o}{N_0} \frac{E_1^o}{N_0^o} = \frac{1 - \lambda^r}{\lambda^r} \frac{E_1^r}{N_0^r} \frac{N_0^r}{N_0}$$

or

$$(1 - \lambda^r) n_1^o = \frac{1 - \lambda^r}{\lambda^r} n_1^r \lambda^r \rightarrow n_t^o = n_t^r = n_t$$

The marginal utility of consumption for both Ricardian and RoT consumers is obtained from the following conditions,

$$\lambda_{1t}^o = \lambda_{1t}^o = \frac{1}{(P_t^c/P_t)(1 + \tau_t^c)} \left(\frac{1}{c_t^o - h^o c_{t-1}^o} - \beta \frac{h^o}{c_{t+1}^o - h^o c_t^o} \right)$$

$$\lambda_{1t}^r = \lambda_{1t}^o = \frac{1}{(P_t^c/P_t)(1 + \tau_t^c)} \left(\frac{1}{c_t^r - h^r c_{t-1}^r} - \beta \frac{h^r}{c_{t+1}^r - h^r c_t^r} \right)$$

The shadow price of an additional worker for the firm, λ_t^{nd}, can be computed using the free-entry condition affecting the creation of vacancies:

$$\lambda_{ft} = \frac{\kappa_v v_t}{mat_t} \tag{A5.1}$$

With κ_v being the flow cost of an open vacancy, v the number of vacancies and *mat* the number of new matches. The flow cost of an open vacancy has been estimated assuming that, on average, the overall cost of posted vacancies in the economy, $\kappa_v v$, represents 0.5 per cent of GDP (see Andolfatto, 1996).

To obtain the shadow price of a new job match one may use the expression:

$$\frac{1 - \lambda^r}{\lambda_{1t}^o} \lambda_{ht}^o + \frac{\lambda^r}{\lambda_{1t}^r} \lambda_{ht}^r = \frac{\lambda^w}{(1 - \lambda^w)} \frac{(1 - \tau^l)}{(1 + \tau^{sc})} \lambda_{ft} \tag{A5.2}$$

This expression, which concerns the derivation of the equilibrium wage, equates to the marginal utility of a new match for firms and workers. To pin down λ_{ht}^o and λ_{ht}^r, we impose the restriction that Equation (A5.2) has to be satisfied. Thus we use the following estimators:

$$\lambda_{ht}^r = \frac{\lambda^w}{(1 - \lambda^w)} \frac{(1 - \tau^l)}{(1 + \tau^{sc})} \lambda_{ft} \lambda_{1t}^r \tag{A5.3}$$

$$\lambda_{ht}^o = \frac{\lambda^w}{(1 - \lambda^w)} \frac{(1 - \tau^l)}{(1 + \tau^{sc})} \lambda_{ft} \lambda_{1t}^o \tag{A5.4}$$

Time series for Tobin's q have been constructed from the following expression:

$$q_t = \left(1 + \phi \left(\frac{j_t}{k_t} \right) \right) \tag{A5.5}$$

This behavioural equation, which is derived from the household maximisation problem, states that the amount of investment net of adjustment costs, j_t, is undertaken to the extent that the opportunity cost of a marginal increase in investment in terms of consumption, $1 + \phi\left(\frac{j_t}{k_t}\right)$, is equal to its marginal expected contribution to household utility. The adjustment costs parameter, ϕ, has been set at 5.5, which is the value estimated for Spain in the QUEST II model.

Capital stock is modelled as a composite of physical capital and energy, according to the following CES technology:

$$ke_t = \left[ak_t^{-\rho} + (1-a)e_t^{-\rho}\right]^{-\frac{1}{\rho}} \tag{A5.6}$$

As is standard in the empirical literature, we rely on a Cobb–Douglas production function to residually compute an indicator for total factor productivity, A_t. The production function in levels is given by:

$$Y_{it} = \left\{\left[aK_{it}^{-\rho} + (1-a)E_{it}n_{it}^{-\rho}\right]^{-\frac{1}{\rho}}\right\}^{1-\alpha} (A_t E_{it} l_{i1t})^\alpha \left(k_{it}^p\right)^\zeta \tag{A5.7}$$

where E represents the employed population and k_{it}^p appears in efficiency units. The same expression in per capita terms can be written as:

$$\tilde{y}_{it} = \left\{\left[a\tilde{k}_{it}^{-\rho} + (1-a)\tilde{e}_{it}^{-\rho}\right]^{-\frac{1}{\rho}}\right\}^{1-\alpha} (A_t n_{it} l_{i1t})^\alpha \left(\frac{K_{it}^p}{A_t N_t}\right)^\zeta \tag{A5.8}$$

and clearing for A_t :

$$A_t = \left(\frac{\tilde{y}_{it}}{\tilde{k}_{et}^{1-\alpha}(n_{it}l_{i1t})^\alpha \tilde{k}_t^{p\zeta}}\right)^{\frac{1}{\alpha-\zeta}}$$

where $n_t l_t$ represents overall hours worked and y_t reflects (per capita) gross output, which includes gross value added, imported energy and the (time-varying) fixed costs weighing on non-competitive firms. Furthermore, in the calibration exercise we break A_t down into a permanent and a transitory component (z):

$$\ln A_t = \overline{\ln A_t} + z_t \tag{A5.9}$$

where the permanent component is used to obtain variables in efficiency units.

Finally, we ascertain the value of the marginal cost series by using the expression for the marginal value for the firm of an additional employment; that is,

$$\lambda_{ft} = \alpha mc_t \frac{y_t}{n_t} - w_t(1+\tau_t^{sc})l_{1t} + (1-\sigma)\frac{1+\pi_{t+1}}{1+r_{t+1}^n}\lambda_{ft+1} \tag{A5.10}$$

whereby optimality requires the marginal contribution of a newly created job to the firm's profit being equal to the marginal product of labour net of the wage rate plus the capital value of the new job in $t+1$, corrected by the job destruction rate between t and $t+1$. Leaving the marginal cost series aside, any variable in the expression above is taken to the data in our calibration procedure, meaning that the former can be expressed as a function of the latter. More precisely, π, r^n, y, w, τ^{sc}, l and σ match respectively the actual values of the inflation rate, nominal interest rate and gross output as defined above, the hourly real wage, the payroll tax rate, the number of working hours per employee and the exogenous rate of job destruction.

Appendix 6
Tax Reforms and Economic Performance: Transitional Dynamics

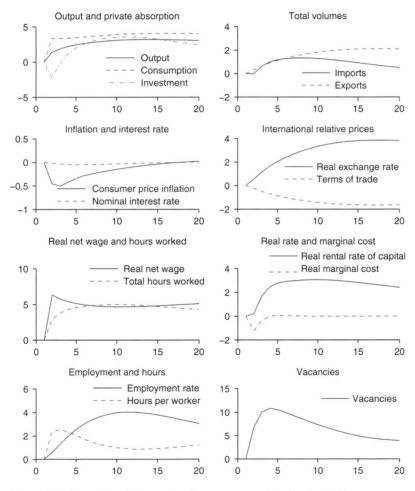

Figure A6.1 Transitional dynamics after a permanent reduction in the consumption tax rate

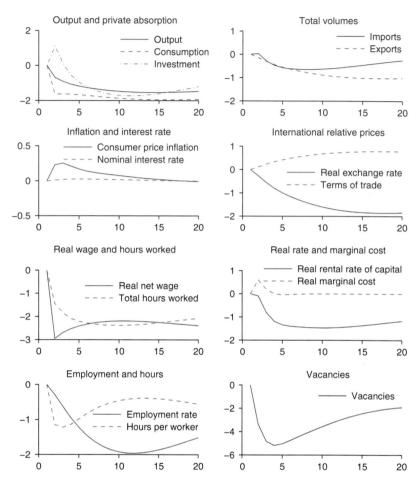

Figure A6.2   Transitional dynamics after a permanent increase in labour tax rate

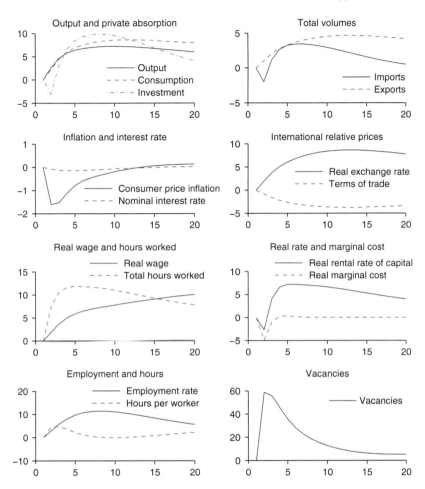

Figure A6.3 Transitional dynamics after a permanent reduction in social security contributions

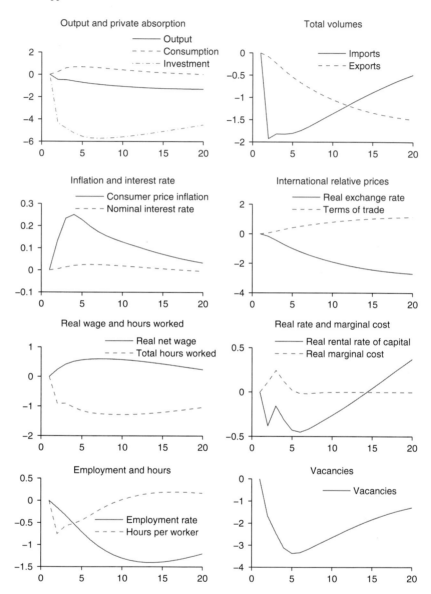

Figure A6.4   Transitional dynamics after a permanent increase in capital tax rate

References

Aaron, H. (1990) Discussion of 'Why Is Infrastructure Important?' in A. Munnell (ed.), *Is There a Shortfall in Public Capital Investment?*. Conference Series No. 34, Federal Reserve Bank of Boston, June, pp. 51–63.

Abbas, S. M. A., J. Bouhga-Hagbe, A. Fatás, P. Mauro and R. C. Velloso (2010) 'Fiscal Policy and the Current Account'. Working Paper 10/121. IMF.

Adolfson, M., S. Laséen, J. Lindé and M. Villani (2007) 'Evaluating an Estimated New Keynesian Small Open Economy Model', Working Paper Series 203, Sveriges Riksbank.

Aguirregabiria, V. and C. Alonso-Borrego (2009) 'Labor Contracts and Flexibility: Evidence from a Labor Market Reform in Spain', Universidad Carlos III de Madrid, Working Papers 09-18, Economic Series (11).

Albala-Bertrand, J. M. and E. C. Mamatzakis (2001) 'Is Public Infrastructure Productive? Evidence from Chile', *Applied Economics Letters*, 8, pp. 195–8.

Alesina, A. and F. Giavazzi (2006) *The Future of Europe: Reform or Decline*, Cambridge, MA: MIT Press.

Álvarez, A., L. Orea and J. Fernández (2003) 'La Productividad de las Infraestructuras en España', *Papeles de Economía Española*, 95, pp. 125–36.

Álvarez, L., E. Dhyne, M. Hoeberichts, C. Kwapil, H. Le Bihan, P. Lünnemann, F. Martins, R. Sabbatini, H. Stahl, P. Vermeulen and J. Vilmunen (2006) 'Sticky Prices in the Euro Area: A Summary of New Microevidence', *Journal of the European Economic Association*, 4(2–3), 575–84.

Andolfatto, D. (1996) 'Business Cycles and Labor-Market Search', *American Economic Review*, 86 (1).

Andrés, J. (1993) 'La Persistencia del Desempleo Agregado: una Panorámica', *Moneda y Crédito*, 197, 91–127.

Andrés, J. and R. Doménech (2006) 'Automatic Stabilizers, Fiscal Rules and Macroeconomic Stability', *European Economic Review*, 50(6), 1487–1506.

Andrés, J., P. Burriel and A. Estrada (2006) 'BEMOD: A DSGE Model for the Spanish Economy and the Rest of the Euro Area', Banco de España Research Paper, No. WP-0631.

Andrés, J., R. Doménech and A. Fatás (2008) 'The Stabilizing Role of Government Size . *Journal of Economic Dynamics and Control*, 32, 571–93.

Andrés, J., J. E. Boscá, R. Doménech and J. Ferri (2010a) 'Creación de Empleo en España: ¿Cambio en el Modelo Productivo, Reforma del Mercado de Trabajo, o Ambos?',*Papeles de Economía Española*, 124.

Andrés, J., S. Hurtado, E. Ortega and C. Thomas (2010b) 'Spain in the Euro: A General Equilibrium Analysis', *SERIEs, Journal of the Spanish Economic Association*, 1(1–2), 67–95.

Antolín, P. (1995) 'Job Search Behaviour and Unemployment Benefits in Spain during the Period 1987–1991', *Investigaciones Económicas*, 19(3), 415–33.

Argimon, I., J. M. González-Páramo and J. M. Roldán (1994) 'Productividad e Infraestructuras en la Economía Española', *Moneda y Crédito*, 198, 198–246.

212   *References*

Arnold, J., A. Bassanini and S. Scarpetta (2007) 'Testing Growth Models Using Panel Data from OECD Countries', Documento de Trabajo ECO/WKP(2007)52, OECD.

Arpaia, A. and G. Mourre (2005) 'Labour Market Institutions and Labour Market Performance: A Survey of the Literature', ECFIN/E/3/REP/55806-EN. Directorate-General for Economic and Financial Affairs, European Commission.

Aschauer, D. (1989) 'Is Public Expenditure Productive?', *Journal of Monetary Economics*, 23, 177–200.

Bajo, O. and S. Sosvilla (1993) 'Does Public Capital Affect Private Sector Performance? An Analysis of the Spanish Case 1964–88', *Economic Modelling*, 10, 179–85.

Bajo, O. and A.G. Gómez-Plana (2005) Simulating the Effects of the European Single Market: A CGE Analysis for Spain. *Journal of Policy Modeling*, 27(6), 689–709.

Ball, L. and N. G. Mankiw (2002) 'The NAIRU in Theory and Practice', *Journal of Economic Perspectives*, 16(4), 115–36.

Baltagi, B. and N. Pinnoi (1995) 'Public Capital Stock and State Productivity Growth: Further Evidence from an Error Components Model', *Empirical Economics*, 20, 351–9.

Barrios, S., S. Deroose, S. Langedijk and L. Pench (2010) 'External Imbalances and Public Finances in the EU', *European Economy Occasional Papers*, 66, Directorate-General for Economic and Financial Affairs.

Barro, R. J., N. G. Mankiw and X. Sala-i-Martin (1995) 'Capital Mobility in Neoclassical Models of Growth', *American Economic Review*, 85, 103–15.

Baxter, M. (1995) 'International Trade and Business Cycles', in G. M. Grossman and K. Rogoff (eds), *Handbook of International Economics*, Vol. 3, Amsterdam: North-Holland.

BBVA (2009a) 'Three Structural Reforms for the Spanish Labour Markets,' *Spain Watch*, March, 26–41.

BBVA (2009b) 'Ten Years of Inflation Differential between Spain and EMU,' *Spain Watch*, March, 18–23.

BBVA (2009c) 'Spain's Potential Growth: The Effects of the Crisis,' *Spain Watch*, November, 22–23.

BBVA (2009d) 'Structural Changes in Spanish Public Accounts,' *Spain Watch*, November, 26–33.

Bean, C., R. Layard and S. Nickell (1986) 'The Rise in Unemployment: A Multi-country Study', *Economica*, 53, S1–S22.

Benigno, P. (2001) 'Price Stability with Imperfect Financial Integration', CEPR Discussion Paper No. 2854.

Bentolila, S. and J. F. Jimeno (2006) 'Spanish Unemployment: The End of the Wild Ride?', in M. Werding (ed.), *Structural Unemployment in Western Europe, Reasons and Remedies*, Cambridge, MA: MIT Press.

Bils, M. and P. Klenow (2004). 'Some Evidence on the Importance of Sticky Prices', *Journal of Political Economy*, 112(5), 947–85.

Blanchard, O. (1997) 'The Medium Run', *Brookings Papers on Economic Activity*, 2, 89–157.

Blanchard, O. (2004) 'The Economic Future of Europe', *Journal of Economic Perspectives*, 18, 3–26.

Blanchard, O. (2006) 'European Unemployment', *Economic Policy*, 45, 5–59.

Blanchard, O. (2009) 'The State of Macro', *Annual Review of Economics*, 1, 209–28.

Blanchard, O. and J. Galí (2006) 'A New Keynesian Model with Unemployment', MIT Department of Economics, Working Paper No. 06-22.

Blanchard, O. and F. Giavazzi (2003) 'Macroeconomic Effects of Regulation and Deregulation', *Quarterly Journal of Economics*, 118, 879–07.

Blanchard, O. and C. M. Kahn (1980) 'The Solution of Linear Difference Models under Rational Expectations', *Econometrica*, 48, 1305–11.

Blanchard, O. and J. Wolfers (2000) 'The Role of Shocks and Institutions in the Rise of European Unemployment: The Aggregate Evidence', *Economic Journal*, 110-(462), 1–33.

Bom, P. and J. Ligthart (2008) 'How Productive is Public Capital? A Meta-Analysis', CESifo Working Paper No. 2206.

Boscá, J. E., A. Bustos, A. Díaz, R. Doménech, J. Ferri, E. Pérez and L. Puch (2007) 'The REMSDB Macroeconomic Database of the Spanish Economy', Working Paper WP-2007-03, Ministerio de Economía y Hacienda.

Boscá, J. E., A. Díaz, R. Doménech, J. Ferri, E. Pérez and L. Puch (2010) 'A Rational Expectations Model for Simulation and Policy Evaluation of the Spanish Economy', *SERIEs, Journal of the Spanish Economic Association*, 1–2, 135–69.

Boscá, J. E., R. Doménech and J. Ferri (2009a) 'Tax Reforms and Labour-Market Performance: An Evaluation for Spain using REMS', *Moneda y Crédito*, 228, 145–88.

Boscá, J. E., R. Doménech, and J. Ferri (2009b) 'Search, Nash Bargaining and Rule of Thumb Consumers', Working Paper No. 0901, IEI, University of Valencia.

Boscá, J. E., J. Escribá and M. J. Murgui (2002) 'The Effects of Public Infrastructures on the Private Productive Sector of Spanish Regions', *Journal of Regional Science*, 42(2), 301–26.

Boscá, J. E., J. R. García and D. Taguas (2005) 'Tipos Efectivos de Gravamen y Convergencia Fiscal en la OCDE: 1965-2001', *Hacienda Pública Española*, 174(3), 119–41.

Boucekkine, R. (1995) 'An Alternative Methodology for Solving Non-Linear Forward-Looking Models', *Journal of Economic Dynamics and Control*, 19(4), 711–34.

Breuss, F. and H. Badinger (2005) *The European Single Market for Services in the Context of the Lisbon Agenda: Macroeconomic Effects*, Final Report, December, Study commissioned by the Federal Ministry of Economics and Labour of the Republic of Austria.

Buigues, P., F. Ilzkovitz and J.F. Lebrun (1990) 'The Impact of the Internal Market by Industrial Sector: The Challenge for Member States', *European Economy*, Special Issue.

Burnside, C., M. Eichenbaum and S. Rebelo (1993) 'Labor Hoarding and the Business Cycle', *Journal of Political Economy*, 101(2), 245–73.

Burriel, P., J. Fernández-Villaverde and J. F. Rubio-Ramírez (2010) 'MEDEA: A DSGE Model for the Spanish Economy', *SERIEs, Journal of the Spanish Economic Association*, 1(1–2), 175–243.

Cadiou, L., S. Dées, S. Guichard, A. Kadareja, J. P. Laffargue and B. Rzepkowski (2001) 'Marmotte. A Multinational Model by CEPII/CEPREMAP'. CEPII Working Paper No. 2001-15.

Calvo, G. (1983) 'Staggered Prices in a Utility Maximizing Framework', *Journal of Monetary Economics*, 12, 383–98.

Campa, J. M., and Á. Gavilán (2006) 'Current Accounts in the Euro Area: An Intertemporal Approach', Working Paper No. 0638, Bank of Spain.

Carlstrom, C. T. and T. S. Fuerst (2001). 'Timing and Real Indeterminacy in Monetary Models'. *Journal of Monetary Economics*, 47, 285–98.

Caselli, F. (2005) 'Accounting for Cross-Country Income Differences', in P. Aghion and S. Durlauf (eds), *Handbook of Economic Growth*, Vol. 1, ch. 9, 679–741.

Cassou, S. P. and K. J. Lansing (1998). 'Optimal Fiscal Policy, Public Capital, and the Productivity Slowdown', *Journal of Economic Dynamics and Control*, 22, 911–35.

Causa, O. (2008) 'Explaining Differences in Hours Worked Among OECD Countries: An Empirical Analysis', OECD Economics Department Working Paper No. 596.

Cavallo, M. (2005) 'Understanding the Twin Deficits: New Approaches, New Results', FRBSF *Economic Letter*, No. 2005-16.

Cavallo, M. (2007) 'Government Consumption Expenditures and the Current Account', *Public Finance and Management*, 7 (January), 1.

Chari, V. V., P. J. Kehoe, and E. R. McGrattan (2009) 'New Keynesian Models: Not Yet Useful for Policy Analysis', *American Economic Journal: Macroeconomics*, 1(1), 242–66.

Chow, G. C. and A. Lin (1971) 'Best Linear Unbiased Interpolation, Distribution, and Extrapolation of Time Series by Related Series', *The Review of Economics and Statistics*, 53, 372–75.

Christiano, L., M. Eichenbaum and S. Rebelo (2009) 'When Is the Government Spending Multiplier Large?', NBER Working Paper No. 15394.

Christoffel, K., G. Coenen, A. Warne (2008) 'The New Area-Wide Model of the Euro Area: A Micro-founded Open-Economy Model for Forecasting and Policy Analysis', ECB Working Paper No. 944.

Coenen, G., P. McAdam, and R. Straub (2008) 'Tax Reform and Labour-Market Performance in the Euro Area: A Simulation-based Analysis Using the New Area-Wide Model', *Journal of Economic Dynamics & Control*, 32 (2008), 2543–83.

Cogan, J. F., T. Cwik, J. B. Taylor and V. Wieland (2009) 'New Keynesian versus Old Keynesian Government Spending Multipliers', *Journal of Economic Dynamics and Control*, 34, 281–95.

Cohen, D. and M. Soto (2007) 'Growth and Human Capital: Good Data, Good Results', *Journal of Economic Growth*, 12(1), 51–76.

Conde-Ruiz, J. I., J. R. García and M. Navarro (2008) 'Inmigración y Crecimiento Regional en España', Documento de Trabajo 2008–08, FEDEA.

Conesa, J. C. and T. J. Kehoe (2005) 'Productivity, Taxes and Hours Worked in Spain, 1970–2003', Manuscript, University of Minnesota.

Conway, P., D. De Rosa, G. Nicoletti and F. Steiner (2006) 'Regulation, Competition, and Productivity Convergence', OECD Economics Department Working Paper No. 509.

Copenhagen Economics (2005) *Economic Assessment of the Barriers to the Internal Market in Services: Final Report*, Copenhagen.

Corsetti, G. and G. Müller (2007) 'Twin Deficits, Openness and the Business Cycle', Working Paper 2007/20, EUI.

Corsetti, G. and G. J. Müller (2009) 'Twin Deficits: Squaring, Theory, Evidence and Common Sense', *Economic Policy*, 597–638.

Corsetti, G., A. Meier and G. J. Müller (2006) 'Fiscal Stimulus with Spending Reversals', CEPR DP No. 7302.

Corsetti, G., A. Meier and G. J. Müller (2010) 'When, Where and How does Fiscal Stimulus Work?', Mimeo.

Costain, J., J. F. Jimeno and C. Thomas (2010) 'Employment Fluctuations in a Dual Labour Market', Working Paper No. 1013, Bank of Spain.

Courtney, H. G. (1985) *The Beveridge Curve and Okun's Law: A Re-Examination of Fundamental Macroeconomic Relationships in the United States*, ch. 4. B.A. Economics, Northwestern University.

Cwik, T. and V. Wieland (2009) 'Keynesian Government Spending Multiplier and Spillovers in the Euro Area', CEPR Discussion Paper No. 7389.

Dabán, T. and A. Lamo (1999) 'Convergence and Public Investment Allocation', Documento de Trabajo D-99001, Dir. Gral. de Análisis y Programación Presupuestaria, Madrid: Ministerio de Economía y Hacienda.

Dabán, T., F.J. Escribá, M.J. Murgui and A. Díaz (2002) 'La Base de Datos BD.MORES', *Revista de Economía Aplicada*, 10(30), 165–86.

Davig, T. and E. M. Leeper (2009) 'Monetary–Fiscal Policy Interactions and Fiscal Stimulus', NBER Working Paper No. 15133.

Davis, S. J. and M. Henrekson (2004) 'Tax Effects on Work Activity, Industry Mix and Shadow Economy Size: Evidence from Rich-Country Comparisons', NBER Working Paper No. 10509.

de Bruijn, R., H. Kox and A. Lejour (2006) 'The Trade-Induced Effects of the Services Directive and the Country-of-Origin Principle', ENEPRI Working Paper No. 44.

de la Dehesa (2009) *La Primera Gran Crisis Financiera del Siglo XXI*, Madrid: Alianza Editorial.

de la Fuente, A. (2002a) 'The Effect of Structural Fund Spending on the Spanish Regions: An Assessment of the 1994–99 Objective 1 CSF', CEPR Discussion Paper No. 3673.

de la Fuente, A. (2002b) 'On the Sources of Convergence: A Close Look at the Spanish Regions', *European Economic Review*, 46 (3), 569–99.

de la Fuente, A. (2009) 'Infrastructures and Productivity: An Updated Survey', Mimeo, Instituto de Análisis Económico, Barcelona: CSIC.

de la Fuente, A. and R. Doménech (2006a) 'Human Capital in Growth Regressions: How Much Difference Does Data Quality Make?', *Journal of the European Economic Association*, 4(1), 1–36.

de la Fuente, A. and R. Doménech (2006b) 'Capital Humano, Crecimiento y Desigualdad en las Regiones Españolas', *Moneda y Crédito*. 222, 13–56.

de la Fuente, A. and R. Doménech (2008) 'Human Capital, Growth and Inequality in the Spanish Regions', in U. Stierle, M. Stierle, F. Jennings and A. Kuah (eds), *Regional Economic Policy in Europe*, Cheltenham, UK: Edward Elgar.

de la Fuente, A. and R. Doménech (2010) 'Ageing and Real Convergence: Challenges and Proposals', in J. F. Jimeno (ed.), *Spain and the Euro. The First Ten Years*, Madrid: Bank of Spain.

Dew-Becker, I. and R. J. Gordon (2008) 'The Role of Labour Market Changes in the Slowdown of European Productivity Growth'. NBER Working Paper No. 13840.

Díaz, A. (2007) 'Obtención de las Variables del Mercado de Trabajo en la Ecuación de Matching del Modelo REMS', Mimeo, Ministerio de Economía y Hacienda.

Dolado, J. J., F. Felgueroso and J. F. Jimeno (2001) 'Female Employment and Occupational Changes in the 1990s: How Is the EU Performing Relative to the US?', *European Economic Review*, 45, 875–89.

Dolado, J. J., M. Sebastián and J. Vallés (1993) 'Cyclical Patterns of the Spanish Economy', *Investigaciones Económicas*, XVII(3), 445–72.

Doménech, R. and J. R. García (2008) 'Unemployment, Taxation and Public Expenditure in OECD Economies', *European Journal of Political Economy*, 24, 202–17.

Doménech, R. and J. R. García (2010) '¿Cómo Conseguir que Crezcan la Productividad y el Empleo, y Disminuya el Desequilibrio Exterior?', in J. Herce (ed.), *Claves de la Economía Mundial*.

Doménech, R. and V. Gómez (2005) 'Ciclo Económico y Desempleo Estructural en la Economía Española', *Investigaciones Económicas*, XXIX(2), 259–88.

Doménech, R. and V. Gómez (2006) 'Estimating Potential Output, Core Inflation and the NAIRU as Latent Variables', *Journal of Business and Economic Statistics*, 24(3), 354–65.

Doménech, R. and E. Pérez (2006) 'Fiscal Structure and Equilibrium Unemployment', Mimeo, Universidad de Valencia.

Doménech, R., A. Estrada and L. González-Calbet (2008) 'El Potencial de Crecimiento de la Economía Española', in J. Velarde and J. M. Serrano (eds), La España del Siglo, XXI.

Doménech, R., M. Ledo and D. Taguas (2002) 'Some New Results on Interest Rate Rules in EMU and in the US'. *Journal of Economics and Business*, 54(4), 431–46.

Economic Bureau of the Prime Minister (2006) *Inmigration and the Spanish Economy*, Madrid.

Eichengreen, B. (1992) *Should the Maastricht Treaty Be Saved?*, Princeton Studies in International Finance, No. 74, Princeton University.

Eichhorst, W., M. Feil, and C. Braun (2008) 'What Have We Learned? Assessing Labor Market Institutions and Indicators', IZA DP, No. 3470, IZA.

Elmeskov,J., J. P. Martin and S. Scarpetta (1998) 'Key Lessons for Labour Market Reforms: Evidence from OECD Countries' Experiences', *Swedish Economic Policy Review*, 5-(2), Autumn.

Enflo, K. S. (2009) 'Productivity and Employment – Is There a Trade-Off? Comparing Western European Regions and American States 1950–2000', *Annals of Regional Science*, DOI 10.1007/s00168-009-0315-6.

Erceg, C. J., L. Guerrieri and C. Gust (2005) 'Expansionary Fiscal Shocks and the US Trade Deficit', *International Finance*, 8(3), 363–97.

Erceg, C. J., L. Guerrieri and C. Gust (2006) 'SIGMA: A New Open Economy Model for Policy Analysis', *International Journal of Central Banking*, 2(1), 1–50.

Estrada, A. and D. López-Salido (2004a) 'Understanding Spanish Dual Inflation', *Investigaciones Económicas*, 28-(1), 123–40.

Estrada, A. and D. López-Salido (2004b) 'Sectoral and Aggregate Technology Growth in Spain', *Spanish Economic Review*, 6(1), 3–27.

Estrada, A., J. F. Jimeno and J. L. Malo de Molina (2010) 'The Performance of the Spanish Economy in EMU: The First Ten Years', in J. F. Jimeno (ed.), *Spain and the Euro: The Ten First Years*, Bank of Spain, pp. 83–138.

European Commission (2004) 'Do Labour Taxes (and Their Composition) Affect Wages in the Short and the Long Run?' European Economy, Economic Papers No. 216, European Commission, October.

Evans, P. and G. Karras (1994b) 'Are Government Activities Productive? Evidence from a Panel of US States', *Review of Economics and Statistics*, LXXVI-(1), 1–11.

Everaert, G. and F. Heylen (2001) 'Public Capital and Productivity Growth: Evidence for Country-Region Belgium, 1953–1996', *Economic Modelling*, 18, 97–116.

Faggio, G. and S. Nickell (2007) 'Patterns of Work Across the OECD', *The Economic Journal*, 117 (June), 416–40.

Fang, L. and R. Rogerson (2009) 'Policy Analysis in a Matching Model with Intensive and Extensive Margins', *International Economic Review*, 50, 1153–68.

FEDEA (2009) 'A Proposal to Restart the Spanish Labor Market', Grupo de Discusión de Economía Laboral, FEDEA. Available at: *http://www.crisis09.es/economialaboral*.

Fernald, J. (1999) 'Roads to Prosperity? Assessing the Link Between Public Capital and Productivity.' *American Economic Review*, 89(3), 619–38.

Fernández, R. B. (1981) 'Methodological Note on the Estimation of Time Series', *The Review of Economics and Statistics*, 63, 471–8.

Fernández de Córdoba, G. and R. J. Torregrosa (2005) 'Efectos de una Sustitución de Impuestos Sobre el Trabajo por Impuestos Sobre el Capital: el Caso de España', *Hacienda Pública Española*, 175(4/2005), 9–23.

Fernández-Villaverde, J. and L. Ohanian (2010) 'The Spanish Crisis from a Global Perspective', FEDEA Working Paper No. 2010-03.

Flores de Frutos, R., M. Gracia-Diez and T. Pérez-Amaral (1998) 'Public Capital Stock and Economic Growth: An Analysis of the Spanish Economy', *Applied Economics*, 30, 985–94.

Ford R. and P. Poret (1991) 'Infrastructure and Private-Sector Productivity', *OECD Economic Studies*, 17 (Autumn), 63–88.

Fujita, S. (2004) 'Vacancy Persistence', Federal Reserve Bank of Philadelphia, Working Paper No. 04-23.

Galí, J. (1999) 'Technology, Employment and the Business Cycle: Do Technology Shocks Explain Aggregate Fluctuations?', *American Economic Review*, 89(1), 249–71.

Galí, J. (2008) *Monetary Policy, Inflation, and the Business Cycle: An Introduction to the New Keynesian Framework* Princeton, NJ: Princeton University Press.

Galí, J. and J. D. Lopez-Salido (2001) 'Una Nueva Curva de Phillips para España'. Moneda y Crédito, 212, 265–304.

Galí, J. and P. Rabanal (2004) 'Technology Shocks and Aggregate Fluctuations: How Well Does the RBS Model Fit Postwar U.S. Data?', NBER Working Paper No. 10636.

Galí, J., M. Gertler and J. D. Lopez-Salido (2001) 'European Inflation Dynamics', *European Economic Review*, 45, 1237–70.

Galí, J., J. D. Lopez-Salido and J. Vallés (2007) 'Understanding the Effects of Government Spending on Consumption', *Journal of the European Economic Association*, 5 (1), 227–70.

García-Milà, T., T. McGuire and R. Porter (1996) 'The Effects of Public Capital in State-Level Production Functions Reconsidered', *Review of Economics and Statistics*, 78(1), 177–80.

Garibaldi, P. and P. Mauro (2002) 'Anatomy of Employment Growth', *Economic Policy*, 17(34), 69–113.

Gavilán, A., J. F. Jimeno, P. Hernández de Cos and J. Rojas (2010) 'Fiscal Policy and External Imbalances: A Quantitative Evaluation for Spain', Mimeo, Banco de España.

Gianella, C., I. Koske, E. Rusticelli and O. Chatal (2008) 'What Drives the NAIRU? Evidence from a Panel of OECD Countries', OECD Economics Department Working Paper, No. 649.

González-Páramo, J. M. and I. Argimón (1997) 'Efectos de la Inversión en Infraestructuras Sobre la Productividad y la Renta de las CC.AA.', in E. Pérez Touriño (ed.), *Infraestructuras y Desarrollo Regional: Efectos Económicos de la Autopista del Atlántico*, Madrid: Editorial Civitas, Colección Economía

González-Páramo, J. M. and Á. Melguizo (2008) 'Who Bears Social Security Taxes? A Meta-Analysis Approach', Mimeo.

Gordon, R. J. (1995) 'Is There a Tradeoff between Unemployment and Productivity Growth?', NBER Working Paper No. 5081.

Gramlich, E. M. (1994) 'Infrastructure Investment: A Review Essay', *Journal of Economic Literature*, 32, 1176–96.

Granger, C. and P. Newbold (1974) 'Spurious Regressions in Econometrics', *Journal of Econometrics*, 2, 111–20.

Griliches, Z. (1980) 'R&D and the Productivity Slowdown', NBER Working Paper No. 0434.

Groshen, E. L and S. Potter (2003). 'Has Structural Change Contributed to a Jobless Recovery?', *Current Issues in Economics and Finance*, Federal Reserve Bank of New York, 9(8), 1–7.

Hall, R. (2009) 'By How Much Does GDP Rise if the Government Buys More Output?', *Brookings Papers on Economic Activity*, Fall, 183–231.

Harrison, R., K. Nikolov, M. Quinn, G. Ramsay, A. Scott and R. Thomas (2005) *The Bank of England Quarterly Model*, London: Bank of England.

Harvey, A. C. (1989) *Structural Models and the Kalman Filter*, Cambridge, UK: Cambridge University Press.

Hernando, I. and S. Nuñez (2004) 'The Contribution of ICT to Economic Activity: A Growth Accounting Exercise with Spanish Firm-Level Data', *Investigaciones Económicas*, 28(2), 315–48.

Holtz-Eakin, D. (1994) 'Public Sector Capital and the Productivity Puzzle', *Review of Economics and Statistics*, 76(1), 12–21.

Hosios, A. J. (1990) 'On the Efficiency of Matching and Related Models of Search Unemployment', *Review of Economic Studies*, 57, 279–98.

Huang, H-C. and S-C. Lin (2008) 'Smooth-Time-Varying Okun's Coefficients', *Economic Modelling*, 25, 363–75.

Hulten, C. and R. Schwab (1991) 'Is There Too Little Public Capital? Infrastructure and Economic Growth', Paper delivered at Conference 'Infrastructure Needs and Policy Options for the 90s', Washington, DC, February.

Izquierdo, M. and J. F. Jimeno (2005) 'Inmigración: Desarrollos Recientes y Consecuencias Económicas', Banco de España, *Boletín Económico*, Banco de España, February, 41–71.

Izquierdo, M., J. F. Jimeno and J. A. Rojas (2010) 'On The Aggregate Effects of Immigration in Spain', *SERIEs, Journal of The Spanish Economic Association*, 1(4), March, 409–32.

Jackman,R., R. Layard and S. Nickell (1996) 'Combatting Unemployment: Is Flexibility Enough?'. Discussion Paper No. 293, Centre for Economic Performance.

Jimeno, J. F. and R. Sánchez (2006) 'La Productividad en España: Una Perspectiva Macroeconómica', in J. Segura (ed.), *La Productividad en la Economía Española*, Madrid: Ramón Areces Foundation.

Jorgenson, D. (1991) 'Fragile Statistical Foundations: The Macro-Economics of Public Infrastructure Investment', Paper delivered at Conference 'Infrastructure Needs and Policy Options for the 90s', Washington, DC, February.

Juillard, M., (1996) 'Dynare: A Program for the Resolution and Simulation of Dynamic Models with Forward Variables through the Use of a Relaxation Algorithm', CEPREMAP Working Paper No. 9602.

Kamps, C. (2006) 'New Estimates of Government Net Capital Stocks for 22 OECD Countries, 1960–2001', *IFM Staff Papers* 53(1), 120–50.

Karagedikli, Ö., T. Matheson, C. Smith and S. Vahey (2009) 'RBCs and DSGEs: The Computational Approach to Business Cycle Theory and Evidence', *Journal of Economic Surveys*, 24(1), 113–36.

Kavanagh, C. (1997) 'Public Capital and Private Sector Productivity in Ireland, 1958–90', *Journal of Economic Studies*, 24, 72–94.

Khemraj, T., J. Madrick and W. Semmler (2006) 'Okun's Law and Jobless Growth', Schwartz Center for Economic Policy Analysis, Policy Note 3.

Kilponen, J., A. Ripatti and J. Vilmunen (2004) 'AINO: The Bank of Finland's New Dynamic General Equilibrium Model of the Finnish Economy', *Bank of Finland Bulletin*, 3/2004, 71–7.

Kim, S. and N. Roubini (2008) 'Twin Deficit or Twin Divergence? Fiscal Policy, Current Account, and Real Exchange Rate in the US', *Journal of International Economics*, 74(2), 362–83.

Knoester, A. (1986) 'Okun's Law Revisited', *Weltwirtschaftliches Archiv*, 122, 657–66.

Kox, H. and A. Lejour, (2005) 'Regulatory Heterogeneity as Obstacle for International Services Trade', CPB Discussion Papers 49, CPB Netherlands Bureau for Economic Policy Analysis.

Kox, H., A. Lejour and R. Montizaan (2004) 'The Free Movement of Services within the EU', CPB Document 69, CPB Netherlands Bureau for Economic Policy Analysis.

Kremer, J., L. Giovanni, L. von Thadden, and T. Werner (2006) 'Dynamic Stochastic General Equilibrium Models as a Tool for Policy Analysis'. *CESifo Economic Studies*, 52(4), 640–65.

Krugman, P. (1993) 'Lessons of Massachusetts for EMU', in F. Torres and F. Giavazzi (eds), *Adjustment for Growth in the European Monetary Union*, Cambridge, UK: Cambridge University Press.

Kumar, K., R. G. Rajan and L. Zingales (1999) 'What Determines Firm Size?', NBER Working Paper No. W7208.

Laffarque, J. P. (1990) 'Résolution d'un Modèle Macroéconomique avec Anticipations Rationneles', *Annales d'Economie et Statistique*, 17, 97–119.

Layard, R., S. Nickell and R. Jackman (2005) *Unemployment: Macroeconomic Performance and the Labour Market*, 2nd edn, Oxford, UK: Oxford University Press.

Lee, J. (2000) 'The Robustness of Okun's Law: Evidence from OECD Countries', *Journal of Macroeconomics*, 22, 331–56.

Ligthart, J. (2000) 'Public Capital and Output Growth in Portugal: An Empirical Analysis', IMF Working Paper No. 00/11, Washington, DC.

Lindé, J., M. Nessén and U. Söderström (2004) 'Monetary Policy in an Estimated Open-Economy Model with Imperfect Pass-Through', Working Paper Series 167, Sveriges Riksbank.

Lores, F. X. (2001) 'Growth and Cyclical Fluctuations in Spanish Macroeconomic Series', Working Paper, 2001–09, Universidad Carlos III.

Mamatzakis, E. C. (1999) 'Testing for Long-run Relationships between Infrastructure and Private Capital Productivity: A Time Series Analysis for the Greek Industry', *Applied Economics Letters*, 6, 243–6.

Mas, M., J. Maudos, F. Pérez and E. Uriel (1993) 'Capital Público y Productividad de la Economía Española', Mimeo, Instituto Valenciano de Investigaciones Económicas, Valencia.

Mas, M., J. Maudos, F. Pérez and E. Uriel (1996) 'Infrastructures and Productivity in the Spanish Regions', *Regional Studies*, 30(7), 641–9.

Merz, M. (1995) 'Search in the Labor Market and the Real Business Cycle', *Journal of Monetary Economics*, 36, 269–300.

Molinas, C., C. Ballabriga, E. Canadell, A. Escribano, E. López, L. Manzanedo, R. Mestre, M. Sebastián and D. Taguas (1990) *MOISEES: un Modelo de Investigación y Simulación de la Economía Española*, Barcelona; Antoni Bosch.

Munnell, A. (1990a) 'Why Has Productivity Declined? Productivity and Public Investment', *New England Economic Review*, Federal Reserve Bank of Boston, Jan/Feb., 3–22.

Munnell, A. (1990b) 'How Does Public Infrastructure Affect Regional Economic Performance?', in A. Munnell (ed.), *Is There a Shortfall in Public Capital Investment?*, Boston, MA, Federal Reserve Bank of Boston, pp. 69–103.

Munnell, A. (1992) 'Infrastructure Investment and Economic Growth', *Journal of Economic Perspectives*, 6(4), Fall, 189–98.

Murchison, S., A. Rennison and Z. Zhu (2004) 'A Structural Small Open-Economy Model for Canada', Working Paper 04-4, Bank of Canada.

Nickell, S. (1997) 'Unemployment and Labour Market Rigidities: Europe versus North America', *Journal of Economic Perspectives*, 11(3), 55–74.

Nickell, S. (2004) 'Employment and Taxes', CEP Discussion Paper No. 634.

Nickell, S. (2006) 'Work and Taxes', in J. Agell and P. B. Sorensen (eds), *Tax Policy and Labour Market Performance*, Cambridge, MA: MIT Press.

Nickell, S. and R. Layard (1999) 'Labour Market Institutions and Economic Performance', in O. Ashenfelter and D. Card (eds), *Handbook of Labour Economics*, Vol. 3, Amsterdam: North-Holland.

Nickell, S., L. Nunziata and W. Ochel (2005) 'Unemployment in the OECD Since the 1960s: What Do We Know?', *The Economic Journal*, 115, 1–27.

Nicoletti, G. and S. Scarpetta (2003) 'Regulation, Productivity and Growth: OECD Evidence', *Economic Policy*, 36, 10–21.

Nicoletti, G., S. Golub, D. Hajkova, D. Mirza and K.-Y. Yoo (2003) 'Policies and International Integration: Influences on Trade and Foreign Direct Investment', OECD Economic Department Working Paper No. 359.

Nicoletti, G., T. Kozluk, I. Wanner and A. Wölfl (2009) 'Ten Years of Product Market Reform in OECD Countries – Insights from a Revised PMR Indicator', OECD Economics Department Working Paper No. 695.

Obstfeld, M. and K. Rogoff (1995) 'Exchange Rate Dynamics Redux', *Journal of Political Economy*, 103, 624–60.

Obstfeld, M. and K. Rogoff (1996) *Foundations of International Macroeconomics*, Cambridge, MA: MIT Press.

OECD (2003) *From Red Tape to Smart Tape, Administrative Simplification in OECD Countries*, Paris: OECD.

OECD (2008) *OECD Compendium of Productivity Indicators 2008*. Paris, OECD.

Ohanian, L., A. Raffo and R. Rogerson (2008) 'Long-Term Changes in Labor Supply and Taxes: Evidence from OECD Countries, 1956–2004', *Journal of Monetary Economics*, 55, 1353–62.

Okun, A. M. (1962) 'Potential GNP: Its Measurement and Significance', *Proceedings of the Business and Statistics Economic Section*, American Statistical Association.

Otto, G. D. and G. M. Voss (1996) 'Public Capital and Private Production in Australia', *Southern Economic Journal*, 62, 723–38.

Pérez, F., J. Maudos, J. M. Pastor and L Serrano (2006) *Productividad e Internacionalización. El Crecimiento Español ante los Nuevos Cambios Estructurales*, Madrid: BBVA Foundation.

Pissarides, C. A. (2000) *Equilibrium Unemployment Theory*, Cambridge, MA: MIT Press.

Pissarides, C. A. (2007) 'Unemployment and Hours of Work: The North Atlantic Divide Revisited', *International Economic Review*, 48(1), 1–36.

Planas, C., W. Roeger and A. Rossi (2007) 'How Much Has Labour Taxation Contributed to European Structural Unemployment?', *Journal of Economic Dynamics & Control*, 31, 1359–75.

Prescott, E. C. (2004) 'Why Do Americans Work So Much More Than Europeans?', *Federal Reserve Bank of Minneapolis Quarterly Review*, 28, 2–13.

Przybyla, M. and M. Roma (2005) Does Product Market Competition Reduce Inflation? Evidence form EU Countries and Sectors', European Central Bank Working Paper No. 453.

Puch, L. and O. Licandro (1997) 'Are There Any Special Features in the Spanish Business Cycle?', *Investigaciones Economicas*, XXI (2), 361–94.

Ramírez, M. (2000) 'Public Capital Formation and Labor Productivity Growth in Chile', *Contemporary Economic Policy*, 18(2), 159–69.

Ramírez, M. (2002) 'Public Capital Formation and Labor Productivity Growth in Mexico', *Atlantic Economic Journal*, 30(4), 366–79.

Ravn, M. O. and S. Simonelli (2007) 'Labor Market Dynamics and the Business Cycle: Structural Evidence for the United States', CSEF Working Paper, No. 182.

Rezai, A. and W. Semmler (2007) 'Productivity and Unemployment in the Short and Long Run', Policy Note, Schwartz Center for Economic Policy Analysis.

Roeger W., J. Varga and J. in't Veld (2008) 'Structural Reforms in the EU: A Simulation-Based Analysis Using the QUEST Model with Endogenous Growth', European Economy Economic Paper No. 351.

Rogerson, R. (2006) 'Understanding Differences in Hours Worked', *Review of Economic Dynamics*, 9, 365–409.

Rogerson, R. (2007) 'Taxation and Market Work: Is Scandinavia an Outlier?', *Economic Theory*, 32, 59–85.

Rogerson, R. (2008) 'Structural Transformation and the Deterioration of European Labour Market Outcomes'. *Journal of Political Economy*, 116(2), 235–59.

Romero-Ávila, D. and C. Usabiaga (2007) 'Unit Root Test and Persistence of Unemployment: Spain vs. the United States', *Applied Economic Letters*, 14, 457–61.

Sala, H. and J. I. Silva (2009) 'Flexibility at the Margin and Labour Market Volatility: The Case of Spain', *Investigaciones Económicas*, XXXIII(2), 145–78.

Schmitt-Grohe, S. and M. Uribe (2003) 'Closing Small Open Economy Models', *Journal of International Economics*, 61, 163–85.

Seater, J. J. (1993) 'Ricardian Equivalence', *Journal of Economic Literature*, 31(1), 142–90.

Smets, F. and R. Wouters (2003) 'An Estimated Dynamic Stochastic General Equilibrium Model of the Euro Area', *Journal of the European Economic Association*, 1(5), 1123–75.

Smets, F., K. Christoffel, G. Coenen, R. Motto and M. Rostagno (2010) 'DSGE Models and Their Use at the ECB', *SERIEs, Journal of the Spanish Economic Association*, 1(1–2), 51–65.

Suárez, J. (2010) 'The Spanish Crisis: Background and Policy Challenges', CEPR Discussion Paper No. 7909.

Summers, R. and Heston, A. (1991) 'The Penn World Table (Mark 5): An Expanded Set of International Comparisons', 1950–1988, *Quarterly Journal of Economics*, 106(2), May, 327–68.

Tatom, J. (1991a) 'Public Capital and Private Sector Performance', *Federal Reserve Bank of St. Louis Review*, 73, May/June, 3–15.

Tatom, J. (1991b) 'Should Government Spending on Capital Goods be Raised?', *Federal Reserve Bank of St. Louis Review*, March/April, 3–15.

Trigari, A. (2006) 'The Role of Search Frictions and Bargaining for Inflation Dynamics', IGIER Working Paper No. 304.

Turnovsky, S. J. (1985) 'Domestic and Foreign Disturbances in an Optimizing Model of Exchange-Rate Determination', *Journal of International Money and Finance*, 4(1), 151–71.

Wieland, V. (2010) 'Fiscal Stimulus and the Promise of Future Spending Cuts', *International Journal of Central Banking*, 6(1), March, 39–50.

Wölfl, A., I. Wanner, T. Kozluk and G. Nicoletti (2009) 'Ten Years of Product Market Reform in OECD Countries: Insights from a Revised PMR Indicator', OECD Economics Department Working Paper No. 695, Paris.

Woodford, M. (2003) *Interest and Prices, Foundations of a Theory of Monetary Policy*, Princeton, NJ: Princeton University Press.

Woodford, M. (2009) 'Convergence in Macroeconomics: Elements of the New Synthesis', *American Economic Journal: Macroeconomics*, 1(1), 267–79.

Woodford, M. (2010) 'Simple Analytics of the Government Expenditure Multiplier', NBER Working Paper No. 15714.

World Bank (2007) *Doing Business 2008* Washington, DC: World Bank.

Index

aggregate consumption, 39–40, 51–4, 66, 175–6, 183
aggregate employment, 39–40
aggregate resource constraint, 54, 201

Balassa-Samuelson hypothesis, 97–8, 99, 106
behavioural equations, 204–6
Bellman equation, 35, 42
bilateral trade, 110
Bolkenstein Directive, *see* Services Directive (SD)
budget constraint, 32, 34, 49, 54, 180, 201
budget deficit, 140, 147, 149–50, 187
budget surplus, 144, 146, 187
business cycles, 1, 3, 27–8, 183

Calvo hypothesis, 43
capital
    human, 11–12, 14–17
    physical, 11, 12, 15, 18
    private, 42
    private productive capital, 13, 17
capital-output ratio, 14, 19–20, 21, 29n8
capital stocks, 120–7, 186, 190–1
capital taxation, 161, 166, 173, 176, 188, 210
China, 100
Cobb-Douglas production function, 11, 27, 35, 41, 128
competition, 16, 103, 110–11
competitiveness, 97, 106, 108, 112, 114, 115, 185
Computable General Equilibrium (CGE) models, 111
constant elasticity of substitution (CES), 51
consumer price levels, 99
consumption, 51, 52, 53, 69, 88

aggregate, 39–40, 51–4, 66, 175–6, 183
household, 34
private, 22, 25, 27, 28, 69, 146, 153
public, 22, 26, 27, 48–9, 148–50
consumption behavior, 32–3
cost minimisation problem, 41
country of origin principle, 110, 112
crowding-out effects, 153
current account balance, 54, 100, 146, 148–50
current account deficit, 2, 28n2, 70, 144, 156, 182, 187
cyclical regularities, 18–27
cyclical unemployment, 23

deficits, 69, 100, 140, 147, 149–50, 155, 187
    see also current account deficit; external deficit
dynamic general equilibrium (DGE) model, 30, 111
dynamic stochastic general equilibrium (DSGE) models, 31, 91

Economic and Monetary Union (EMU), 1–2, 50, 97, 98, 181
economic growth, 27, 88, 181
    infrastructures and, 127–35
    in Spain, 1–11, 71–82, 183
economic integration, 99–100
education, 14–15, 27
employment
    across sectors, 82
    aggregate, 39–40
    productivity and, 73–5, 163–4
    stability, 183–4
employment growth, 72
    see also job creation
employment rate, 6–7, 19, 33, 163, 178

energy, 53
energy demand, 42
EU-10, 83–7
Europe
  human capital in, 14–15
  labour market in, 12
  productivity in, 2, 181–2
European Central Bank (ECB), 2, 32, 50
European integration, 2
expansionary fiscal policies, 144–59, 187
exporting companies, 100–1
export prices, 53–4
exports, 20, 27, 53–4, 100, 101, 156, 175
external deficit, 28n2, 97, 99–102, 106, 117, 182

factor demands, 40–3
financial frictions, 31
firm-level agreements, 91
firm size, 103
fiscal deficits, 144–6, 149–50, 155
fiscal multiplier, 156–7
fiscal policy, 2, 160, 182
  current account and, 148–50
  expansionary, 144–59, 187
fiscal stimulus, 147, 155–7, 158, 187
Fisher parity condition, 37
foreign assets, accumulation of, 54
foreign direct investment (FDI), 109, 110
France, 100

GDP deflator, 52
GDP per capita, 100
Germany, 100
goods market, 103
government, 48–50
government debt, 27, 48–9, 69
government expenditures, 48–9
government revenues, 49
government shocks, 146–7
Great Recession, 2, 70, 182
Greece, 105
gross domestic product (GDP), 27, 28, 162–3

growth model, 184
  general equilibrium analysis, 87–94
  job creation and, 83–94
  Solow, 66, 182–3

Hodrick-Prescott trend, 19
hours worked, 7–8, 19–20, 47, 160–1, 164, 167–9, 176
household consumption, 34
households
  optimising, 33–40
  rule-of-thumb, 38–9
  savings rate, 144, 145, 147, 187
household utility, 36, 38, 59, 206
human capital, 11–12, 14–17

immigrants, 15, 77
immigration, 2, 29n5, 181
imports, 20, 53–4, 100, 101, 115, 156
impulse-response functions, 148, 151, 153
income per capita, 3–4, 6, 9–10, 98, 99, 160, 162, 182
incorporated technical progress, 12
inflation, 1–2, 45, 50, 70, 97–9, 105–7, 149, 181, 182
information and communication technologies (ICT), 14, 16
infrastructures, 2, 127–35, 186
interest rates, 2, 50, 69, 149, 181, 184
intermediate firms, pricing behaviour of, 43–5
intermediate producers, 40
international dataset, 189–91
international trade, 100, 101, 175
investment, 22, 51, 52, 53, 69, 116, 175
  see also public investment
investment rates, 12, 145
Ireland, 99, 105

job creation, 69–96
  general equilibrium evaluation of, 87–94
  growth model and, 83–7
  Spanish growth model and, 71–82
  stable employment and, 183–4

jobless growth, 95n7
job turnover, 91

labour contracts, 45–8, 91
labour force participation, 2–6, 73, 76
labour income taxes, 152–4
labour market, 10, 12, 22, 31, 45–8,
    69–71, 79, 103
  in EU, 164–9
  proposal for reforming, 90–4
  reforms, 184
  in Spain, 164–70
  taxation and, 160–70
  in US, 164–70
labour market policies, 91
labour productivity
  see also productivity
  determinants of, 11–18
  firm size and, 103
  in Spain, 3, 8–11, 97, 101–8
  taxation and, 162–9
labour regulations, 184
labour supply elasticity, 176–8
law of one price, 54
laws of motion, 34–5

macroeconomic aggregates, 24, 28
macroeconomic performance, 162–9
market competition, 111
maximisation problem, 46–7, 198
MOISEES, 30
monetary policy, 1–2, 32, 50, 157,
  181, 182
money (M1) velocity, 22, 27
monopolistic competition, 43, 53
motion, laws of, 34–5

Nash bargaining, 198–200
Nash maximisation problem, 46–7,
  198
net exports, 27, 28
net foreign asset accumulation, 201–3
new growth model, 83–94
New Neoclassical-Keynesian synthesis
  model, 30
New Phillips curve, 43–5
nominal frictions, 31

Okun's law, 22, 71, 72, 75–81, 89–90
Optimal Currency Areas (OCAs), 111
optimising households,
  33–40
output growth, 72
output shocks, 147

participation rates, 3–6, 75, 76, 164,
  182
per capita GDP, 3, 4, 27, 28n4, 100
per capita income, 1–4, 6, 9–10, 98,
  99, 160, 162, 182
permanent-income hypothesis, 32
Phillips curve, 31, 43–5
physical capital, 11, 12, 15, 18
population growth, 1, 2, 181
positive shocks, 148–9, 151–2
price convergence, 98
price deflators, 52, 53
price formation, 52–3
pricing behaviour, 43–5
pricing-to-market hypothesis, 53
private capital, 42
private consumption, 22, 25, 27, 69,
  146, 153
private productive capital, 13, 17
production, 40, 69–70, 82
productivity
  across sectors, 81–2
  current account deficit and,
    28n2
  determinants of, 11–18
  employment and, 73–4, 75, 163–4
  in Europe, 181–2
  growth of, 74
  infrastructures and, 127–35
  per worker, 74
  Services Directive and, 114
  in Spain, 2–11, 69–70, 73, 81–2, 97,
    101–8, 181–2
  unemployment and, 75–82
  in US, 181–2
product market regulation (PMR),
  103–6, 109
profit margins, 107
public capital stocks, 120–7, 186
public consumption, 22, 26, 27, 48–9,
  148–50

public consumption shock, 62–5
public debt, 69
public investment
  effects of, 120–43
  as fraction of GDP, 122
  as fraction of total investment, 123
  in infrastructures, 127–35, 186
  long-run effects, 135–8
  in OECD, 120–7
  permanent increase in, 135–41,
    186–7
  rate of, 185–6
  short-run effects, 138–41
  temporary increase in, 150–2
purchasing power parities, 12, 28n1

rational expectations hypothesis, 65,
  182
real estate prices, 70
real frictions, 31
regulations, 103–6, 109, 184
REMS (Rational Expectations Model
    for Simulation and Policy
    Evaluation of the Spanish
    Economy), 30–68, 182–3
  accounting identities in the
    economy, 54–5
  conclusions, 65–6
  consumption behavior, 32–3
  expansionary fiscal policies, 147
  external sector, 51–4
  factor demands, 40–3
  general equilibrium analysis, 87–94
  government, 48–50
  introduction to, 30–1
  labour contracts, 45–8
  model solution method, 55
  monetary policy, 50
  New Phillips curve, 43–5
  optimising households, 33–40
  parameterisation, 56–60
  Services Directive and, 109–12
  simulations, 60–5
  tax reform and, 161
  theoretical framework, 31–55
REMSDB (REMS Database), 31, 56,
  192–7
residential investment, 2

reverse causation, 129, 131
Ricardian equivalence, 144, 147,
  149–50, 187
Ricardian households, 33–40
road construction, 130–1
rule-of-thumb households, 38–9

savings rate, 144, 145, 147, 187
schooling, 14–15
Services Directive (SD), 184–5
  economic impact of, 112–17
  effects of, 108–12
  long-run effects, 112–14
  transitional dynamics, 114–16, 118
services market, 103
small firms, 103, 104
small open economy, 30, 31, 51,
  146–7
Solow growth model, 66, 182–3
Spain
  economic growth in, 3–11, 183
  impact of Services Directive in,
    112–17
  job creation in, 69–96
  production structure of, 71–82
  productivity in, 2–11, 69–70, 73,
    81–2, 101–8, 181–2
  public investment in, 120–43
  tax reform in, 169–76
Spanish economy
  cyclical regularities of, 18–27
  growth of, 69–70, 181
  long-run and business cycle factors
    of, 1–29
Spanish growth model, 71–82
structural unemployment, 6–7, 103,
  104, 163
subprime financial crisis, 183

taxation, 71, 152–4, 160–1, 162–9
tax burden, 7
tax reform, 188
  economic performance and, 160–80,
    207–10
  long-run effects, 170–3, 177
  sensitivity analysis, 176–9
  transitional dynamics, 173–6,
    207–10

technical progress, 12
technology, 77, 167
technology shock, 60–2, 63,
    88–9
temporary contracts, 91
temporary workers, 184
total factor productivity (TFP), 11–12,
    16–18, 27, 29n7, 76
trade, 100, 101, 110, 175
trade balance, 54
trade deficit, 157–8
trade unions, 71
twin deficits, 144, 149–50, 187
twin divergence, 144, 158

unemployment, 45, 70
    cyclical, 23
    output growth and, 72
    productivity and, 75–82
    structural, 6–7, 103, 104, 163
unemployment benefits, 71, 167
unemployment protection, 71, 91,
    167

unemployment rate, 2, 6–7, 22, 23,
    33, 69, 71–3, 77, 86, 88,
    108, 182
United Kingdom, 100
United States, 100
    current account deficit in,
        28n2
    human capital in, 14–15
    labour market, 160–1,
        164–9
    per capita income in, 9–10
    productivity in, 2, 8–9, 16–18, 28n2,
        181–2

wages, 46, 47, 73
women, 2, 6, 77
workers' bargaining power, 46–7,
    155
working-age population, 5, 46, 163,
    167

youth, 77